KIM CHERNIN was born in New York in 1940, and grew up there and in California. In 1965 she graduated magna cum laude from the University of California. Since then she has taught creative writing as well as concentrating on her own writing. She is the author of *Womansize: Reflections on the Tyranny of Slenderness*, and has published a collection of poetry, *The Hunger Song*. She is currently at work on two books, a novel and a non-fiction work. She has a daughter, and lives in Berkeley, California.

Kim Chernin spent seven years writing *In My Mother's House: A Daughter's Story*. In this remarkably woven account of four generations of Chernin women, she speaks as herself but also creates the extraordinary voices of her past – a past of intense political and personal conflict, of confrontation and finally, reconciliation and love.

In My Mother's House

Kim Chernin

Published by VIRAGO PRESS Limited 1985
41 William IV Street, London WC2N 4DB

Copyright © 1983 by Kim Chernin

First published by Ticknor & Fields,
New Haven and New York 1983

All rights reserved

British Library Cataloguing in Publication Data
Chernin, Kim
  In my mother's house.
  1. Chernin, Rose   2. Chernin, Kim
  3. Communists—United States—Biography
  I. Title
  335.43'092'2   HX84.C57

  ISBN 0-86068-563-2

Printed in Great Britain by
Anchor Brendon Ltd, Tiptree, Essex

For my mother, Rose Chernin.
For her mother, Perle Chernin.
And for my daughter, Larissa Chernin.

Contents

Part Three: The Survivor

PART ONE

Wasn't I Once Also a Daughter?

The Proposal

July 1974

She calls me on the telephone three times the day before I am due to arrive in Los Angeles. The first time she says, "Tell me, you still like cottage cheese?" "Sure," I say, "I love it. Cottage cheese, yogurt, ricotta . . ." "Good," she says, "we'll have plenty."

The second conversation is much like the first. "What about chicken? You remember how I used to bake it?"

The third time she calls the issue is schav — Russian sorrel soup, served cold, with sour cream, chopped egg, and onion, large chunks of dry black bread. "Mama," I say. "Don't worry. It's you I'm coming to visit. It doesn't matter what we eat."

She worries. She is afraid she has not been a good mother. An activist when I was growing up, Communist Party organizer, she would put up our dinner in a huge iron pot before she left for work each morning, in this way making sure she neglected no essential duty of a mother and wife. For this, however, she had to get up early. I would watch her, chopping onions and tomatoes, cutting a chicken up small, dicing meat, while I ate breakfast, sitting on a small stepladder at our chopping board.

Now, thirty years later, she's afraid she won't be able to give whatever it is I come looking for when I come for a visit. I'm laughing, and telling my daughter about her three calls, and I am weeping.

"What's schav?" my daughter asks me as we get off the plane in Los Angeles. "There's Grandma," I say, "ask her," as I wave to my mother, trying to suggest some topic of conversation for this eleven-year-old American girl and the woman in her seventies who was born in a small Jewish village in Russia.

My mother catches sight of us and immediately begins talking in an excited voice over the heads of people in line before us as we come through the disembarcation lane. I love this about her, this extravagance of feeling, the moodiness that goes along with it.

"Mama," I call out, waving excitedly, while my daughter looks at her feet and falls back with embarrassment as I push forward into my mother's arms.

She takes me by the elbow as we make our way toward the baggage, giving me sideways her most cunning look. What does she see? I look at myself with her eyes. Suddenly, I'm a giant. Five feet, four and a half inches tall the last time I measured myself, now I'm strolling along here as if I'm on stilts. She has to tip back her head to look into my eyes. This woman, whose hands were once large enough to hold my entire body, does not now reach as high as my daughter's shoulder.

We are all trying to think of something to say. We hurry past murals on the terminal walls. Finally, it is my mother who speaks. "Who are you running from?" she says, tugging me by the arm. "Let me get a look at you."

She stops and looks into my eyes. Then she looks at Larissa. Deeply perceptive, this look of hers. Assessing. Eyes narrowing. "A beauty," she whispers to me as Larissa goes off to stand near the baggage chute. But then she straightens her back and tilts her head up. "It's good you came now," she whispers. "It's important."

She comes up close to me, her shoulder resting against mine. "There's something I didn't tell you."

"You don't have to tell me," I say as quietly as possible. "I already know."

"You know?" She looks doubtful, but only for a moment. "Hoie," she sighs, "you were always like this. Who can keep anything from you?"

"Is she in pain?"

"Pain, sorrow, who can distinguish? There is, let me tell you, a story here. If you would write it down in a book, nobody would believe you."

I know better than to ask about the story. In my family they hint and retreat and tell you later in their own good time.

"But this is not for now," she says, turning her head sharply. "She won't last long, that much I know."

"What do the doctors say?"

"I should wait for doctors to tell me about my own sister?" Her voice has an edge to it, an impatience. But I know her by now. With this tone she attempts to master her own pain.

I want to put my arms around her, to comfort her for the loss of Aunt Gertrude. But I'm afraid she'll push me away, needing her own strength more than she needs my comfort.

"You know doctors," she continues, softening. "For every one thing they tell you, there are two things hidden under the tongue."

"And you?" I ask, because it seems to me she'll let the question come now. "How are you?"

She gestures dismissively with her hand and I know what will follow. *"Gezunt vi gezunt,"* she snorts, with her grim, shtetl humor: "Never mind my health, just tell me where to get potatoes."

Larissa waves. She has been making faces at me, as if the luggage is much too heavy for her to carry; she drags it along, wiping her forehead with an imaginary rag.

"What's this?" my mother calls out. "We leave the child to carry the luggage?"

But I am wringing my hands. I have put my fists against my temples, rocking myself with exaggerated woe. My mother looks at me, frowning, puzzled. There is a playfulness between Larissa and me, a comradeship she does not understand. When I was pregnant with Larissa I used to dream about running with her through the park, a small child at play with a larger one called the mother.

But now my mother cries out, "Wait, wait, we'll help you, don't strain like this."

She is confused by our sudden bursts of wildness; she frowns and seems to be struggling to understand the meaning of playfulness.

"It's a joke, Mama," I have to tell her, "a game we play."

Then, with hesitation, she smiles. But it is here I see most clearly the difference in our generations. Hers, with its eye fixed steadily on survival. Mine freer, more frivolous, less scarred and, in my own eyes, far less noble.

Now she has understood what Larissa is doing.

"Another one, look at her," she calls out, shaking her hands next to her head, leaning forward. "Both crazy."

We take up the suitcases and walk out toward the car. Larissa is carrying the two small duffel bags that make it clear we have come for only a few days.

But my mother has not overlooked this symbolism. And now, refusing my hand when I reach out for her, she says, "Three and a half years you haven't been to visit. You think you're living in the North Pole?"

"Berkeley, the North Pole, what's the difference?" I say, irresistibly drawn into her idiom. "It would take a team of huskies to drag me away from my work."

"Your work," she says, with all the mixed pride and ambivalence she feels about the fact that I live alone with my daughter, supporting both of us as a private teacher, involved in a work of solitary scholarship and poetry she does not understand.

"Still the same thing?" she asks, a tone of uncertainty creeping into her voice. "Mat-ri-archy?"

Reluctantly, I nod my head. But it is not like us to avoid a confrontation. "Tell me," she says, in a hushed, conspiratorial tone, as if she were making an alliance with my better nature. "Tell me, this is serious work you are doing?"

Once, years ago, coming down to visit I grew so angry that when we reached home I called a taxi and returned to the airport again.

"Mama," I say, my voice already too vehement, "listen to me." Larissa falls back and walks beside me. "In doing this work I am breaking taboos as great as those you broke when you became a Communist."

I know that my daughter wants me to lower my voice. Her face is puckered and worried. I put my hand on her shoulder, changing my tone.

"Believe me, where women are concerned, there are still ideas it is as difficult to think as it was once difficult for Marx to understand the fact that bourgeoise society was built upon the exploitation of the workers."

Since I was a small girl I have been fighting with my mother. When the family was eating dinner some petty disagreement would arise and I'd jump up from the table, pick up a plate and smash it against the wall. I'd go running from the room, slamming doors behind me.

By the age of thirteen I insisted that Hegel was right and not Marx. "The Idea came first," I cried out from the bathroom, which had the only door in the house that locked. "The Spirit came before material existence."

In the afternoons I read books. I started on the left side of the bookcase, at the top shelf, and thumbed my way through every book in the library. *The Classics of Marxism, Scottsboro Boy, State and Revolution* by Lenin, a story about the Huck Bella Hop in the Philippines, stories about the Spanish civil war.

I understood little of what I read, but I built a vocabulary, a mighty arsenal of weapons to use against my mother.

Then, when she came into the house, I was ready for her. Any opinion she uttered, I took the opposite point of view. If she liked realism, I preferred abstract art. If she believed in internationalism, I spoke about the necessity to concentrate on local conditions.

Twenty years later nothing has changed. We still refuse to understand one another, both of us still protesting the fact we are so little alike.

Her voice rises; she has clenched her jaw. "You're going to tell me about the exploitation of the workers?"

I answer belligerently, shaking with passion. "There is the same defiance of authority in the scholarship I do, the same passion for truth in the poetry I write as there has been in your life."

"Truth? We're going to discuss truth now?"

"And it changes, doesn't it? From generation to generation?"

The silence that follows this outburst is filled up through every cubic inch of itself by my shame. We are not even out of the airport and already I've lost my temper. And this time especially I had wanted so much to draw close to her. Surely, it must be possible after all these years.

"Mama," I say, throwing my arm around her shoulders with the same conspiratorial appeal she has used in approaching me. "You know what I found out? Marx and Engels, both of them, believed there was once a matriarchal stage of social organization. Yes, I'm serious. I'll tell you where you can read it."

"Marx and Engels?" she says. "You don't say. Marx and Engels?"

But now she sighs, shaking her head. "So all right, I am what I am, we can't be the same person. But I don't like to see you spending your life like this, that much I know."

She pauses, looking over at me, and I can see in her eyes the same resolution I have made.

"Let it go, I don't want to quarrel with you. But when I think . . . a woman like you. So brilliant, so well-educated. You could contribute to the world. With your gifts, what couldn't you accomplish?" Then, in her most endearing voice she says, "You're a poet. I accept this. But now I've got something to say to you. And I don't want you to say no before you give it some thought."

I look down at her face, so deeply marked with determination. "Tell me," I say, in spite of myself, for I know she won't tell me now, no matter what I do.

She looks around her. She has always liked a little suspense. She looks over at Larissa, she looks down at our bags. She reaches in her purse and feels around for her keys.

And then finally, taking my arm, she says, confidingly, almost with humor, "So, what's the hurry? We've got time."

~ ~

At dinner Larissa toys with her food. Who can blame her? From the moment we entered the house my mother has been feeding her. In the first ten minutes she brought out a plate of cookies baked for us by Aunt Sara, my father's brother's wife. Since then, I've seen my mother standing at the kitchen door, her hands at her waist, watching my daughter. "A good eater," she says to no one in particular as Larissa accepts a slice of Jell-O mold. "This is what you used to be like," she adds, turning to me, "before you took it in your head to get so thin."

In the kitchen, lined up on the counter, there are several large platters wrapped in tin foil. They are the gifts brought by my various aunts when they heard I was coming down for a visit. Raisin strudel from Aunt Anne, rolled cinnamon twists from Sara Sol's, a bowl of chopped liver, kugel in an oval pan.

I have always been held in high esteem by my family. "A *chochma*, a wise one," they'd say about me even as a child. "Born with a clear star over her head," his oldest sister would say to my father. "A golden tongue," they'd murmur when I burst out in some extravagant childhood story.

Even to this day, in spite of the fact that I have brought home to them so few tangible signs of worldly fame, they admire me.

They manage to forgive me for my two divorces. They struggle to understand the way I live.

"We never had a poet in the family before," my father's oldest brother said to me before he died. "We're proud of you. If you were born a son, you maybe would have become even a rabbi."

Their family traces itself back to the Vilna Goan, a famous rabbinical scholar of the eighteenth century. But my mother, whenever she heard this, would always snort. "Hach, little people, trying to make themselves feel important."

Her own family was more radical, more violent in its passion, more extreme in its life choices. Each side has always expected me to carry on its tradition. As it is, I have inherited my mother's fierce, revolutionary fervor, my father's quiet inclination for scholarship, and someone else's wild, untutored mystical leanings. They all worry about me because I have become too thin. But the food they have brought me, in love and in tribute, today has been eaten by my daughter.

Larissa moves her food over to the side of her plate, shovels it back toward the center, and makes fork marks in the baked squash.

My mother casts a disapproving glance at her. "Chopped liver she doesn't like. Schav she doesn't like. So eat a mouthful of chicken. Chicken they are eating also among the fifth generation born Americans."

At this, my mother's sister, Aunt Gertrude, who is sitting next to me, throws back her head and emits a dry, conciliatory laugh. It is impossible to recognize in this frail, withdrawn woman, the aunt of my childhood, the woman who joined the Peace Corps at the age of fifty-three, and went off to serve as a nurse in Ethiopia. I have heard that one day she rode a donkey over the mountains, taking supplies to villages of the interior. The image of her has lived on with me, an aging woman with gaunt face and brilliant eyes, her white hair beginning to yellow, the habitual smoker's cough, the clop of the animal's hooves and she rides, talking, smoking, gesturing, over the bad roads of the mountains of Ethiopia.

When I lean close to her I can smell the acrid sweetness I have known since childhood, when my sister was dying. It makes me want to run toward her, to grab her so tight death cannot get hold of her, and it makes me want to run away. I glance toward her from the corner of my eye, knowing she would not like to be stared at. And she, growing conscious of my tact, presses my foot beneath the table.

Her touch is so light I can scarcely feel it, but it has the power to jog my memory. Profoundly moved, I recall the games we used to play together when I was a child visiting at her house, little pokings and pattings, accompanied by puffs from her cigarettes, perfect rings of smoke, the smell of caffeine and the good odor of soap.

She had some secret sorrow, never spoken of, never completely hidden from me. But I knew, even as a small girl, that if you loved this woman you should pretend to believe that she was happy.

"There you be, cookie," she'd say in her husky voice when she came looking for me. I would jump up and throw my arms around her neck, charmed by her gruff tenderness.

She worked hard; she grew old early. "Something's eating her," my mother would say to my father. And I watched the wrinkles gnawing at her face, deepening perceptibly every time I saw her.

Silence comes to our table. Gertrude sipping her black tea, my mother tapping her fork against her plate, my own chair shifting restlessly as it attempts in all futility to establish itself in some permanent niche in the world.

And suddenly I know precisely what my mother has been hinting at since I arrived in Los Angeles. It comes to me from the silence as if it had been clearly and distinctly uttered. Now, in front of my aunt and my daughter, she is going to ask me something impossible to refuse.

She takes a deep breath, looks around the room as if she has misplaced something, and then delivers herself of one of those weighty utterances which have been troubling the atmosphere all day. "Do you know why I'm alive today?" she says, as if it were a question of her own will that she has lived to be an old woman. "Do you want to know why I'm still living?" And then, when Larissa looks toward her expectantly: "Because," she says, "there's still injustice in the world. And I am a fighter."

My mother's conversation frequently assumes this rhetorical tone. It comes, I suppose, from the many years she has been a public speaker. Even her English changes at such moments. It loses its Yiddish inflection and her voice rings out as if she were speaking through a megaphone. But today I know that all these statements are intended for me.

"Never mind how old I am," she says. "Never mind when I was born. Or where, or to what mother. There's only one important fact about a life. And that one is always a beginning. A woman who lives for a cause, a woman with dedication and unbreakable devotion — that's a woman who deserves the name of woman."

Has she been rehearsing this little speech? I ask myself. Has she been going over it again and again in her mind, as she waited for me at the airport?

As we leave the table she looks out the window, bends her knees slightly, and tips back her head, trying to catch sight of the moon. "Not yet," she mutters and walks toward the room where Larissa has been building a fire.

Here, everything has a story. The charcoal sketch of Harriet Tubman, given to her by Langston Hughes. The book of Tina Modotti's photographs, a gift from a young radical woman. And now I realize there is something new in this room, which she has been wanting me to notice. It is visible in the light from the small lamp attached to an oil painting of my sister in her red Komsomol scarf. It says:

TO ROSE CHERNIN FOR 25 YEARS OF MILITANT LEADERSHIP TO THE COMMITTEE FOR THE DEFENSE OF THE BILL OF RIGHTS. IN APPRECIATION OF YOUR LIFELONG DEVOTION AND STRUGGLE ON BEHALF OF THE FOREIGN-BORN AND ALL VICTIMS OF POLITICAL AND

RACIAL OPPRESSION. PRESENTED AT THE 25TH ANNUAL BANQUET, JANUARY 18, 1974.

She watches me as I study the plaque, unconsciously reciting the words aloud to Larissa. Then she waves at it with a disparaging shake of her hand. "So what else could they say? You think someone would write: 'To Rose Chernin: A Mean Person'?"

She is standing next to the fire, her foot on the rocker of Gertrude's chair. They are twisting newspaper into tight coils. Larissa pokes at the glowing coals with a wire hanger. But my mother has been waiting to speak with me. And now she says, "My mother knew how to read and to write. Isn't it so, Gertrude? Mama was a literate woman."

This fact makes no impression upon my daughter. She has no context for wondering at this achievement, so rare, so remarkable in a Jewish woman of the shtetl. On me, however, these words make a tremendous impression. The tone in which my mother speaks them moves me even to tears. "Mama was a literate woman," she repeats with a strangely wistful pride. Now she looks significantly at me and I know that we have come finally to the end of all this hinting.

"You are a writer," she says. "So, do you want to take down the story of my life?"

I am torn by contradiction. I love this woman. She was my first great aching love. All my life I have wanted to do whatever she asked of me, in spite of our quarreling.

She's old, I say to myself. What will it take from you? Give this to her. She's never asked anything from you as a writer before. Give this. You can always go back to your own work later.

But it is not so easy to turn from the path I have imagined for myself. This enterprise will take years. It will draw me back into the family, waking its ghosts. It will bring the two of us together to face all the secrets and silences we have kept. The very idea of it changes me. I'm afraid. I fear, as any daughter would, losing myself back into the mother.

I sit down on the edge of the gray chair that used to be my father's favorite reading place. It occurs to me that I should reason with her, tell her how much it means to me now to go my own way. "Mama,"

I say, intending to bring everything out into the open. And then she turns toward me expectantly, a raw look of hope and longing in her eyes.

~ ~

I learned to understand my mother's life when I was a small girl, waiting for her to come home in the afternoons. Each night I would set the table carefully, filling three small glasses with tomato juice while my father tossed a salad. Then we would hear my mother's car pull up in front of the house and I could go into the living room and kneel on the gray couch in front of the window to watch her come across the lawn, weighed down with newspapers and pamphlets and large blue boxes of envelopes for the mailing I would help to get out that night.

She was a woman who woke early, no matter how late she went to bed the night before. Every morning she would exercise, bending and lifting and touching and stretching, while I sat on the bed watching her with my legs curled up. Then, a cold shower and she would come from it shivering, smelling of rosewater, slapping her arms. She ate toast with cottage cheese, standing up, reading the morning paper. But she would always have too little time to finish her coffee. I would watch her taking quick sips as she stood at the door. "Put a napkin into your lunch," she'd call out to me, "I forgot the napkin." And there was always a cup with a lipstick stain standing half full of coffee on the table near the door.

Later, the Party gave her a car and finally she learned how to drive it. But in the early years she went to work by bus. Sometimes when I was on vacation I went downtown with her.

In her office she took off her shoes and sat down in a wooden chair that swiveled. Always, the telephone was ringing. A young black man. Framed on a false murder charge. And so she was on her feet again, her fist clenched. By twelve o'clock she would have made friends with the young man's mother. And for years after that time some member of his family would drive across town on his birthday to pick up my mother and take her home to celebrate.

It was the invariable pattern of her life, as I learned to know it when I was a little girl, still hoping to become a woman like my mother. To this day I rise early, eat a frugal meal, take a cold shower and laugh as I slap my arms, bending and stretching, touching and reaching.

But I cannot describe my day with these bold, clear strokes that sketch in her life. This strange matter of becoming a poet, its struggle so inward and silent. How can I tell her about this life that has so little to show for itself in the outer world?

But I should never underestimate my mother. Since I was a child she has been able to read my thoughts. And now she turns from the bookshelf where she has been showing my daughter the old books she brought back during the thirties from the Soviet Union. She looks at me with that serious, disapproving gaze which taught me, even as a small child, always to lie about myself. And now she comes toward me, in all the extraordinary power of her presence, to touch me with her index finger on my shoulder.

"I went to Cuba last year," she says. "I took with me ... what was it? Twenty-five people. All of them younger than myself. And you know what they did at night? Did I tell you? They went to sleep. Now could I sleep in a place like that? I ask you. So I took this one and that one, we went out into the streets, we walked, we went into restaurants. I don't care what the doctors tell me. I'm not going to rest. Do I have to live to be a hundred? What matters to me, so long as I'm living, I'm alive."

For me, these words have all the old seductive charm I experienced as a small girl, learning to know this woman. I loved her exclamation of surprise when someone came to our door, her arms flying out, her pleasure at whoever it was, dropping in on the way to a meeting. It was open house at our house on Wednesday nights. We never knew who might drop in. We'd pull up an extra chair, my father would go off to add lettuce to the salad, I'd pour another glass of tomato juice, and my mother would climb up on a stepladder to bring down a tin of anchovies. Every Wednesday morning she prepared a big pot of beef stroganoff or a spaghetti sauce with grated carrots and green pepper, which I would heat up, to simmer slowly, when I came home from school.

But how could I become my mother? She arrived in this country as a girl of twelve. An immigrant, struggling for survival, she supported her family when her father ran off and deserted them. To me she gave everything she must have wanted for herself, a girl of thirteen or fourteen, walking home from the factory, exhausted after a day of work.

What she is grows up out of her past in a becoming, natural way. She was born in a village where most women did not know how to read. She did not see a gaslight until she was twelve years old. And I? Am I perhaps what she herself might have become if she had been born in my generation in America?

This thought, although it remains unspoken, startles my mother. She looks over at me as if I have called her. And now she reaches out and pats my face, her hand falling roughly on my cheek.

She clears her throat. There comes into her voice a strangely confessional tone. "I'd come into your room at night," she says, "there you'd be. Looking out the window." She breathes deeply, shaking her head at some unpleasant impression life has left upon her. "I thought, this one maybe will grow up to be a *Luftmensch*. You know what it means? A dreamer. One who never has her feet on the ground."

She stops now, looking at me for understanding. She is vulnerable, uncertain whether she can continue. "We were poor people. Immigrants. For everything we had to struggle." I do not take my eyes from her face. And then the words rush from her, their intensity unexpected, shattering both of us. "The older I get the more I think about Mama. Always I struggled. Never to be like Mama. Never like that poor, broken woman . . ."

Larissa has been taking books out of the bookshelves, stacking them up on the floor, overturning the stacks. She seems surprised at the crash as her face turns toward her grandmother, who nods conciliation, as she never did to me, the child of her anxious years.

My grandmother could not adjust to the New World. I have heard this all my life. She was sent to a mental hospital. She attempted suicide. My mother would talk about the beautiful letters she wrote. "A Sholom Aleichem," my mother would say. "The most heart-breaking stories," my aunt echoed. Then she added, "She must have wanted to become a writer."

She, too, was a dreamer and she lived through most of her days in that sorrow of mute protest which in her generation was known as melancholia. My mother, her daughter, was obsessed by the fate of her mother and this obsession has descended to me. But who could have imagined these old stories would awaken my child to an interest in the family? She is growing up, I say to myself, she is becoming conscious, my heart already stirred by the magnitude of this, she is entering the mythology of this family.

The twilight comes into the room. It spreads itself out on the stacks of magazines, the lacquered Chinese dish, the little carved man with a blue patch in his wooden trousers. Everyone begins to look as if they have been brushed with understanding. For here finally is the clear shape of the story my mother wants me to write down — this tale of four generations, immigrants who have come to take possession of a new world. It is a tale of transformation and development — the female reversal of that patriarchal story in which the power of the family's founder is lost and dissipated as the inheriting generations decline and fall to ruin. A story of power.

My mother has stopped talking. She raises her eyebrows, asking me to respond to her. Soon I know if I hold silence she will take a deep breath and straighten her shoulders. "Daughter," she will say, in a voice that is stern and admonishing, "always a woman must be stronger than the most terrible circumstance. You know what my mother used to say? Through us, the women of the world, only through us can everything survive."

An image comes to me. I see generations of women bearing a flame. It is hidden, buried deep within, yet they are handing it down from one to another, burning. It is a gift of fire, transported from a world far off and far away, but never extinguished. And now, in this very moment, my mother imparts the care of it to me. I must keep it alive, I must manage not to be consumed by it, I must hand it on when the time comes to my daughter.

Larissa tugs at my sleeve. She is pointing to the window. I wonder why I feel such shame that I am crying, why I want to hide my face in my hands. I see my mother standing by the window, the dark folds of the drape gathered on either side of her. And there, above her head, where my daughter is now pointing, we see the slender cutting of a sickle moon, as my mother stands in silence, her arms folded upon her breast.

My mother sighs. But even in this expression of weariness or sorrow, I feel the power of the woman, as she straightens her shoulders, strides back into the room, sits down on the coffee table in front of me, and takes my hands.

"You never knew how to protect yourself," she says, "You never knew. I would stand there and watch you weep. You wept for everything. The whole world seemed to cause you pain. And I would say to myself, This one I will strengthen. This one I will make a fighter. And you, why can't you forgive me I wanted to teach you how to struggle with life? Why can't you forgive?"

My head moves down. I cannot restrain myself any longer. I know what I am going to do and I must take the risk. I feel my own lips, cold, unsure of themselves, pressed against my mother's hand. Very softly, whispering, I say to her, "Mama, tell me a story."

She lifts her head, her breast rises. "Good," she says. "From the mother to the daughter."

And so, eagerly now, I surrender. Deeply moved, I shall do what she has asked. I sit down on the floor, leaning against the knees of a white-haired old woman. And yes, with all the skill available to me as a writer, I will take down her tales and tell her story.

She was born in the first years of this century, in that shtetl culture which cannot any longer be found in this world. Her language is that haunting mixture of English, Yiddish, and Russian, in which an old world preserves itself. It is a story that will die with her generation. My own child will know nothing of it if it is not told now.

How could I have imagined that I, who am one of the few who could translate her memory of the world into the language of the printed page, had some more important work to do?

It grows dark as she is talking. "Today I will tell you about my life as a child," she says. "But the beginning, who can tell you? I don't know even the day I was born." No one moves to turn on the light. Far away, there is the sound of barking. And now, from a darkness no one of us wishes ever to visit, a wolf lifts its head and begins to howl. But none of this matters to me now. I am safe here in this little house. A cock crows at the edge of the village. The goat coughs in the cellar and on the windowsill there is a baked potato, cut in half and holding a candle someone has just lighted.

"When we were coming to America we made up the date for my birth. 'Rochele, Rochele,' my mother would say, pointing to me.

'First born. A daughter.' Then she would take hold of her ear. 'Do you remember, Papa? She was born when there was standing no more wheat in the field.' "

For a moment she catches her breath; her eyes dart uncertainly from me to the picture of my sister, above the fireplace, and back to me again.

But I — I am the one who has been chosen to set these stories down.

"And so they reconstructed. My grandfather picked out a date. September 14, 1903. You think this will do for a beginning?"

The First Story My Mother Tells
Childhood in Russia (1903–1914)

W hen I was a girl we lived with my grandfather in a town called Chasnik, in the Russian Pale of Settlement. What was the Pale? It was the area, inside greater Russia, where the czar made Jews live. If there were Jews who wanted to live or to work in any area outside the Pale, they had to get a special permit. Well, on the same street with us lived a peasant family. I used to visit them every day and I played with their children. But one day I came home singing a song. Here, however, I must say something about my singing. My grandfather always used to say, *"Rochele, zingen kenst du nit. Rochele, du bist a teiyere maidele, ober zingen kenst du nit."* (Rose, you can't sing. Rose, you are a dear girl but you just can't sing.)

I liked to sing. After all, I didn't have to listen to it. So I began singing a song and it went like this: *"Tsar Nikolai sidit na stoyle kak cabakou na svinye."* I looked up at my grandfather and instead of saying, Rochele, you can't sing, his face turned to stone. He was a very good-natured man. But this time he said sternly, "Where did you learn this song?" "From Masha," I said. "Rochele, this is a revolutionary song," he answered. "Don't you ever dare sing it again unless you want us to go to Siberia."

Now no child, no Jewish child, ever had to be told twice what Siberia was, because people would warn us, "Be careful, you'll go to Siberia." And without knowing exactly what they meant, to us it was a horrible place. What was that song? That song translated says, "Czar Nicholas sits on a throne like a dog sits on a pig."

I never sang that song again. But this is one of my first memories.

My grandfather was to us what a father is to most children. By that time we didn't have a father. He had gone to America. But even when we lived with him we were afraid of him. He bought grain for a mill in the next town. When he came home we were put away to sleep because he was always a very unpleasant man. I was six when he went to America. I don't recall the earliest days and I don't remember him going away. But I always heard, as children do, "Papa is in America." When they talked about him they used to remember his bad temper. We wondered why Mama married him. We always used to ask her, "Why did you ever marry a man like this?"

But my grandfather was to us perfection. He had a kind face. A long, gray beard. He was very tall. And he was always ready to laugh. He, too, used to be away during the week. He would buy grain from the peasants in the villages and sell it to the contractors. That's how he made a living. He used to go away on Sunday and come back early on Friday, in time for the Sabbath.

We used to ask our mother all the time, "How many more days until Friday?" The younger ones asked and Zipora and I, who were older, asked, too. My mother was a very good-natured woman and she knew what we meant. "You're waiting for Zayde (Grandfather)?"

We were waiting for Zayde, believe me, because it was really fun when Zayde was with us. Well, Friday would come around as Fridays do and that was the longest day of the week. But finally it would begin to get dark and Mama used to say, "Put on your coats and your shawls and go out to meet Zayde at the gate."

The gate was locked. It was very heavy; there was a big bolt on the inside. Our mother would say, "Stay on this side of the gate. It's too late to go outside." So we stayed until we heard Zayde talking to his horses. He would say, "Slow now, we're home now, slow." We'd all pull that bolt; it took all four of us and the gate would swing back. He would drive in and honest to goodness we thought he was a hero in a chariot. We'd lock the gate and we'd run to the house while he took the horses into the stable. Then he'd walk in and say to my mother, *"Gut Shabbas,* Perle," with so much love to my mother. And she'd say, *"Gut Shabbas,* Father. You're tired." And he'd say, "No, no." Then playfully, winking at her, "But where are all the children?" Mama would say, "Papa, here they are. Papa, you can see them." Each week it was the same thing. And always she would be so surprised when we'd all shout: "Here we are, Zadye." So he'd count, "Rochele, Zipora, Gita, Mikhail. Yes, all here. But I must tell you, I had a very bad week this week, very bad. There wasn't an apple in the village. Not an apple."

Those days in the shtetl we didn't see any fruit. Only in the peasant villages were there apples or pears. So he would bring us something when he came home for the Sabbath and that's why we lined up. But he would always say, teasing us, "There was no fruit. None. The peasants didn't even have one apple." And we would look so disappointed.

"But," he said, "you don't have to be disappointed. Next week will be better and I'll bring apples." At the same time he would unwind his sash. You know how the Russian men tied their heavy coats with a sash? He'd open it and the apples would just scatter on the floor. Can you imagine! I remember the howling and the screaming as we picked up the apples. But then he'd say, "And where is one for the mama?" We'd look up at him, questioningly. We hadn't thought of Mama. "Find it, children, it's somewhere on the floor." And then we would hand one to him, naturally.

He would wash his hands and we would have the Sabbath meal. Mama would light the candles because of course our grandfather was a religious man. That's why he didn't like Papa. Our papa was already an atheist. But now that he was gone to America we had a very happy childhood, especially on the Sabbath. We had a wooden table, candle holders, linen for the Sabbath, and oil lamps. I thought we lived in a big house but children can't measure. We lived in poverty.

Zayde was a showman. He had the horses, of course, which were necessary for his livelihood, and for this he had an ordinary wagon. But then, he also had a very nice sled that was painted with bright colors. Every week he'd dress up. A long black coat. The fur hat. His jacket buttoned up high. And a white shirt, showing only at the collar.

I had a black dress. Lace around the neck. Everything made for us by Mama. But this dress had buttons up the back and these buttons I remember caused trouble. Every time we put on the fancy dress Zipora would break out in crying. What could my mother do? She'd try to reason with her. "Zipa," she'd whisper, "little bird. What is to cry about? She's taller than you are. The dress is longer. So, an extra button."

But Zipora was always like this, from the first years already wanting what somebody else had. And this you should remember. You'll see why later. I loved her, why not? She was my sister. But already she had a certain kind of nature.

So, we would get dressed up. Mama would take along a blanket. It was very cold in the winter in the sled. I remember the bells. Zayde would drive us right through town to the public bath and there he'd go inside with my brother Mikhail. He gave us a sack of candy and we sat there, Zipora, Gita, and Mama and I. Suddenly Mikhail would come out from the bathhouse. He would be all wrapped up in his heavy coat. And his cheeks? I'll never forget it. Fiery. Like two red coals.

The shtetl was so beautiful in the winter; the snow covered all the mud. The horse shook its head, the bells rang, I looked around me and I saw a world in light. We had a study house in our shtetl and a school. There were maybe two hundred houses, all of them old. They were made of wood and they would lean sideways. The street went in every direction. And then suddenly back they would come on themselves. There were shops in the ghetto: a little tailor shop, a weaver, a cobbler. There was the rabbi, of course, and the schoolteacher and whatever else was needed. But everything was in the very lowest form of social organization. People lived by their wits because Jews, as you know, weren't allowed to take on any work that would compete with the peasants or the Russian tradesmen. They weren't even allowed to learn a trade. This was the ghetto.

The peasants had their own village surrounding our shtetl. It was different in other places but in Chasnik, where we lived, there was a good relationship between the peasants and the Jews. We knew the peasant children. We played with them and they would come into our house. On Friday night, the eve of the Sabbath, we weren't allowed to do work and we would freeze to death if the peasants didn't come in to light the stoves for us; a peasant woman would come to our house, my mother would give her bread for her children.

The peasants were as poor as we were, but none of this meant anything to us because we thought everybody in the world lived the way we lived. I thought everyone was either a peasant or a Jew.

In our shtetl the girls went to school; we learned Russian and Yiddish both, from a Jewish teacher, of course. But it wasn't much of a school. It had one room, we were maybe fifteen children and we sat on benches. Our teacher was very strict; he told us that we, the girls, were very fortunate to get an education. He used to talk to my mother about me; I know what he said because I was listening: "She has a good head. But she won't apply herself." I remember just the way he used to say it. "She could do so well but she's always reading. She doesn't want to work."

My mother would nod; she would wipe her hands on the apron and she would say to him, "A girl who likes to read!"

My mother was very fond of us. She was a gentle woman and I remember her best always embroidering. When she wasn't cooking and baking she would sit and stitch. She also wrote letters for people. She wrote to the husbands who were in America. When we would come home from school we sometimes found her sitting and crying bitterly. She and another lady would be there, at the table. They would weep and my mother would be writing a letter to America.

But this I better explain to you. In the shtetl, because of the poverty, who knew how they would live from one year to another? If the tax would be higher, if a horse would get lame, this was trouble. And so the people there were thinking always about America. If somebody heard about California you can be sure it was a place where it never rained, where children never got sick. And of course by this time everybody in the shtetl had someone in America. We, as you know, had our papa there. Down the street was a lady whose husband went away.

So why would this lady and our mama be crying? Naturally, in our shtetl there was hardship enough. But for the real hardship Mama and the other woman were not weeping. For this, no one had tears to waste. Our mama made up stories for the letters to America. And it was these stories, that didn't happen, that made them cry, Mama and the other woman, when we came home from school.

On a Sabbath she would take a walk and we would tag after her. We would go through fields of rye outside the shtetl. In Russia bluebells grow in the rye. We would pick the bluebells and make chains with them. Zipora and Gita would wear them in their hair. Mama would sing, she carried Mikhail in her arms and we three girls walked behind her, picking flowers. But we would, with our walking, ruin the fields of rye. The peasants would complain to my grandfather and this, too, I remember.

My mother seemed happy then. Whether she missed our papa or not who can say? She loved Zayde and she was like a wife to him. She took care of him and she managed his house. He used to bring her presents like he did to us. He would sit and tell her how much her sister misses her and loves her and wants her to visit. He was always tender and gentle with her and maybe for this reason she was so attached to him. She never did go to visit her sister, or her brother, who lived in Riga. She preferred to stay home.

But then one day my grandfather remarried and he brought this woman to our home. I can see her in front of my eyes now. She was a nice-looking woman, with a big shape, very prepossessing. Kids see everything. When this woman came into the house we knew that Mama was no longer in control. As I told you, our mama was very good-natured, easygoing, very gentle. And my grandfather's wife could lord it over her.

So it bothered us to see her pushed aside like this in her own house. Mama could not stand up for herself. We had to fight for her.

We made my grandfather's wife's life miserable! When she would bake bread and it would be rising, we would put our fingers in it! We whispered about her and we made plans. We, the older ones, Zipora and I, were the perpetrators. And I most of all. Gita was still a little girl. But she was very mischievous and I used to tell her what to do, and she would do it and we would make trouble.

We told Gita to steal the salt when my grandfather's wife was cooking, or we put sugar into something that wasn't supposed to be sweet. I don't think my mother minded. She would look at us and when we looked at her she turned away, as if she didn't see us. We used to break this woman's dishes. We would spill the soup that was ready for Zadie's dinner. And finally she left him. It might have taken a month or more, but finally we drove my grandfather's wife out of the house.

And then we felt good. Mama was restored. We would come in from school, Mama was baking, she made *zudhartkes* (little cinnamon twists), the bread was ready, cooling on the table, but the *zudhartkes* she would take right out of the oven. She'd say, "Careful children. They're still hot." And we smiled at each other because now Mama was back in control.

Zayde never said anything about it. I never remember him saying anything harsh to us. But when I think about it now it must have been hard for him to lose a woman. He was maybe fifty years old or fifty-five. That is a young man, as I see it today. But to us, as children, he was just a wonderful old man.

He was always very fond of me because I was the eldest; I would sit on his knees and reach down into his pocket. There was always something for me, hidden away in a corner: a sweet or a small piece of fruit. And one day he took me to a bazaar. On Christian holidays, four or five times a year, the peasants would have a bazaar. This was something special.

It was a big event to go out of our shtetl. I'm not like my mother, who was always afraid to go away from home. I loved the idea of going to another place.

My mother got up early and made a fire in the stove. I got wrapped up, always wrapped up, I don't remember summer except for the bluebells and the dust, but I remember the winters. We dressed, we drank hot milk, and we went off in the middle of the night. I sat near Zadie, very close to him, because I was terribly afraid. There were wolves howling, it was dark, but my grandfather was his usual self, singing as we went through the woods.

When I was ten, the year before we left for the United States, I went to the big city in Latvia. My grandfather told me that I would go much farther than we had gone to the bazaar. He told me that I was going to a big city and that I would see things I never even heard of before.

I went to visit my aunt and uncle, who lived in Riga. My uncle was a rich man because he was in the lumber business. You know, of course, that a Jew couldn't be in business by himself. My uncle had a partner, who was a Latvian. They were floating timber from the woods into Riga.

My uncle was a rough man — he came from our shtetl. He wasn't mean but he didn't have polished manners. He came from poor folks, but when he grew up he went to Riga and met my aunt. I remember her vividly. She was an educated woman, refined, and she liked me very much. I thought she was very high in the world. She dressed up in a hat when she went out; she put on gloves and took an umbrella. When she went shopping a servant went along with her. We would go to a wonderful market where she would pick out the food, by pointing, and the maid would carry it in a basket. I had never seen anyone buy so much food before. And all in her white gloves.

We didn't stay in the city the whole time. The family had a *dacha*, a country house, on the Baltic shore. The house stood away from the beach and we went through a garden; we opened the gate and went down to the sea. It was the first time I saw an ocean, the first time I saw a country house. I remembered our shtetl and I thought that there were two worlds in the world. And I could hardly believe it. Now I had got out into the bigger one.

My aunt taught me how to read Latvian. By the time I went to Riga I could read very well in Russian and Yiddish, but I preferred Russian. I learned quickly and my aunt was very pleased with me. I thought that I was a very grown-up person who had traveled in the world. I had been to a bazaar, I had been to Riga, and now I was living in a *dacha* on the Baltic Sea.

~ ~

In the autumn I went home but the following year we came again to Riga, all of us, on the way to Libaba, to leave for the United States.

My father had sent for us. We were excited, but also we were sorry to leave my grandfather. We used to talk, Zipora and I. And we'd say, "If only Zayde would come."

We asked him why he didn't come with us. "There's no room for old people in America," he said.

We had known, all those years, that some day my father was going to send for us. We never thought that we would go without Zayde. But now that the time came I was very excited. I was so happy that

I didn't mind leaving Zayde behind. In childhood nothing is forever.
I thought I would see him again. But when we were in America he
wrote to my mother. "Perle, I'm so lonely. I could die of loneliness."

And in fact he died. Two years later he died.

We went from Libaba to Liverpool on a small boat. In Liverpool
I saw two things that I had never seen before. In the place where we
stayed I saw the first thing. At home we only had kerosene lamps and
candles. Even in Riga I saw only kerosene lamps. But in the hotel
I saw something marvelous — light coming from the ceiling,
brighter than any light I'd ever seen. I stared at it and people said
it wasn't a kerosene lamp, it was a gaslight.

And the other new thing which I'll never forget: In Liverpool in
1914 I ate a banana for the first time.

From Liverpool we traveled steerage. Mama was very sick on that
boat. People were vomiting. It was hard to breathe. I remember how
crowded it was. Zipora and I were on one narrow cot and we slept
most of the time. We never saw the ocean and like Mama used to
say: "We barely came through."

But now I must tell you, that is all I remember about my childhood
in Russia. This I remember but nothing else. . . .

Oy, My Enlightenment

My mother's face is the face of a child. It refuses to give up its sense of the marvelous. She looks up, as if she could still see that light coming from the ceiling. Her white hair is curled and tousled. Her head tilted to one side, she seems to be listening to the echo of her own voice. And then, without warning, something happens to her face. To me, it seems that a great convulsion passes over her features. She does not move, even her breathing seems to have stopped and now, very slowly, a single tear moves down her cheek. She lifts her hand, wipes impatiently at this tear, and suddenly she is an old woman again.

But I cannot escape so easily from the past. I imagine myself walking through muddy streets. I carry heavy books beneath my arm; around the corner is a study house. And she says, interrupting my thoughts, "You are a woman. Don't you understand? In that world, you think you would have become a scholar?"

When I glance down I notice that my hands are taut, stretched out, straining. But something elusive is passing away from us. We cannot hold it, we are being driven into the present. I sense that something irretrievable has been lost. My mother wipes crumbs from the table into an ashtray. Gertrude, without saying a word, gets up and walks from the room. I shake myself past the feeling of desolation that tries to settle on me. And Larissa stretches out her legs, uncurling from the story's rapture. "Mama, I'm tired," she says, with a trace of irritation in her voice. And now my mother and I, uneasy, guilty mothers both of us, because we do not make our children the center of our lives, bustle into activity.

And so we enter the present together, making up the couch into a bed for Larissa and me to sleep in. My mother, invigorated by the story she has been telling, has regained that self I remember from my childhood, making this work into a game, organizing everything, going out of the room and returning with Larissa beside her, their arms piled high with pillows and sheets and blankets, marching as my mother chants, *"Raz, dva, tre, cheteri, piat, vwishel seitchik pagulyat,"* correcting Larissa's pronounciation, calling out to me, "Translate. Translate for your daughter."

"One, two, three, four," I shout, obedient to her high spirits, "the hunter went out hunting for a hare."

Now we are making the bed together, smoothing the sheet and tucking it with careful folds at the corners, while my mother discourses upon women and the making of beds. Listening, half-listening to her, I observe the way she never loses an opportunity for giving instruction. "My own mother," she says, "told me not to learn to cook or to sew. 'You'll marry a rich man? then you won't need it. If he's a poor man, better you don't know how to become his slave.' "

Now she is telling us, as the blanket flaps up into the air, and, laughing, we take hold of the corners and spread it out, the way the world is ordered by these smoothings and tuckings. The way, as I remind her, I needed her there at night when I was a child because no one else could tuck me in tightly enough. How, when she was arrested during the McCarthy time and went to jail, it seemed that my father, no matter how hard he tried, could not make the bed covers smooth, and could not braid my hair so that the braids were tight enough. The way, without her, things always seemed to come undone.

Now we pull the corners taut and slip them under the mattress. My mother passes her hand over the blanket and I recall how much I loved this gesture when I was a girl, believing it made sleep possible and kept it peaceful.

Larissa has been eager to join this conversation. She turns her head from me to my mother, watching our lips, waiting for an opportunity. The moment she begins to talk I restrain an impulse to reach out and clap my hand over her mouth.

"Grandma," she is saying, "Grandma, you know what Mama used to say?" My mother looks over at her with a heartbreaking eagerness, delighted that this reserved child is now so willing to confide in her. "It was a hot day," says Larissa. "Mama was helping me make my bed. But I didn't want to. I hated it, didn't I, Mama? And Mama said, 'Larissa, when I have to do something I don't like, I tell myself that if I take the right care with this work, and do it patiently, even this humble task could show me the way to enlightenment.'"

She looks up at us, her eyes full of the knowledge that she has become a storyteller for the first time in her life.

But my mother does not smile down at her as Larissa has expected. Instead, a silence comes up and we all fidget and feel uncomfortable. That word *enlightenment!* And I am embarrassed, too, by the way I am like and not like my mother, always seeking opportunity for instruction but drawing from it such different morals.

Larissa is growing angry. She looks up at me — I should take her side. And I realize just how hard it is to become a daughter of this family, never knowing when some chance word or expression will suddenly transform a happy mood and create this terrible abyss, the silence.

My mother says, "So this is the way you are raising your daughter?" But she does not wait for me to answer. Leaving us now with a quick kiss good-night, eager to avoid any friction between us, any disagreement, however slight.

Larissa is sitting straight up in bed. She is hurt and angry, I can tell, as she tugs on her red nightgown and turns her back to me, socking the pillows into place beneath her head. But when I sit down next to her I see that deep look in her eyes, which at such times are so much like the eyes of my mother. "Mama," she says, forgiving me, "do you think she was strange?"

"Who?" I ask, knowing perfectly well whom she means.

And then, because of this dishonesty, she casts a baleful look at me. "You know," she says, the judgment implacable, "who I mean."

These eyes run in our family. In the older world, my mother says, they were known as the eyes of the *macheschaefe,* the witch. But then,

I suspect, the word was never used lightly and I wonder what it means that my grandmother used it of my own mother, who has frequently used it of me.

"Well, do you?" she insists, as if this were a simple question. Was my grandmother peculiar already in the old country? Is that why her husband left her and went to America? Is that why she stayed so close to her father and never really wanted to leave home?

"It's not so easy," I say finally, hearing even more in this question than she asks. "When I was a little girl, growing up in the Bronx, I used to look for her every day on the park bench even though I knew she was already dead. You see what I mean? There was, in that woman's life, some feeling about the world that our own time has lost."

I watch her face as the words settle. She does not at first know what they mean, but she is comforted by the fact that I am being philosophical. Then, the words seem to reach a place where her understanding is larger than she is. For an instant she glances again into my eyes, touching a carefully guarded place few people are able to reach. And then something closes inside her, locking the words away. Later, they will become her conscious knowledge. For now they are simply the guarantee that understanding is possible.

She shakes herself, swallows once or twice, and begins to hum. She is folding a small piece of paper, her hands skillful the way the hands of my mother and myself have never been. She seems to have forgotten completely about me and looks up surprised at my gasp of astonishment as she unfolds a perfect bird from the scrap of newspaper with which she has been working. It is a skill her great-grandmother might have taught her, sitting next to the tiled stove in that vanished house in the little village, telling her how the windows must be left open at night so that the restless evil spirits can escape.

These old stories, which she has never heard, live in her eyes. Looking at her I understand why I must have frightened my mother when I was a child. We all have eyes that see into the far side of things which people prefer to keep hidden.

Absorbed in her folding and tearing, Larissa moves her lips silently as she creates these elusive paper beings who have made a menagerie of our bed. The bird with its bemused, quizzical expression; the grave innocence of this angel who seems to know everything although he has experienced nothing; the little house that stands at the edge of a crease that stands for a river. Is she creating a little shtetl on our bed, into which we ourselves can now enter, so that I shall not have to continue to feel this loneliness, this futile nostalgia, this sense of loss?

She lifts her head. For an instant I see my mother's face, turned to the ceiling, beholding light. "Not yet, not yet," I whisper absurdly to myself, afraid that she will wake up from her reverie and become an old woman. But she does not reach up impatiently to cast away her childhood. Very carefully, setting down a rocking chair next to the little house wobbling on her bed, she says to me, "Tell me, Mama," with precisely the tone and expression I used as a child. "Tell me," she repeats, musing so deeply, "could someone living now do something as great as Einstein did?"

"Well," I say, "yes, I suppose so." But suddenly her question impresses me through its urgency.

"Could I, Mama? Is it still possible? Could I, do you think?"

This girl sleeps with a picture of Einstein over her bed, riding his bicycle through the stone courtyard at the California Institute of Technology.

And so I think, urgently now, does one feel in this girl that capacity she asks of? And then I give up trying to reach this knowledge. I let something in myself which knows these things answer her. "Yes," I say to her, "it is possible for you." And I see, in the look she casts into me now, that a lie here, the slightest failure to know or to report truly, would have cost me this closeness with her forever.

"Good," she says, reaching out to smooth a village square in front of the synagogue where the angel rests haphazardly. "I hoped it would be."

It is one of those moments between people, and I have known them frequently, when something is asked, something tested, a barrier falls and one passes or fails, is deemed worthy, or is closed out from this sort of vulnerable communion forever. That is the kind of girl she is. And I am the same sort of woman.

She puts her head on my lap. "Perle," she says in that dreamy voice she has not used for years. "And after Perle came Rochele. And after Rochele, Elke. And then came Larissa."

She stretches out, turning over the little house in the shtetl, crushing the innocent angel, pinching the wing of the quizzical bird I have wanted to keep forever, out of the reach of this sort of holocaust. And now, satisfied that her future will be large enough to accommodate the forces she feels stirring inside her, she reaches out and flattens the rocking chair, wiping away a past that has always refused to belong to me. But I understand her. I put my hand on her head and in a moment she is asleep.

But now, of course, my mother comes back down the hall. The door opens, she peeks in and nods vigorously, pleased that I, too, have not been able to sleep. She sits down next to me on the bed, careful not to disturb Larissa. "My mother," she says and then drops her voice to a whisper, "my mother used to start first thing in the morning with the beds." The memory, pushing against some obstacle I cannot see, passes furiously over her face. She gazes around her absently for a moment or two and then picks up the crumpled pieces of paper that so recently were a world. Very carefully now she begins to smooth them out, unfolding them, returning them to their state of pure potential.

"That," she says, her voice rising, "was after we left the shtetl. So forgive me, I am ahead of my story. Then, when we were living in Waterbury, she had not only our beds, and Lillian's bed, but she had also the beds from the boarders. So think. What would it mean to this woman if you would say to her, Do every little task in that certain way which makes it perfect? Of course, maybe I don't know what you mean by enlightened," she says, interrupting herself and looking at me with an expression intended to leave no doubt she knows perfectly well what this word means to me. "But I can tell you," she continues, "just what an oppression this would be to my mother, who was still working on those beds when we got home from school. And maybe she tried to cook dinner for us, maybe she tried to clean the house, and of course it was hard for her, she never liked it and now she was always confused. And so those beds, I tell you, were always there . . ."

Larissa ceases to pretend that she is still asleep. She sits up in bed, throws her arms around my mother, and begins to rock her in her arms. My mother looks down at her, startled, suspicious and then, as she takes in the expression on her face, triumphant. "Ha," she says and picks up a corner of the blanket. She holds it up in the air and gazes at it reverently. "Oy, my enlightenment," she chants, winking at my daughter, "how shall I fold you so that you will never come out from your fold again?"

Larissa loves it. Ignoring me, she shakes the pillow out of its case and wags her head at my mother. "Oy, my enlightenment," she chokes out, bent double with laughter.

I sit here, waiting to argue for my point of view, wanting to keep my mother from winning over my daughter, but knowing if I remain serious now, I shall look even smaller, more absurd. And finally, it does not seem to matter so much as I watch them undoing this bed we made up so carefully an hour ago. It was, after all, for this I brought her to visit my mother, was it not? This girl who, less than a year ago, did not know her grandmother was born in a shtetl.

"Oy, my enlightenment," Larissa is chanting wildly to herself, shaking a pillow over her head. And now, glancing quickly from my mother to me, she picks up her cue. "Grandma," she says, in a voice grown fully conscious of the part it is to play; "Grandma, tell me a story," she shouts, lost to all memory of reserve and caution, as we settle down together in the fine disorder of the bed.

The Second Story My Mother Tells
America, the Early Years (1914–1920)

*D*id I ever tell you about my Papa? Did I ever tell you about that man? To this day, I think about him and I make a fist.

We came to the United States through Ellis Island. There, for the first time in five years, we put our eyes on him. My brother Mikhail had never seen him. How could he know who this man was? He was born a few months after Papa left us. And the rest of us didn't remember. We just looked at him and we waited to see what would be. To us he was a stranger. Mama said, "Here is your papa." And we looked.

When we cleared customs he took us to the Jeromes, who were his distant cousins. If I told you they were living in a mansion you wouldn't believe me. And you would be right. They were just poor people living in Brooklyn. But I thought we had walked into a palace for the czar.

I remember we had chopped herring and something that was red. It was cut up and none of us knew what it was. But I, as the eldest, took a taste of it. The herring I knew and remembered. But the other thing, the red thing, made me want to vomit. I was ashamed to vomit. I couldn't swallow it. It was a tomato.

Then my father took us to our home, in Staten Island. That was a nice apartment and we had come to live now in the United States.

I remember the first night in America. There was a bedroom for my mother and father and one for the four children. In our room there were only three cots. Your Aunt Gertrude was supposed to sleep with me. But she wanted to sleep with my mother, the way she had always done. She was a spoiled child and very ill-tempered. If somebody crossed her she threw herself on the floor and screamed. And Mama, who could never say no to anyone, would always give her whatever she wanted.

But that time my father took one look at her, gave her a beating, and threw her into our room. She went to sleep sobbing in my bed. I felt very sorry for her, but what could I do? She fell asleep. And I am witness to this: she has never lost her temper again. He broke her spirit. Never again in childhood, never again in adulthood. She never stood up to anything or anybody. And I tell you this, you my children, I date her character back to this first night. After that, she was a good girl, self-denying, always giving to others.

I was happy with America. No, it was something more. I was enamored. In the apartment there was running water, a toilet inside. My father bought us clothes. In America everything was new. There were pavements on the street. It was just like Zayde said: there were no old people in America. There was more sun in America. Everything was painted in America. We were in love with this shining world.

Then I went to school. You remember, I could read and write in Russian and Yiddish. I knew a little Latvian. But here in America I was put in the first grade. Before now, always, I was proud of my learning. I knew arithmetic, I knew history, I knew many things. But none of this I knew in English. There I was sitting, eleven years old, in a room with six-year-old children. I felt ashamed.

My father gave us American names. Now we were Rose and Celia, Gertrude and Milton. We put away Rochele, Zipora, Gita, and Mikhail. Can you imagine? Calling a Rochele a Rose? I didn't recognize myself. I didn't know who this Rose was. But it passed, all of it, very quickly. I had a teacher at school, Miss Sullivan, who started to teach me English. I imagine she felt sorry for me and she said, "Stay after school, I'll speak to you and you'll learn."

After that, Russia vanished. Everything from before went out of my life. I went from the first grade into the seventh.

In Staten Island, during those years, there weren't many Jews. We could never understand why my father went to live there. When we arrived he had a horse and carriage and he was selling kerosene. My mother stayed in the house. My father never took her out with him, never. So how could she adjust to life in the United States? Everything was new to her and there was nobody to show her anything. She didn't know how to do the housework. Everything was different, she had no one to speak with, she was overwhelmed. All this that to us seemed a paradise, to her was a living hell. The cousins Jerome were very critical of her. They looked down upon her. They called her "the green one." I think she suspected that one woman there, in Brooklyn, was in love with Papa. Mama was so unhappy that she attempted suicide. She tried to drink kerosene; they took her to the hospital and she was gone for a long time.

We weren't told it was suicide, but we knew. Children know. I especially as the oldest knew. My father's sister, our Aunt Gita, who was a single woman, came to take care of us. When my mother came back from the hospital, we preferred Gita, our aunt. She knew how to do things. She could cook and she knew how to press. In America my mother seemed completely helpless. She missed her father and her life in Russia. She came here and she was a nobody. Nobody cared about her and Papa hated her. We kids were mean to her, too. We couldn't sympathize with her; we preferred our aunt and our aunt encouraged us against our mother. From the time we came to this country it was unmitigated misery in our home.

But children get used to their conditions. We forgot it could be different. We already had forgotten Zayde. With our new clothes and our new names should we go weeping into the past? That we left to Mama.

We discovered a way to make joy. Sometimes, on a Sunday, my mother or my aunt would pack a lunch for us. Five cents for the trolley bought us a transfer to the ferry that crossed into New York. It went past the Statue of Liberty. No American, born in this country, could know the impression seeing this beautiful woman for the first time. We would crowd to the side of the boat, each time, to see her again. We felt she had been put there for us, we thought she was ours. There was a band on the boat and we could stay there the whole day. We went back and forth, all Sunday, from nine o'clock in the morning until three in the afternoon.

We easily got used to life in America, but the misery in our home we could never get used to. My father beat my mother. Always he would yell at her. There were terrible scenes. My father would tell her to make breakfast and she would make breakfast for him. If he didn't like the way the coffee tasted he'd throw all the dishes off the table. She would never sit down and eat at the table with him. She ate afterwards. She tried to cook only the way he liked. But he beat her for the least thing. She was a gentle person and he broke her spirit. He broke her mind.

She was the sort of woman who could not stand to hear raised voices. The only thing she would ever say to us was, "Children, stop, my head is coming apart from your shouting." We were four kittens, so we'd play hard, we'd fight and wrestle and she'd say, always gently, "Shah, Papa's coming." And then we were quiet.

That we turned out, each of us, the way we did is a tribute to our fortitude. We could have gone any old way. Nobody would care. My mother couldn't care anymore. In two years she was destroyed.

We stayed in Staten Island for only three years and then my father decided to move. He wanted to send Mama and Celia and me back to our grandfather in Russia. It was his decision and Mama agreed. The tickets were bought and then we couldn't travel because of the First World War. The whole family went to Connecticut instead. We were children; no one consulted us. But speaking for Celia and myself, we would have gone back happily to Russia. We already hated my father. The longer we knew him the more there was to hate.

We went to a small city called Waterbury. It was a war manufacturing city, a brass city. It went into the war industries and became very prosperous. Papa got a store and sold dry goods to the workers. By that time I was already fourteen years old. I had graduated from public school, and I went to work in the factory. I got workers papers and went to work as an inspector on the assembly line.

No one questioned the necessity of working for a living. Coming from our background, we were happy when we could find work. This was good fortune, the reason we came to America. But I didn't like it. I could not accept the factory for my life. I tried going to school at night but after ten hours in the factory I would fall asleep in my class. We always had to help Mama at home. She could never manage by herself. From the moment I woke up, early, early in the morning, there was something to do.

We never stopped, we never rested. In the factory they were pushing us, trying to keep the war production going at a fast pace. I would look up from the assembly line; I saw all those people bending over it, their hands flying. Nobody walked, everybody scurried. I, too, hurried; I rushed back from the factory, I helped my mother at home with the younger children, I grabbed something to eat, I went off to night school. By then I'd been on my feet, rushing, working, hurrying through the day, for more than twelve hours. I was fourteen years old.

Finally, I had to give it up. But I couldn't forget the idea of going to school. The idea never left me. My father, of course, did not want me to go to school. But I had already learned not to be intimidated by my father. He might beat my mother but I would never let him lay a hand on me.

My mother found it easier when I started to work. I was earning twenty-nine dollars a week. The wages were high for those times. There were no deductions, except for war bonds. They were a form of savings. So, I was taking home about twenty-five dollars a week for five and a half days' work. Naturally, I gave the money to my mother for the family. "Now we can live a little," she said.

I loved my mother, I wanted to help her. I would lie awake at night and remember those fists beating at her, breaking her down. Destroying her. And I knew it would not be me. I would not be my mother and no child of mine would be my mother. I would see to it. But that work was eating up my life. I never thought of playing, my childhood was over, school was over, I was afraid I would forget how to read. Each night, before I went to bed, I made certain I read something. A page, two paragraphs. Only not to forget.

The factories in Waterbury at that time were producing ammunition twenty-four hours a day. Mama rented out our bedrooms to the night-shift workers. When we would get up in the morning they would go into our beds. The months passed, our lives took on a pattern.

In bed I would sit with my book, falling asleep on the first pages.

I remember, one night, I saw my sister asleep. What time was it? Not yet eight o'clock. Suddenly, I was filled with anger. I could not accept this life.

"Celia," I said, shaking her by the shoulder. "Wake up. Read. We can't afford to sleep."

Here, you might ask, what did I know about another way to live? Among us, everybody lived that way. Maybe, even, I should be happy to have this work, so that Mama and the children wouldn't starve. Then came my break. Because of the shortage of labor, they needed high-school children in war industries. They shortened the school day so the students could get out by one o'clock from school and still put in a full day at the factory. It was a grueling schedule, let me tell you. But when I heard about it I knew my chance had come. There were other girls in the factory who could have had this same break. But they didn't take it. This fact I think about even today.

So I went down to register at Crosby. It was the college-preparatory high school. Very high up. I put on my best clothes. From Celia I borrowed gloves. When I got there I talked to the principal. "I'm a factory worker," I said. "I want to go into the high school." But then suddenly I lost my nerve. He was looking at me. "Maybe," I said, "I should go over and register at Welby." Welby was the commercial school. I felt I was stepping beyond myself.

Meanwhile, he's giving a long look at me. And he says, "Go into Crosby."

I will never forget it. I looked up at him. I said, "I don't have money for college."

"Listen to me, young lady. You came to this country in 1914. (This was 1917.) If you can learn English the way you did, you don't know what will happen in four years. You're an intelligent girl. Go to school. Maybe some good luck will make it possible for you to go to college."

I, Rose Chernin, go to college? Think who I was. An immigrant girl, fourteen years old, a factory worker, without a future. But now I stood there. In the office of an American high school. I heard the possibility I might go to college.

I didn't mind the factory, believe me, after that. But I was still hurrying. I had fifteen minutes to cross the gate. I used to run and eat my sandwich and cross the gate as the whistle blew. The man who was at the gate would say, "I couldn't hold it a minute longer. I knew you were coming. Now we can close the gate."

In this way I went to school and I could still earn the twenty-five dollars a week. You think my father gave us money? We never knew what he did with his money and by that time, let me tell you, we never cared. All we wanted was for him to leave Mama alone. One day, finally, I said to him, "If you ever hit my mother again I am going to hit you back."

He looked at me; he was not a big man but he had mean eyes.

I said, "If I hold a knife at that time you'll get it if you lay a hand on her." In that moment I knew I could do anything.

"Just try," he said. "Just you try it."

But I saw something in his eyes. It moved, behind the eyelids. Fear? My father afraid of me?

I made a big fist out of my hand. "Papa," I said, "don't you worry. You lift up again a hand against Mama and I will lift up my hand against you."

After that childhood everything was easy. Nobody could break me. I knew, even as a child, that this would be so. Mama used to say, "We don't have to worry. Let the ones worry who are up there. We are way below and we can't fall farther."

By that time I had already met your father. He and his brother Max were in the same school with my sister Celia and me. We all lived on the same block and often we went to school together. There was no dating in those days, but Max Kusnitz and Paul Kusnitz and their cousins the Milenkis and Celia and I would walk to school.

Paul Kusnitz was three years older than me, already a senior in high school when I was a freshman. And a senior doesn't bother much with a freshman, of course. But because we were neighbors and we were Jewish, and our families both came from Russia, and because my mother was a friend of his mother, this walking together occurred. We very seldom talked together. The girls walked by themselves and the boys walked alongside or in back of us.

But one day Paul Kusnitz suddenly asks me if I'd be interested in reading something. He came right up to me and gave me some material. It was the *New York Call.* He stood next to me and he said, "You ought to read this."

So I said, "What kind of paper is this?"

"It's a socialist paper," he told me and then he was gone, into the school with the Milenkis. The next time I saw him he was silent again.

So I read the paper. Why not? It made sense to me. For the first time I learned that there were classes. I found out that there were people struggling for a better system than capitalism. I told Paul Kusnitz what I thought and he gave me a pamphlet by Upton Sinclair. I read it too and I thought, Is this socialism? To me, socialism was just common sense.

By that time I had already noticed that your father had a twinkle in his eyes. He was a very handsome boy. All the Kusnitz boys were good looking. And they liked to have fun. Their father owned a butcher store and all the brothers used to work in it. You could walk by outside and hear them laughing. To me, this was something very special. A happy family.

I thought of myself as a very homely girl. I never had an explanation for why Paul Kusnitz paid attention to me. Even today what would I say? Maybe he thought I was intelligent? But when you think about it, how would he know? There we were, Celia and I, two Jewish girls walking together to school. And Celia was a beauty. So why should he talk to me and not to Celia?

One day I overheard my mama talking. She had some friends; there was tea and she had made some cookies and I was listening from my own room. She was telling her friends, *"Bei mir iz di schenste di letzte."* (In my family the good looking ones are the last born.) She meant Gertrude and Celia. I listened to this and I started to cry. When the people went away she says to me, "Why are you crying?"

"Because of what you said. That I'm no beauty."

And she says, *"Ober du bist a kluge."* (You're an intelligent girl.)

And I said, sobbing, "I don't want to be clever; I want to be a beauty."

Well, one day Paul Kusnitz comes again. This time he asks me to go with him to hear a conscientious objector who would lecture, a woman speaker named Kate Richards O'Hare, who had served some time in prison. She was coming to speak in the workers' hall and I decided right away I would go with him. From the moment Paul Kusnitz mentioned this woman I thought about nothing else. I felt,

Something is coming here, something from the world, to this little town.

Finally, the night arrived. And there came with it one of those moments. That was how long ago? Sixty years? But still I remember. Even the yellow sweater Paul Kusnitz wore. It was the excitement that made this memory. The terrible excitement.

All my life people have asked me how or why did I become Communist. They ask you questions like that, they really wonder. And sometimes you think they are asking, How did you become this monster? And you want to be able to answer them, to tell them about this proud life you have lived, this life as a Communist. But I have never really known how to answer them. Even to you, my daughter and my granddaughter, what can I say? It just made sense.

So the night arrived. We walked into that meeting and it was packed. It was the first time in my life I heard the voice of a radical woman. It stirred me. I sat at the edge of my seat. I held my breath. I didn't want to miss a word. Who ever heard of such a woman before? I wanted to be just like her. And I thought I could be. Her dedication. This struggle to make a better world for people. That interested me all the time I was in high school. I could not stand any injustice. In the pamphlets Paul Kusnitz gave me I began to see how the people were exploited. I found out something could be done about it. Kate Richards O'Hare became for me the symbol of what I wanted to be. A woman who stands up to injustice. I sat there, and I thought, why shouldn't I be a woman like this? What is to stop me?

And she said, "Considering that we are political prisoners, we are treated terribly. Some conditions in American prisons might well compare to those in Russia."

That was Saturday night. On Sunday the Waterbury papers wrote up the story. They said that Kate Richards O'Hare was in town and had said that the prisons of this country were worse than the Russian prisons of Siberia.

On Monday, our principal, Mr. McDonald, called an assembly. When he came in and started speaking, we knew what was going to be. He said there was a radical socialist, a subversive woman, an ex-convict, who came to our town and spoke in the workers' hall. He said some high-school students were in the audience. And he assumed they were from Crosby High. He went on, "It is a disgrace to have high-school students go to this kind of a meeting."

I sat silently, letting him talk. But then he said, "And do you know what they do at these socialist meetings? This woman had the gall to say that the prisons in America are worse than those in Siberia."

That I couldn't stand anymore. I couldn't sit still. I raised up my hand; everyone turned to look at me. I stood up: "Mr. McDonald, she did not say this."

He looked at me with astonishment: "Were you there?"

"Yes, I was there."

"Who else was there?"

"I didn't see anybody else."

"You didn't see any students from Crosby?"

"I don't know all the Crosby students. But I am here to tell you the papers did not tell the truth about Kate Richards O'Hare."

That was a moment. In it what comes after is already there. Character shows itself. At the time you have no idea of this. Thinking back you realize. Was it for nothing Paul Kusnitz came up to you? Was it for nothing you responded to the *Call?* Was it an accident you stood up there in the school assembly? An immigrant girl, standing up to the principal?

So of course, after the assembly, we are going back to class and everyone is looking at me as we are going down the hall. And the word spreads: "Rose, he wants you in the office."

I went over there; I thought the doorknob was very large, it was stiff and I could hardly turn it. But I went in and I talked to him. At first, he just asked me who else was there at the meeting. But I wouldn't tell him. So he started asking me what Kate Richards O'Hare had said. I told him what I had heard at the meeting and he asked me, "So why do you think the papers didn't report it this way?"

"What do I know? Who believes what they read in the papers?"

He told me he was going to suspend me from school. And he added, "I'm really disappointed in you. A girl who could come to this country, go through public school, and learn English in three years. You should know better than to support a subversive. You are suspended. Bring your father to school."

Bring my father to school? My father? I figured it was all over. I would be in the factory forever. What could I do? Not for anything, not even for school, would I give him the names from the others.

I ran home. I waited for my father. In our house he was always complaining. We would hear him whenever anything was going wrong. "My daughters," he would say, "my daughters had to get an education." You would think our education was something we were doing against him, to shame him maybe. The minute he comes into the house I go up to him. I was desperate. What did I have to lose? But now, what do you think? He comes to school with me, right then, before the day is over. And he is boiling, with his bad temper, really boiling.

He said, "That's the kind of country it is. They talk about their free speech. And if you went to a Ku Klux Klan meeting would you be suspended then?"

My father was not a radical man. He was bitter, disappointed with his life. It is not this which makes a radical. Because for that you need to believe in something.

And so we came to the principal and I am asked to wait outside. He goes in there, and he is hitching up his trousers the way he does when he is angry. He is blowing his nose. But still I did not expect what was to happen. And then I hear my father screaming. I can't hear a word of what the principal is saying but my father's voice is coming down the hall: "You're going way out of your responsibility here, Mr. McDonald. Don't you assume responsibility for my children when they're not in school. Maybe you think I'm only an ignorant man. What do I know about America, you think? This much I know. I gave her permission to go. And let me tell you, this girl is an A student. Unless you prove to me and to the authorities she isn't a good student you are not going to suspend her. And this you wouldn't be able to prove."

It was the only time in my life I felt affection for my father. The first time I saw his terrible temper turned to help me. Why did he come to school? For this nobody could give you an answer. He walks home with me and under his breath I hear him grumbling. "My daughter," he is saying, "my daughter had to get an education."

We had a straw vote in our class during election year. We voted secretly, of course, the way you must in America, but the teacher reported the voting in this way: "Seventy students are Republicans," she said. "Thirteen are Democrats and Rose Chernin is a socialist."

I leaped to my feet. I said to her, "Pardon me, Miss Smythe, but you sure believe in the secret ballot, don't you?"

Well, a few months after this it was said in our yearbook that Rose Chernin will surely run for president.

One day my father left us. He sold his store to an auctioneer and left for Pennsylvania where those Jerome relatives were living. He never wrote to us, he never made an effort to contact us. By then, a fourth girl, Lillian, was born in our family. There were five children at home now and Lillian was only a baby. At first, it was just terrible, and especially for me as the eldest. Onto my shoulders came now the responsibility for Mama and the children. How long had we been in the country by then? Five years? So consider.

Mama had to take in work that could be done at home. She was making handles for suitcases. Each morning she went out and brought back the raw materials from the factory. We would help her wrap the handles. But then something happened. In our house suddenly it became pleasant. The kids came in from the neighborhood, they would go sit down at a big gray table and help with the handles. My mother would go down into the cellar and bring up some apples and milk. We told jokes, we laughed. The work got done. Mama began to seem better now that Papa was away.

When my father was gone, Mama would sit down with us and tell stories. She had a special way of talking, her own wisdom. We never knew this about our mama when my father was there. "Children," she'd say, "you see this apple? This apple is the same one from which Eve gave to Adam a bite to eat." "Mama," we'd shout, "how can you say this? You know how long ago this was? You think this really happened?" "Don't tell me," she'd answer. "Just listen. In every weed is growing the garden of Eden. You only should have the eyes to look."

So time passed. We were managing to live. We were growing older. Celia and I were thinking already about what will be after high school. But what could we do about Mama and the children? Gertrude, next to us in age, was still a girl. From her, of course, was never a word of complaint. She helped Mama in the house, she took care of Milton and Lillian. By this time already she kept nothing for herself. A piece of fruit came into her hand and right away, what did she do? She slipped it into the pocket of one of the children. So how could we go off and leave the family to Gertrude?

Then, one day I learned that Papa was in Canonsville. Right away I went to see him. I looked, after all this time, into that mean face of his. "So what's new," he says to me. By then I knew my way around in America.

I said, "You take back the family or you're going to jail."

If he didn't care for me, that was a small feeling next to the way I thought about him. And so we stood there. It wasn't the first time.

"You're going to jail," I said. "Here, in America, is a law. I will send you to jail. Do you hear me? I will do it if you don't come back and take care of them."

What can you do with such a man? If I threw him into jail would that help Mama?

"Take them to Canonsville," I said. "You are the responsible one. You want to bury Celia and me with the responsibility for the family?"

He says nothing. He stands there and he thinks maybe if he stands there long enough I'll go out the door. I stand there too. He's not looking at me. Finally, I said, "That's settled then. You'll take them."

Still nothing. "But don't think," I start to shout, "I'm coming to Canonsville with them. Celia and I are going to stay in high school. We won't interrupt our high school. You understand? We won't interrupt."

Well, he took the family to Canonsville and that was my mistake. I should have done what I did not know how to do. I should have made him give support and keep away from us. But maybe I did what was easier for me? I want to be honest. Here we sit, three generations. I want to be truthful with you. There was a lot involved in my going to Canonsville. I could have given up school. Celia could have given up school. We could have managed after my father left. But we wanted to continue with our life. We wanted nothing to interfere with our education. We felt that unless he came back and took his responsibilities with his family, we would be trapped forever.

Do you know what it's like, ten hours a day, looking at shells in a noisy, dirty plant? You turn over a shell, this way, that way, until your mind goes blank. And always you're waiting for the break, the five-minute break to go to the toilet. This became the one meaningful thing in the ten hours of the day. You felt that there had to be another way. I thought, with the naïveté of a child, that to get an education, a high-school education, would give me a job in an office. In an office! When we crossed the yard into the factory, we passed the offices. I looked at those girls, sitting there, cleanly dressed at their desks. And I thought, There is another world.

After the family moved to Canonsville, Celia and I went to live with some classmates. And now let me tell you in this house we were happy. But soon we began to learn that in Canonsville Mama had hell on earth. A few years after she arrived there, the Ku Klux Klan burned a cross on the hill opposite my father's store. They didn't want Jews in that town. For Mama, it was the same story all over again. For her it was again like leaving Russia and moving to America. In Waterbury she had the other immigrant women. She knew her neighbors, she could talk Yiddish. On our street she was admired for her stories, for the jam she made. But in Canonsville my mother broke down and my father committed her to the insane asylum. And now I'll tell you, you who are a writer. She had tried to commit suicide again. She drank ink.

Our lives were separate from the family now. Mama's life was terrible. But ours? Ours was just heaven on earth. We accepted this. We were young then. Do you blame me? A young person doesn't think so much about these things. I never said to myself, Maybe I put myself before Mama so that Celia and I could have our own life. This home we were living in with the Milenki girls, it was what we had never known before. It was the same thing you could imagine from the Kusnitz family if you went into the butcher store. Here there was a piano, classical music was an ordinary part of the day. You might ask, what did I know about music or a piano? It is a good question. Celia and I had no experience of culture at the time. Yet somehow I recognized this was a finer thing. When I lived in that house I had the same impression I once had, years before, when I went to visit the family in Riga. And I knew that nothing would ever make me go back to the family. Do you blame me? Not even Mama's letters. Not even what he was doing to Mama. No, I tell you. Not even that. . . .

Do This for Me, Rose

*T*here is coughing in the back of the house, that unnerving wheeze and gasping for breath of the smoker who suffers from emphysema. My mother looks at me with an unguarded, imploring expression, a movement into helplessness I have not seen in her face before. And now she slips her hand through my arm. She reaches out to take Larissa's hand, murmuring "Larochka, darling." She needs our support for what confronts us at the back of the house.

"Oy," she says, as we walk down the corridor, "what did she do to deserve it? This one, a saint, giving everything she had to others."

It is Larissa who enters first. I see her striding in ahead of us, carried by the wave of feeling that rose up out of my mother's story. But suddenly her whole body seems to contract itself and to spring violently together as she stops a safe distance from her great-aunt's bed, terrified of the skeletal arm that lies visibly withering on the quilt.

My mother stands behind me as I sit down on the edge of Gertrude's bed. The skin around her throat is puckered and yellow, with a dry, dull look to it, as if in this part of herself she had already died. It is difficult now for her to draw a single clear breath. When she exhales, the bones in her chest rise up, prematurely skeletal. But it is her hands that betray the greatest eloquence. They are, unmistakably, the hands of a nurse and they carry the story of her life's long sacrifice. In them, I see the history of beds turned, heads lifted, pillows straightened, bedpans emptied, all the patient heroisms of her compassion. This is a woman I have loved since I was a small girl. Now she is dying and I am afraid.

Gertrude's hand tightens on the cover. The knuckles turn white and my mother reaches out convulsively. Moving swiftly, I catch my mother's hand. And now we see Gertrude opening out her arms; very, very slowly, they begin to rise until they come to rest a few inches above the bed. "Like Mama," my mother mutters beneath her breath. And then she turns her head away, as this whole, trembling gesture of adoration suddenly collapses, shaken down by another violent spasm of coughing.

Fascinated, I look down, watching the expressions that flow over my aunt's face. For a moment, it seems to me that she is very lonely, as she lies there with her eyes closed, the lashes quivering. But then the loneliness turns into a rapt and violent watching.

"Gita," my mother says, in a soft voice, uncertain if she is sleeping. But I know that my aunt is looking intently at something she does not with to share with us.

Is it possible to be curious about death? No one ever told me it was possible. Larissa comes to stand next to me, a few inches from Aunt Gertrude's bed. I regard this daughter of mine with some surprise, her face set and determined, that grim line tightening around her mouth which one day will make her look like my mother. She leans forward to give my aunt the pink tablets that will suppress her coughing.

My mother twists the cloth napkin she has picked up from Gertrude's bedside table. She stands helpless, wishing to say something, her hand fluttering over to my shoulder. She, too, is passing through a confrontation with death; she, too, will be altered by it. But it is I who hold the eyes of my aunt when they open and begin to search our faces, moving anxiously from one face to the next.

Time changes, it slows perceptibly and then it vanishes. My aunt's eyes fix me with interrogation. In silence she asks, in silence I answer. My eyes say, willing this: "I'm here. Try me."

Now Aunt Gertrude looks up at my mother. She looks so imploringly into her face that I see she believes my mother has the power to impart to her some of her own life force. And my mother, overcoming her fear, which makes her stand rigid a few inches behind me, bends down. She takes Gertrude's hand from mine and presses it against her own breast, in one of those gestures which remind me just how deeply feeling a heart moves this woman of iron discipline.

We are not crying; we are unwilling to allow ourselves that relief. Aunt Gertrude's body is wracked with another spasm of violent coughing. My mother reaches out for a glass of water, and my aunt's hand tightens so fiercely against my own I must battle within myself not to cry out in protest.

And now we have surrounded her with love; the glass of water is at her lips, a hand is clasped in a hand, a head supported, eyes meet and hold, the head that is dying is brought into a living circle of care. Comforted, she lies back upon the pillow again and her eyes move from one face to the next, still searching for someone who should be there and is not.

My mother bends down and whispers something to her. It seems to me I hear my name and then I hear the name Vida. And now I see the effect of these words pass across Gertrude's face. It looks as if someone had been hacking away at a knot in her, trying to make it bleed so that the life force can then flow on beyond this obstruction. My mother is a brave woman; she will say what everyone is terrified of hearing and this utterance will often prove to be everyone's release. For a moment the look on Gertrude's face is so terrible I close my eyes. And when I open them again Gertrude has sunk back into indifference. Now it is my mother's face, turning toward me, which makes me want to look away. She is trying too hard, she is offering Gertrude something impossibly difficult for her to give, she is being exhausted by this death and does not have the temperament to deal with it.

When I look at her now, her face pinched, her dark eyes huge and staring, I see a small girl. It is for only an instant and the vision is gone. But there remains in my mother's face, as she looks down at her sister, all that the little girl once saw when she was still too young to fight against it. Terrified, she watches her mother lift up her arms over her head, crying out for help, while her father moves down upon her. And she, this child who grew up to become a Communist, stands there helpless.

We go out into the hall. My mother says to me, "She wants you to have the Indian bowls she brought back from Chile. She loves you so much, you know." And I begin to understand the hidden tragedy that is occurring here. For where is she? Vida. This daughter who was always so close to her mother. What does it mean that she is absent now as her mother lies dying? My eye falls upon the rubbing from a temple door in Thailand. And yes, my mother says, "She wants you to have this, too. She knows how much you would cherish it."

Here we stop and look at one another; I see that I am supposed to understand what she is not supposed to tell me. And Larissa says, as if she were party to some privileged source of information: "Grandma has given you to Aunt Gertrude."

For a moment, stunned, I am aware of nothing but my daughter's brilliance. But then, glancing at the acknowledgment in my mother's face, I become fully aware of what has just happened.

I, the storyteller, have become the daughter to this dying woman. It is I now who will take up the burden of memory. I will tell the stories her daughter would have told, if she could afford to remember.

But now Aunt Gertrude calls out, her voice strong and vigorous, as if she had by some supreme effort of will suddenly put death on hold. "Tell her, Rose," she shouts, "tell her the story of our sister Celia." And then she says, in a voice grown dreadfully weary, so that I imagine her whole life now repeats its sacrifice, its typical gesture, "Do this for me, Rose. Do this for me."

The Third Story My Mother Tells
A Larger World (1920–1928)

Why she wants me to tell you about Celia who can say? For all of us my sister was the most fascinating person. Gertrude we admired. Milton was a brilliant boy. And Lillian, for us, was always the baby. But Celia was like no one else. When I was leaving Waterbury, going off to New York, the hard part was leaving Celia.

My sister was a beautiful girl. Elegant. From our little salary (and of course we were still sending money to Mama) she would always manage to save out a bit. This she spent, all of it, on clothes. How, you might ask, would this immigrant girl from a small town know about fashion? Somehow she knew. She'd come out of the factory and put on her gloves. She had a little round hat, tipped to the front of her head. Like a queen she went. If Mama would catch sight of her she'd say, "This one somebody put by mistake into my cradle."

Now I was going to New York. Celia was to live with the family in Canonsville, to finish her education and get a teacher's certificate. Of course we intended she would come to join me later. But Celia, naturally, didn't want to go back to the family. The last night in Waterbury she said, "Rose, take me with you. We'll work. We'll get an apartment. I can't go back to them; I'm not like you, Rose, I can't fight with Papa. Let me go, too."

"Celia," I said, "you listen to me. If you go to New York you'll never finish high school. What will become of you?"

With this, of course, nobody could argue. We were in our room, lying each in her own bed. After a while I turned away from her and put out my light. But I did not sleep one minute all that night.

Why did I tell you this story? This is why. If I would let myself feel sorry for my mother, if I would let myself feel sorry for my sister, would I have gone out of that little town? You draw the conclusion. This is what it took for a girl like me to leave the family and go to New York.

New York was something everybody talked about. Everyone knew someone there; and in those days a cousin was someone you could go to. They lived in one room? They put up a curtain. They had a potato for dinner? They cut it in half for you. It wasn't sentiment. It was survival. So everyone was talking, after school, at work in the factory, someday they are going to New York. Someday they are going.

Now it's a funny thing, and this you should think about. Because not everyone went. I was the first in our little circle of friends; and Celia came after me.

But now what follows is not really about Celia. Gertrude, I know, wants you to hear about her. What I became, what she became, it's all one story. And why Gertrude wants you to know is part of the story, too. But to you I say, if you want to understand my sister's tragedy, you have to know the choices I, as the eldest, was making. I left Waterbury, I left my mother with my father, I left my sister behind. I put aside everything to go after my own life. If you have sisters, and one of them lives a story, the others listen. That is what my mother used to say. And you know what she meant? What one sister does, the others will follow. Oy, but will it come out the same?

So now, if you want to understand Celia's story, and why Gertrude wants me to tell it, come back into my life. It was, by then, 1921. I was eighteen years old, I had graduated from high school. At the time a high-school education was a very big thing. Especially among the workers where we lived. I graduated in the top ten people of my class and my principal insisted I take the exams for Hunter College. When I passed, with very high marks even, I went into his office. I saw him standing there, a tall man, behind his desk. From the first sight I knew why he called me there. He didn't say anything. Not a word. He reached out his hand.

For me, life was opening up. The First World War was over. We had already heard in Waterbury about William Foster's strike with the steelworkers. William Foster was the head of the Communist Party and all over the country the workers were beginning to struggle for conditions. People remembered the Triangle Shirtwaist Factory. Over a hundred workers were burned there in the fire. We knew there was something going through the world, the Ladies Garment Workers Union organizing, the furriers becoming militant. And of course the Russian Revolution had occurred.

But here I have something to tell you about the Russian Revolution. This story takes us back to my childhood when I was still going to public school. So for Celia, please, I ask you, just be patient. "What is in the background," my mother used to say, "this matters also to the story."

One day I was coming home from school and I noticed the headline in the paper. The headline covered a quarter of the front page: CZAR NICHOLAS ABDICATES. I wasn't sure what abdicate meant. I walked over to the newsstand and I figured out that the czar did something so that he was no longer czar. In my home I always heard that this was the thing to be hoped for. But they also said that it would never happen, that the czar was too powerful.

I went up to the newspaperman and I said to him:

"What does abdicate mean?"

"No more czar. No more czar," he said. "But what do you care?"

I was terribly excited by that time. I grabbed the paper and ran all the way home. I kept looking at it and I knew now: no more czar. Can you imagine? No more czar. I reached home and I hollered, "Pa, Pa," but I couldn't say more because by that time I had no breath left.

My father came to the head of the stairs and hollered back:

"What happened?" But I couldn't talk, I couldn't tell him; I sat down, pointing, gasping for breath. He looked at the paper and he snorted, "Is that what you're so excited about?"

I thought he would be so glad. I hoped it would get him into a better mood.

"But, Papa, aren't you glad there's no more czar?"

He said — I remember it — he said, "Rochele, how many times did I tell you that you can't believe what you read in the Hearst papers?"

So it didn't happen, it didn't happen. The czar was still there. I felt squelched and I said to myself, It was too good to be true. It had to come later. It is not for my life.

Six weeks later my father's Yiddish paper, the *Morning Journal*, arrived in the mail. And Yiddish papers we could believe. It said the czar had abdicated, that a revolution had taken place. My father said, "For once. For once the Hearst paper told the truth."

You see what this means? We ran from the czar. In Russia, the czar had been the torment of the Jewish people. He had always been there. How could we imagine the people would be able to drive away the czar? Think only. If this could happen to the czar, what now could not happen in a person's life?

~ ~

My father had a cousin named Sonia Chernin, who lived in New York. She was a very poor woman, of course, married to a furrier. I went to live with her, in a small worker's flat, a walkup, on the sixth floor. There was a little bit of a kitchen, two small bedrooms, a bathroom in the apartment. My room had a window that looked out on a brick wall.

This, I admit, you would not call a palace. So what? I was happy in this place. I had to support myself and this was a problem. Conditions were very bad in the country at that time. There was a lot of unemployment, there were not many places where a girl of my preparation could find work. So this was the first thing, to look for a job, to start working. Only then I could go over to register at Hunter College.

There was a young man, a neighbor I met. He was a music buff and he had the most wonderful voice. When he would open the windows in his apartment we could hear him singing. He would sing arias from operas, in Italian and German. I would stand there. Who could believe this was my life? This you wouldn't find in Waterbury.

I used to go out with this man and walk in the park. We'd stroll through the botanical gardens and we would talk. He, too, was

Russian-born; I felt he was a person like myself, only more developed. At the time he was out of work and I got the distinct impression he liked the idea of not working.

A few weeks went by and he invited me to the Russian Club, of which he was a member. In this club there were young people who had readings of Russian poets, there were lectures on the Soviet Union, discussions about socialism and communism.

I can't tell you what it was like for me to see this place. It was not like anything I had ever seen before. The walls were all painted in bright colors; there were slogans and posters everywhere. On Fridays there were lectures, on Saturdays dancing, there were literary evenings and in one corner of the room there was a buffet, where women were serving tea and cakes. And there was also a little stage someone had built, where the poets could read or someone could give a talk about the Soviet Union. When they would hold dances the people would just spill out of the club into the street outside.

Who could have imagined a group like this? They were cultured and educated young people. They were workers, like myself. They were very excited about what had happened in the Soviet Union; there were debates and discussions and arguments until all hours of the night.

We generally walked home, blocks and blocks away. We would be dancing in the street because there was hardly any traffic and because it was wonderful to be alive.

After a few weeks in New York I registered at Hunter College. I started attending classes and I loved it. I loved everything about it. Every day when I put my foot on the campus, I'd say to myself, Rose, look where you are.

Soon, however, I was running out of money. When I left the factory in Waterbury I had five hundred dollars in war bonds; it was a large savings and could have lasted for a year or two. But my father needed the money for his store in Canonsville. I couldn't care less if the whole store went bankrupt and I told him so. But then my mother went past him. She said, "I never thought you would be the kind of child who wouldn't care whether we eat or we don't."

I took what I needed to start life in New York and left the rest of my savings with my father. I got a job in a perfume factory. I didn't like this work; the smell bothered me and most of the day I felt dizzy.

I found it hard to concentrate on my schoolwork. In the beginning I blamed the job. But now, looking back, what would I say? Maybe it was not the job which caused the trouble. It was all the distractions of New York, my social life which I was enjoying and which took my time.

I had the Russian Club, the debates and discussions, the dances at night and the politics which this club was involved in. The people in the club wanted me to take more responsibility, they wanted me to become an organizer, to be more involved. The time came to make a decision, to choose one thing or another. I decided to quit school. I was so sure I could go back again. It was a mistake. I never went back and this I have regretted all my life. But who knows?

New York was the dream of every young person who lived in Waterbury. It was for us what Moscow was for the three sisters in Chekhov's play. The parks were there, the theater was there, the concerts were there. The subway was there and you could get onto it with a nickel fare. Think of the library! The Forty-second Street Library. To be young, this was an education. To be in New York, to walk the streets, to talk and argue was an education. I never looked back. I didn't care about the heat in the summer, the cold in the winter. My life was sweeping me along and every day was something new.

You have to realize what was happening in New York at that time. The workers were becoming very militant and the Russian Club was involved in all of this. There was a very radical faction of the Ladies Garment Workers Union and people used to go down to help them guard their headquarters. There you would see the whole of New York. There were women from the Bronx, Communists were there, and students from the colleges all over the city. And of course the trade unionists, everyone coming to support these workers. Sometimes there were just hilarious goings-on. A union meeting would be called and if a woman didn't like what was happening, or maybe it was a right-winger talking too long, she'd just fall right down on the floor. There were whole brigades of these women, who would stand up and faint at the union meetings if the discussion wasn't taking the right direction. These were the fainting brigades. And so of course everyone would rush about and begin talking at once and the business would be completely disrupted. Or if someone they didn't like came by in the street, the women would spit into the gutter. The women, too, were becoming very militant at that time and of course all this affected me. You'd hear about a boss in the sweatshops bothering one of the women workers. Maybe she was a beauty and he was interested in her. So he'd make a pass or say something under this breath and the woman would get offended. This had been going on for how many thousands of years? But now the woman would speak out and the other women would take her side. Someone would stand up and shout, someone else would go over to the window and throw the sewing machine into the street. Or they would pick up the scissor and hold it there, with the pointed edge, next to the machine, facing up to the bosses.

This, of course, will remind you of my sister. And you are right, Celia was such a woman, wherever she went somebody would be making a pass at her. When she finished high school and got her teacher's certificate, she went to work in a school, right there in Canonsville. But you know who came into this school? Farmboys, big ones, in the rough clothes. They were five, six years older than Celia. They took one look at her and what did they do? Half the time they didn't know how to read. They'd sit there, with this beautiful girl for their teacher and what can you expect? She was lucky she got out of there without being raped.

You think maybe you invented the struggle for women. But this struggle we knew, believe me, already in our time.

~ ~

About the struggle of the furriers I knew something too, because my father's cousin Sonia was married to a furrier. And the men in this union were the most militant fighters in New York.

There was then a special squad of the police department; it was known as the Industrial Squad. They'd come down armed to break up strikes and harass the workers. And so the furriers started to fight back, Jewish and Greek workers together, against the police, against the armed thugs, against the right-wingers in the union. And they were tough, let me tell you, always ready to defend themselves. They were the real rank and file and they won some important victories.

They had a very violent strike, maybe it was 1925 or 1926. They
fought with knives and pipes and they won real benefits, wage in-
creases and the forty-hour week.

So what do you think? Was this something worth knowing about?

On Seventh Avenue, if you would go down there at lunch time,
there would be Ben Gold. He was an organizer of the fur union.
Without even a microphone, he'd get up to address the workers in
the streets of the garment district. He was a small man, very fiery and
he'd boom out at them, in Yiddish and English, about the injustice
of the capitalist system.

Here's a song, written by a Socialist, an anti-Communist who was
called Al Levy. But this song is poking fun, it is his idea of what the
Communist union would sing.

> Oh, the Cloakmakers' Union is a no-good union
> It's a company union for the bosses.
> Oh, the right-wing cloakmakers and the socialist fakers
> Are making by the workers double crosses.
> For the Hillquits, Dubinskys, and the Thomases
> Are making by the workers false promises.
> They preach socialism but they practice fascism
> To preserve capitalism for the bosses.

Are you laughing? But I say, what's so funny? This is what the
Communists believed about the Cloakmakers. The workers then had
very strong feelings.

I remember that in Yankee Stadium fifty thousand workers from
the garment makers' unions gathered. There was a stoppage of work,
thousands and thousands of workers left the shops. They came into
the streets, they crowded into the halls to hear the union speakers.
The Communists were very active in all of this, relating everything
to the class struggle all over the world, to what had happened
in the Soviet Union. What could Hunter College offer that could
compete?

We had culture, we had politics, we were learning what was
possible for a worker, we had our own books and newspapers, and
some of these newspapers, like the *Freiheit,* were very radical. This
was the Jewish paper that had broken away from the *Forward.* It was
against religion and it never lost an opportunity to attack the tradi-

tion. I admired this. In New York at the time it was generally agreed that a Yiddish paper would not be published on the holidays. But the *Freiheit* you would see even on Yom Kippur, the holiest day of the year. To you this may not sound like anything very much, but to us it was the world turning upside down.

~ ~

One day I met a poet and writer by the name of David Thorne. He came from a theatrical family. His father was a famous Jewish actor. His brother, August, was an actor as well and he played at that time in a very popular play called *Abie's Irish Rose.* I met David's family. I walked into their home and I could not believe what I was seeing: a theatrical family, a real theatrical family.

In those years in New York there was a great activity in the Yiddish theaters. It was part of the education. And this, too, is part of Celia's story. I remember the whole thing together. Who can separate? We had professional theaters and little theater groups supported by the Workmen's Circle. Here there was always something very extravagant, great sorrow, great laughter. You could see everything. Sholom Aleichem, Chekhov, Shakespeare, Yiddish plays. Companies would come over from Europe, from Vilna or Moscow. There were comedians and great actresses appearing. There was a man named Jacob Adler, he was a Russian Jew, an actor. He did a performance of Shylock in the Yiddish theater and later this went on to Broadway. Adler managed to make Shylock into a very sympathetic character. He was a handsome man, he carried himself with tremendous pride. When he died his coffin was carried through the streets of the East Side and people followed after it.

That was the world David's family came from. You'd go into their house and these were the things they would be talking about. His brother would go off into another room, he'd come back in with a beard and a cloak, and there was Shakespeare, right in the living room.

David was a very handsome man, he was a few years older than me and he knew many people on Broadway. He had friends on *Variety.* When he came to see me he would come in from that world of writers and poets and musicians. He was always telling me stories. And he would take me downtown to a place on Second Avenue which was a restaurant and a club, where actors and writers came. A year before I was a high-school girl working in a factory. Now I was sitting in a literary club on Second Avenue, drinking a glass of wine.

In my life, at this time, I was just following whatever came along. This maybe is what it means to be young. How else would you find out what was in the world? So now I went into this life David Thorne was living. That's how it was. Should I apologize? David and I took an apartment together and I got a job as a saleslady in a store downtown. David was writing. He wanted to become a playwright and from his family you could believe this would be possible. He was, as I said, one of those men who didn't like to work; he would stay up to all hours, drinking tea and putting his hand through his hair, reading again and again a scene that wouldn't fill the cover of a matchbook. But of course the next day he was too tired to do anything else and it was I who had to support us. Nevertheless, for a short time I was very happy. We went to plays, we went in to have a meal with David's family, I was meeting famous people at the literary club, we went to concerts. David would meet me after work and we'd walk on the avenues, looking in the windows. Always talking. He was a great dreamer. What would be, what would become when he had a play produced on Broadway. The clothes he would buy for me. The house we would live in. You know the type of man. But very quickly I began to tire of this life. I began to dislike being in an apartment which was my responsibility, where I had to cook the meals and do the cleaning, and earn the living. And he, meanwhile, would begin to go out and he stayed away sometimes all night. So I left him; I don't know how many times I went away from him. But always he came back.

One night I was in the kitchen at my cousin's apartment. I was in there alone, making a cup of tea. David walks in without even knocking. He gets a look at me and right away he falls down on his knees. I was so surprised I almost dropped the tea on his head. "Rose," he says to me, and he reaches up with his hands, "come back. Come, I can't live without you." Well, you know me. "David Thorne," I said to him, "if I would be willing to come back to you it would not be because of the knees." And then, would you believe it? "Anything," he says, "tell me. I'll do anything." He breaks out in tears. This I had never seen in my life before. A man weeping. I put out my hand to him. What could I do? And he covered it in kisses.

But it couldn't work. How could it work? What was this glamorous world for me? A job in a store, dishes in the sink when I got home. This I could have done in Waterbury. It was not for this I came to New York.

One night I knew I couldn't go on like that any longer. I was in the kitchen. I picked up a plate. "No more, it's all over," I shouted. I smashed the plate against the sink. Right away, I snatched up another. "There's got to be more to life," I shouted. I grabbed a cup. But that was enough. Two plates and a cup and I had my resolution. "A woman," I said, "is not the same thing as a slave."

I would not say I had any ideas at the time about a woman's development. The women I knew lived as I was living. They stayed at home, they took care of a man. Even when they were working women the responsibilities of home life fell on their shoulders. I looked at them and always I blamed myself. Why did I have to be different?

So now I decided we should change our relationship. I insisted and David agreed. He went back to live with his parents and I took a room in one of the houses nearby. We went out together on weekends. He would recite to me the words from his play, still he was dreaming into the future. But I very gradually began to lose touch with him. One weekend there was another young man, a neighbor, who belonged to a trio. We went out walking in the park. Another weekend I would be reading a book. And soon, I was drifting back into the Russian Club. I was reading books, I was thinking again about the class struggle. What did I have to do with those fancy people on Second Avenue?

In the Russian Club we were speaking every day about what happened in Russia. The years passed, the revolution maintained itself. You see what this meant? The people were governing. They were transforming old Russia. They were creating a new world.

The people were doing this. Think of it. The people.

So, that's it. There you have it. Now finally I can tell you the story about my sister. But first, I better tell you how I met your father. Because, why not? This, too, is a part of it.

~ ~

At about this time, when I was twenty-two years old, a young man came to New York. My phone rang one night, I heard a voice asking if I was Rose Chernin. So who else would I be?

The voice said, "I am Paul Kusnitz, from Waterbury." It was he who had given me the socialist material while we walked to school. "Do you remember me?"

"Of course, Paul Kusnitz. Are you still reading the *Call?*"

"I just came to New York a few weeks ago. I graduated from MIT, I'm an engineer. I've been looking for a job but it's not so easy to find anything in engineering."

Now Paul Kusnitz was something special. Not everybody goes to MIT. He got a scholarship to study there, but MIT only admitted so many Jews a year. And they never filled the quota because the Jewish men wouldn't go into engineering. After they graduated they were discriminated against. Paul was living in Brooklyn, with another Crosby student.

I said to him, "Well, do you want to come over?"

"Of course. I'll come on Saturday."

So it began. Paul Kusnitz made a tremendous impression on me. He was a very handsome young man and he dressed in the latest fashion. He wore spats, he had a waxed mustache; he was more mature, of course, but his eyes still twinkled the way they did in Waterbury. This is the kind of man you don't see around much anymore. He was a real character and I wasn't the only person who thought so. He was always telling stories. Jewish stories you heard so many times who could laugh at them anymore? But when Paul Kusnitz began to tell them everyone was rolling on the floor.

I asked him why he had chosen engineering.

"I'm good in math," he said. We were sitting in the kitchen at the table. "I have always liked the idea of building something. I thought that as an engineer I would be able to travel. I want to make a contribution to the underdeveloped countries of the world."

I stopped stirring my tea. This man, I thought, is somebody you look at twice. "So which underdeveloped countries, Paul," I asked.

I remembered he, too, was born in Russia. "Did you have any particular country in mind?"

"I want to go to the Soviet Union."

Here I better give you an explanation. From our circles thousands of people left America and went back to Russia after the revolution. At first we thought, maybe all the Jews in New York will be going back to Russia. But of course that never happens. Some go, the others go on talking. The next day there's a job and you remember only at night this great idea after a cup of wine. But Paul Kusnitz was not this sort of person. Don't ask me how I knew. Right away, from the beginning, he made a different impression on me. If Paul Kusnitz, I said to myself, says he's going to do something, this you can believe.

When we'd go out walking he'd have something in his pockets for the children he met on the street. He liked to take a bag of bread crumbs to feed the birds in the park. This man, I used to say to myself, would never lift up a hand against a woman. He was a real intellectual, a worker-intellectual.

One day he asked me to marry him, but I felt that I was not ready for marriage. Behind me was the example of my father and mother. I had a taste of being a housewife when I lived with David. I was not eager to go into that drudgery again. I felt that there must be more to me than would be developed at a kitchen sink.

Paul found a job as an engineer, working for the city. He came to tell me and he asked me to marry him again. So I agreed, we would marry but we did not decide upon a date. Paul went home to tell his people. He was supposed to stay in Waterbury for a week. But after two days he called up and said to me, "I'm coming home."

I met him at the train, I looked at him and I thought an avalanche had hit him. He was pale and he looked very sad. I asked him what had happened and he said, "Don't ask. My family just let me have it when I told them I was going to marry you."

You can imagine the objection they would have to me. I was a woman living alone, going out with men and doing everything else they could imagine for a girl who lives in New York. I had a very bad reputation in Waterbury for living with David Thorne. Don't ask me how they knew about it. People find out. Who said the world is a big place? The Kusnitz family wanted him to marry a wealthy girl. He and his brother Max were the youngest sons, educated men with professions. The older brothers were all in the meat business. Barney, a butcher. Sol, a butcher. Sam, also a butcher. So naturally the family wanted something very special for Paul. And something very special, in their eyes, certainly was not me.

Well, should I cry about it? "Paul," I said to him, "You didn't marry me yet. I'm not holding you to any promises. You're a free man, Paul Kusnitz. You can change your mind."

You should have seen the look on his face. For this look he won from me a friend for the rest of his life. "You think," he says, "I would ask for their permission?"

Now Paul cut his family off completely. His mother began writing letters right away. But Paul would not answer. He pressed me to set a date for our marriage but I was still hesitating.

And now, in this hesitation, we come back to Celia. Here I can tell you about her, this is the place where she comes in. And I thank you for waiting.

You know, of course, we always planned to have Celia in New York. I imagined she would come straight into my life. Right away, the first day she was in the city I took her to the Russian Club. The next day I took her down to Seventh Avenue to hear Ben Gold. We went over to the headquarters of the ILGWU. She took one look and raised up her eyebrows. She didn't want to have anything to do with these things. She was an American pure and simple, without a past. That is the way she wanted to think about herself.

This always interested me. Here we were, from the same family, the shtetl was behind us, the same mother and father. So you would expect these two sisters would go after the same things. But this is not what happened. I always knew you couldn't go running away, denying the past. With these radical workers and intellectuals was my home.

About Gertrude of course we don't know. She never got a chance to come to New York. After Mama broke down, Gertrude took care of the family. She did the very thing Celia and I didn't want to do.

Celia, as you know, was never a fighter. But Gertrude was even less a fighter. Celia was wild, she had something in her you couldn't understand. In our family maybe even we were afraid of her. But Gertrude would do whatever my father wanted. She had the sweetest nature of us all. And that, if you want to know, was her downfall. That was the ruin of her. And, who knows? This maybe is why she wants me to tell you about Celia. From the time we came to America until Gertrude was fifty-three years old and went off into the Peace Corps, she never did anything for herself. Never anything. Her whole life was for pleasing others.

So there you have it. Three sisters and maybe we were not like the sisters in Chekhov's play. But I used to feel, from our family a writer could make a good story.

Well, Celia and I moved downtown, we shared an apartment. Paul Kusnitz I still saw frequently but the whole question of marriage I didn't think about for now. In these years I was drifting. Why not? Later, I became something. In my own way, believe me, I settled down. But now I was taking in a little bit of everything.

One night I took Celia to the club on Second Avenue where I used to go with David. It was like a duck coming into water. Morrie Schwartz from the Art Theater was there with his cast every night after the theater. People used to say he never slept and you could believe it. He had a tremendous appetite. You never saw him without something going toward his mouth. He was a very clever man. The actor, the director, the stage manager of his company. Everyone hated him, everyone loved him, everyone wanted him to produce a play. What you saw in his theater would just make you weep. It was great Jewish spectacle, very sentimental. It was theater for the people and we loved it. So you will imagine how it was for us to go into this club. Young writers and famous artists came. The gallery was there and one of the people who came with his coterie was Ben Shahn. Peter Blume the painter was there with his friends, and later on, Sonia Bloom, his sister, became my best friend.

Celia took one look at all this and I knew she was in her element. She sits down at a table, in the next minute a young man comes over to buy her a glass of wine. She takes off her hat, she takes off her gloves. When I look again she's got his scarf around her neck. Then I hear her saying something and it really takes me by surprise. She, who has never been inside a theater, what is she saying? You guessed it! My sister tells everyone who will listen that she's come to New York to be in a play. So of course everyone wants to know what play it is. And I meanwhile am thinking to myself, That's it, it's all over.

Why did I have to come here with my sister? But now, what do you know? Words are coming out of her mouth. She's not one bit embarrassed. And so I listen and I hear her making up the most incredible story. It was so fantastic, let me tell you, anybody would have to believe it was a play.

My sister, I told you, was a beautiful woman. I would look at her and marvel that such a beauty had come out of our family. She had a lovely face, with bright eyes that were full of mischief. She had a small, graceful figure and she was always beautifully dressed. As soon as she arrived in New York she got a job working in a tea room; the wages were small but she got very high tips. She had the wonderful ability to pick out an inexpensive dress and wear it as if it were the highest fashion.

I still thought I was a homely person; I was short and my figure was full. I hated to go into a dress shop because I didn't have the figure for the clothes that were being made then. Everybody was supposed to be flat chested and I definitely was not! I was surprised when I would get a dress that fit me. The women were binding their breasts, wrapping tape around them. But I wouldn't hear of it. In the first place, it wouldn't have done any good. In the second place, what sort of person would that make me? I once told my father that I was going out looking for a job. "Don't bother," he said to me. "Why not?" I asked him. "No one will hire you," he said. "You're too short." To me this meant that no one would ever fall in love with me.

David was always telling me that I was a beautiful woman. Now that I had met Paul Kusnitz and heard the same thing from him, I began to think they must see something in me which I could not see. But when Celia came to New York, I knew all the beauty in our family was in her.

She had a mind that was as sharp as a razor. She would pick up any book and read it in two hours. She would read a chapter in the beginning, a chapter in the end, and she had the great facility to read the one important chapter in the middle and know what the book was about. Then she discussed it with anybody who would listen.

She was always flighty. She would go off, at a moment's notice, with absolutely anyone who attracted her. And she could imagine such things. She would tell of her escapades to a group of our women friends and we would sit there with amazement and listen to her by the hour. With Celia it was impossible to tell what was real and what was invented. It was even better than going to the theater. She could tell stories like no one could tell stories.

I used to eat dinner at the tea room where Celia worked. One day she came over to my table and said she wanted to introduce me to a man. But she added, "Don't be surprised at anything he will tell you. Sit at his table with him, keep him company, but don't contradict him, whatever he says."

By then I knew Celia and her stories, so I was prepared for anything. But this man started to talk and I almost dropped dead. He said, "You come from a very interesting family and I am very honored to meet you."

I held my breath. She had wanted me not to give her away. I was loyal, what else? I sat there and he said to me, "It is an honor to meet a member of the royal family of the czar."

That was my sister. I would look at her and I would think: One day maybe she will become a very wealthy woman. That is what my sister wanted. She had a longing to live, to eat and drink, to travel, to buy, to devour. She seemed insatiable. I was sure she would burn herself out at a young age, lose her beauty, accomplish nothing. I was always cautioning her: "Celia, be careful. You are not yet twenty years old. Save a little for your old age. Who knows, you might yet live to be twenty-five."

It was her life itself I wanted her to preserve because she ran with it, squandering it, not holding anything back from the moment she came to New York.

In the evening she would get dressed up and we would go out to a party. Celia would get into the middle of things and within an hour's time all the men would be around her. She was one of those women who have power over men.

A few years went by, I no longer remember how many. Paul Kusnitz and I got married; we went to live in the Bronx. Paul was working by then on the Eighth Avenue subway. One afternoon he took a half day from work, we went down to City Hall and we got married. That's how it happened, completely natural. And for this, believe me, I have been happy all my life. If I kept on drifting, who knows? Maybe I would have ended like my sister.

In those years I still saw Celia frequently, of course. But the day arrived when Celia left New York. She went to live in Los Angeles. She married Harry Horowitz, who had a famous delicatessen store on Forty-sixth Street. He was older than Celia, but a bachelor. He was a decent man. It was I who encouraged her to marry him.

I was very concerned about the way she was living her life. She was a butterfly, a charming butterfly, but you can't maintain that kind of life for long. I thought about what would happen to her when she got older. We lived marginally; it was never easy to find work. I began to think about the future. Harry was a very nice person. He wasn't our kind, he lacked culture, but he was a good man. You felt that you could rely on him, that he would be a good husband and keep his family well.

Maybe I made a mistake here. Who's to say? The insecurity we felt as children comes back. It comes whenever there is an important decision to make. This began to be more and more true as the years passed. Our youth was slipping away and we didn't know many people with a business who would make her a serious proposal of marriage.

I saw the way Harry Horowitz looked at her when we came in the delicatessen.

"Marry him, Celia," I would say. She was my sister, my closest sister. I was constantly worried about where she would end up in a few years.

"Ask her," I'd say to Harry. "What have you got to lose?"

"Rose," he'd say, wiping his hands on the apron. "She'll laugh at me."

"So, Harry, what will happen if she laughs?"

I knew she wasn't madly in love with Harry but I encouraged her. I thought it would be good for her. I thought it would give her a safe life.

Should I blame myself for this? You look back, it's all so clear, from the time we were children in the shtetl. Celia, always the hungry one, wanting more. You remember the story of the buttons? The way she would howl because Mama put a few more buttons on my dress? But who could know, a few years after she married Harry she would run off and leave her little girl? Who could foresee, one day because of this my sister would break down and go into a mental hospital, like Mama? Could I know the future? Could I tell one day Celia would kill herself?

At that time I was very young myself, I wasn't the wisest person. I had so little experience. I didn't know then what I've learned since. I thought it would be a good thing for her to marry Harry.

As you know, ach, children, it turned out not to be.

Three Sisters

*I*t is early in the morning. Larissa is still asleep. My mother and I have come in here to keep Gertrude company through a hard night. The conversation is difficult. We sit in silence.

"I loved her," I say at last, as if this explained everything. But my mother does not like it.

"You scarcely ever visited her during the last years. What sort of love is this?"

"I loved her even before I met her. I loved every word I ever heard about her."

"She was a selfish woman, you know that. All her life she lived completely for herself."

Aunt Gertrude is propped up against the pillows, her hands clenched around the white blanket on her bed. My mother sits a few feet away, her legs curled up in the chair. Facing them, I remember to notice everything. The way Gertrude reaches for a cigarette, glances at my mother, decides not to smoke. The way my mother plucks pieces of lint from the blanket on Gertrude's bed, making a neat pile of cotton fluff in the corner.

But my mother's face has closed itself down. Her look seems to say that I am telling her something she has not heard before. Her silence tells me I should not go on speaking.

"I wish I had known her when she was in New York," I insist, irritated by her refusal to listen. "Now it's almost impossible to imagine her a young woman."

"She was beautiful and spoiled," Aunt Gertrude whispers. "You could not keep yourself from falling in love with her."

She speaks this very slowly, as if each word had to be weighed and considered, to see whether its meaning had changed since the last time it was used. "You could not keep yourself. From falling in love."

My mother interrupts her. "What was the reason for it?" she asks, as if Gertrude has not spoken at all. "Can you tell me?" She is looking over my shoulder, addressing herself to the air, the blank wall, some unseen audience. "This woman," she says, rapping twice with her knuckles on the arm of her chair, as if to call a large, unruly gathering to order, "she had everything, and nothing left to worry about, money enough to outlast her if she lived to be a hundred. Who can understand it?"

Aunt Gertrude raises her head, staring at me so intently that for a moment I imagine her whole life is thrown open before me. I see accusation, then bitterness, and finally contrition in her eyes. And now she says, with the same terribly slow deliberation that is making my mother nervous, "I could not bear. To look at her. In that funeral home. I, who have been. A nurse. All my life. I could not bear."

I, too, found it horrible but I stayed in that room after the others had left. I didn't want to leave her, although the room was so cold and I scarcely recognized her, with her strangely curling yellow hair, her face so much older than I had ever seen her. It was not the least bit peaceful. But I drew closer and closer to her in that freezing room, wondering if I would be able to bend down and kiss her farewell. And then as I touched my lips to her forehead memory came and I saw two women sitting beneath a lemon tree, dappled with shade, two of them. And both were my mother.

It was summer. I had come from day camp, surprised to see my mother's car pulled up in the drive. I ran into the house and heard my mother calling to me from the garden. When I pushed back the door, sitting beneath the lemon tree there were two of her.

I approached with caution at first, but the phantom mother proved to be unquestionably real; she called to me, in a voice with a slight accent, asking if I knew her, holding out her hand. I felt that I was a wispy girl, who would like to run inside and straighten my hair before meeting this aunt so exactly like my mother — only foreign, exotic, wearing a hat, elegantly dressed and so beautiful! Even her perfume was like no perfume I had noticed before and I thought that she would certainly not want to hug me so I sat down abruptly on the ground, quite near to them, looking from one to the other, from this well known and daily and familiar mother to what appeared to be her double, only so much more ideal!

"She was always running from herself," my mother says, standing up and pacing over to the window, where she pulls furiously at the Venetian blind. "Her boys never knew she was a Jew. They grew up, they came to see the family and what did they find here? These European noblemen from a family of Jews."

Gertrude considers this, her fingers twitching. A month ago they would have been reaching for a cigarette. "I visited her in Holland," she says, speaking gravely, as she ponders the significance of this fact. And then suddenly, with all the old spirit I loved in her when I was a child, she begins to laugh her wonderful, husky, smoker's laugh. "One day," she manages to gasp out, "I walked into the living room. There was Hank Doeff, doing Yoga, the way Celia was always after him to do. He was wearing his three-piece suit. I saw the watch chain and the gold watch hanging down from his pocket. He was upside down. A baron, with a family crest on his ring. Doing Yoga and standing on his head."

"Don't tell me," says my mother, rolling her eyes toward the ceiling. She throws her arms around her waist, hugging herself like a small child. "Hank Doeff, standing on his head?" Gertrude is sputtering, holding a handkerchief to her lips. My mother's shoulders are shaking.

"Did I ever tell you about the cakes?" my mother asks.

But she knows perfectly well she has told this story before. We all know this. And she is not waiting for our approval. "Mama made five little cakes," she says. "One for each child. She put them on the table. Of course, she trusted us. She'd say, 'Children, not until dinner. Don't touch the cakes.' She'd go back into the kitchen. And Celia, what would she do? She'd gobble up her cake and reach over and snatch a piece from the little one. Lillian would scream, she'd just howl. So Gertrude, of course, would give Lillian her cake. And this is character, already in childhood. Milton would say nothing, that's Milton. And I'd argue with her. 'Celia,' I'd say, 'how could you do this?' She'd wink at me and sometimes she'd answer. But most often she sat there, smiling in that way she had. That was our sister. . . ."

Joy enters the room. It settles tentatively on the windowsill, waiting to see whether it will be welcome here. "Would you believe it," says my mother. "I never remembered that story before."

"Mama," I shout to her through my laughter, "how many times did you tell that story in your life?"

"Gertrude," she says, looking over to her favorite witness. "Tell her, Gertrude. This story I never remembered."

But Gertrude is not laughing. There is that same deep look in her eyes, accusation, bitterness, contrition. And finally: "Rose," she says and her voice is breaking. "It's true, isn't it, Rose? Celia was always your favorite."

~ ~

I, too, was always in love with my aunt. As a child I saw pictures of her on the veranda of her beautiful home in South America. The men were wearing white suits, servants stood respectfully to one side, holding enormous fans of woven banana leaf and my aunt sat there, in a lace dress, her face slightly averted, as if it were difficult, even then, to turn and face the family to whom the pictures were to be sent. There were other pictures of Celia in our family album. A fashionable woman in a fur coat standing on the deck of a boat; her twins, the two little boys in sailor suits, holding her by the hand, while she glances, always, away from the camera. But it was the woman in the lace dress I remembered when I was seventeen years old and went to visit Celia in Europe. The train drew into the station in Amsterdam. Pressed against the window I saw her again — with what rapture I saw her, my mother, but more beautiful than my mother, familiar and foreign, dearly loved and scarcely known, this woman with whom I felt the deepest possible affinity, to whom I had come to learn about life.

My mother shakes me by the shoulder: "I was very worried when I heard you had gone to stay with Celia. Wasn't I, Gertrude? No good could come of it, I thought. What kind of influence could she be? I was afraid. Maybe, I thought, she would want to bind you to her. To make up for abandoning Ethel. And even today I think she did influence you. Yes, I think she did . . ."

Certainly, I was an enraptured listener as we sat up alone, late into the night, still talking when the milkman arrived to leave yogurt and fresh bread on the stairs in the morning, still in love with this elegant and cultivated woman, whose words turned back obsessively now to the husband she had left, the delicatessen store in Los Angeles, the men playing poker upstairs all day and he stinking of garlic, she said, when he came to bed at night.

But she was young and when she had lived in New York, it had been so different. How could they blame her? She had fallen in love. The young man had come into the store to buy cigarettes. She noticed his accent, the way he was dressed. If only, she thought, it were not too late. He came back again the next day. He wore a beautiful ring with his family crest. And was it too late? Did she have to bury herself in this life? Was it her fault she had married the wrong man? Was it her fault she did not want to raise a child? Was it her fault Rose had persuaded her?

"Some things," my mother says in a strained voice, "even you don't know about Celia. Some things we kept even from you. But now," she murmurs, glancing quickly over her shoulder, "is the time for telling."

"Leave it, Rose," Gertrude whispers. "What do we need it for?"

"Gertrude, Gertrude, who are we protecting?" my mother answers in an impatient voice. "And from whom?"

But I see that she cannot go on. She stands up to straighten the cover on Gertrude's bed, pulls vigorously at the blanket and shoves it under the mattress with a vengeful thrust.

And then she cannot restrain herself any longer. "Take my sister," she shouts, tossing her head to throw off the last of this outmoded family loyalty. "For this life we need a philosopher at least."

Talking rapidly, she paces back and forth in front of Gertrude's bed. "Ethel she abandoned when she was five years old. Five years, would you believe it? Left her daughter, ran off for a love affair. When I heard the news I put my head against the wall. Who could save her now from her own fate?

"So yes, of course, for a time she's happy. Her new husband is an engineer. They go abroad, they live in Venezuela, they live in Indonesia, wherever it's possible for Shell Oil to exploit the people and make money. You know the life of the wealthy colonial. Servants, beautiful clothes, parties. Why wouldn't she be happy? She writes to us, only now she's called Sylvia, no one should know from her name that she's a Jew. She sends pictures of her oldest boys in little sailor suits. That was Pim and Sander, the twins. And then in 1939 another boy, Michael, is born. But of course by now there's a war in Europe. And what happens? The Japanese invade Indonesia, they take the Dutch engineers and the older boys away into concentration camps, and the women and small children they shut up in separate camps. Would you believe it? For years we didn't hear from our sister. But about Indonesia we heard. Concentration camps for Jews in Europe. And in Indonesia a Jewish woman, with a changed name, interned in the camp because she's a member of the Dutch ruling class. You say life has no sense of irony?

"So, after the war they're released; the family is reunited. Celia came out of the camp all skin and bones and did she have stories. She came for a visit, when was it? Maybe 1949. Beautiful as ever, and now for the stories she wanted to tell, who needed exaggeration? But still, somehow, my sister was the same. What can I tell you? Maybe even more than before she was restless, filled with that hunger of hers. Later, when she returned to Holland we began to hear that she would have a breakdown and go into a mental hospital. And somehow we knew it wasn't Indonesia, it wasn't the concentration camp, it wasn't the war. It was Ethel, I tell you, the child she abandoned.

"Believe me, it was not what Celia suffered that broke her. She was a Chernin, a strong person, like all of us. No, I'm telling you, it was the suffering she caused others that tortured her. She couldn't forgive herself. How else could it be?

"So time passes, the years pass. One day she comes back to America to live. A widow, very depressed. Her boys have left home, in Holland she has no friends, her life is empty.

"Thirty-five years have passed . . . and what do you think? Ethel opens the door to her. Nothing's too good for her mother. Celia has nothing to do? She wants work? Ethel opens a dress shop for her. But Celia can't accept, she can't accept. Everything Ethel gives is not right. She can't live with her, she can't live in Los Angeles, she goes up to Berkeley to live with Sander. And then, who knows why, she takes her own life. After the funeral we find out Celia has cut Ethel out of her will."

My mother stops talking and glances at us, her hands on her hips. Her eyes are casting fierce sparks of outrage all over the room. Her lips, tightened down, have become a grim slash of disapproval. Gertrude does not look up at her. She has been folding a handkerchief and she continues with her work. Very carefully, she picks up an edge of the cloth and matches it to a crease at the center.

"Ach, my sister, my sister," my mother explodes, "who can understand this life?"

She paces over to my side, drawn to me because I have always reminded her of Celia. But now her face contracts. "She was like Mama," she whispers. "Did you ever think of it? Like Mama."

Gertrude is looking at her with a startled expression, her eyes hurt, disbelieving. She has known this woman all her life, she has heard every sort of utterance come from her mouth. But this? Is it possible?

"The same stories," my mother insists, impatient because Gertrude has not understood her. "I used to think, if only Celia could have written them down. From these stories could have come an artist."

Now there comes into my aunt's face the first softening she has allowed since we began speaking about Celia. "An artist," she repeats. "But who ever thought . . . she was like Mama?"

Suddenly I am on my feet. "Yes," I say, the words coming fast, "she *was* like Grandma. When she grew old I always saw her back in the shtetl."

My mother looks over at me, scowling a warning. "Yes, yes," I begin to argue, answering her unspoken challenge. "In spite of her fashionable clothes."

Aunt Gertrude nods thoughtfully. She is considering me in a new light. Is this, too, her eyes seem to be saying, an artist?

And so I take heart, sounding each word with care, in an effort to hide the impossible hope, this time I will be able to explain the way I see things. "In the shtetl . . . you see? There, in that world, they would have known what to make of Celia and her stories."

My mother gathers herself to deliver judgment. "Nonsense," she says. "For you everything is a romance. In the shtetl Celia would have been . . . can you imagine? In the shtetl, a woman like this?"

I feel, within me, a familiar sensation, an impulse of rage curiously mixed with despair.

"Mama," I say, "that's not what I mean." But how many times have I said these same words to her before?

Gertrude is looking anxiously from my mother to me. She knows us. And she is desperately searching, as she has done all her life, for a way to placate both of us and keep us from quarreling. Or does she know that my mother has given me to her? I always imagined myself Celia's daughter. But what if Gertrude had been my mother? Could I have told her how all my life their childhood in the shtetl seemed so mythical to me? These stories my mother tells, would Gertrude understand? They have always reminded me of that wonderful, homely tone in the tale of the matriarch Sarah, laughing within her tent when she heard the words of the Lord. And why, after all, was Sarah laughing? Was it because on that day Abraham, who was a warrior and a man, stood conversing with God in the clear light of day the way, through uncounted generations, women had always done? If Celia had grown up in the shtetl, she would have known the way her own embellishments reached back, through an unbroken tradition, to the first tales of the Hebrew people.

But how could I say this to my mother?

Gertrude's eyes rest on my face. She regards me with a proprietary air, as if she is appreciating for the first time the fact that I have become hers. Suddenly her cheeks turn red. Now that she has me, she's going to fight for me. Very cautiously, she clears her throat. "Rose," she says, turning toward my mother and looking her in the eyes, "it's true Rose. In our village Celia's green goats could have danced right up over the rooftops. And no one would have told her, It's impossible, things don't happen like that here."

I say nothing.

But my heart, in its silence, reaches out for Gertrude; fiercely it takes hold of her and fastens itself upon her forever.

My mother stands stiffly, her hands folded on her breast. I watch the play of emotion on her face. But finally, she throws out her arms, lifting her shoulders as if to say: Well, why not do it their way?

"Who can deny it?" she says. But having gone this far she cannot hold back the tide of feeling. "Ach," she whispers, shaking her head.

"A woman without a people behind her. That was her tragedy."

Gertrude's face collapses. A visible trembling passes through her body. And now she makes an effort to pull herself up in bed. She reaches out and touches my mother on the hand.

"She felt. Closer to you than. To anyone Rose. She felt. You understood her. She's dead. Our judgments don't. Reach her."

Exhausted by this speech her body slumps down, trying to pull her back onto the bed, but my mother holds on to her hand. And suddenly I realize that Gertrude fell ill exactly a year to the day after Celia died. Aunt Lillian told me that Gertrude fought with Celia during the last year of Celia's life. "Gertrude," I asked, "fighting?" "Yes," she assured me. "Celia had begun to get on her nerves."

My mother is silent. Very gently, she taps Gertrude on the hand. And then, in a voice which sounds exactly like Aunt Gertrude's: "She was beautiful and spoiled," she says. "You could not keep yourself from falling in love with her."

Gertrude closes her eyes. This softness in my mother, hidden away for a lifetime, eases the tension in her sister's limbs. She breathes deeply, her arms stretching out on the bedcovers.

But my mother feels that she has said too much. She gets up abruptly and walks out of the room. Her steps are heavy down the hall and soon we hear the careful click of her lock as she closes the door to her bedroom.

Aunt Gertrude whispers something to me. I cannot hear it. She whispers again, hastily, as if wanting to tell me before my mother returns to the room. I know that if I do not manage to hear her now I shall wonder for the rest of my life what she is trying to tell me. There is a single, comprehensible word. ". . . possible," she says. And I snatch this word up as if it were the answer to an intolerable question. But then I see that this word is too large, it explains nothing. Was it possible, she thinks, that Celia might not have wanted to die? Possible she might have found something of value to live by if she had stayed alive? Or does the word refer to something within her own life? All the great, untapped possibility she sacrificed to let Celia and my mother go off into the world?

"Gertrude," I say, "what are you trying to tell me?" She reaches out, takes my hand and places it on her heart. Her lips move but no sound comes from them. The urgency in her face is terrifying.

I have the impression that she is willing to speak the secret she has lived, her whole life, in silence.

"Gertrude," I whisper, "I'm here." And I know suddenly, with a confused sense of embarrassment, that I am the one person to whom her urgency could be addressed.

But now, as she moves her lips, shaping inaudible air, I find myself talking. I, who am so fearful to intrude upon another person's solitude, am saying words that would have been unthinkable even an hour ago.

"You're wondering whether it is possible that you, who always seemed to be sacrificing yourself, really led the richer life than Celia?"

Her eyes release me. A delicate pink color comes into her cheeks and for a moment her whole being is suffused with light, as if the life force were visibly passing through her body.

"That's possible," she says, clearly and simply, with that old twinkle in her eyes. And then I remember. These words were her favorite, her most characteristic expression. "That's possible," she'd say, lifting her shoulders and rolling her eyes. How could I have forgotten?

She squeezes my hand. "There," she says, "you understand." And they are the last words she will speak to me directly.

She closes her eyes and I find that I am very peaceful, sitting here beside her. The sorrow she carried, so deeply hidden, was her mother's. Always we thought she lived out her mother's tragedy. But I see now, keeping watch over her death: she was enriched by what she took from her mother.

The door opens, my mother comes toward us. She places a picture of Aunt Celia in a worn cardboard frame on the table before us. I see a look of confusion on the face of my aunt, a woman of forty, even more beautiful than when she was young, looking out at us with bewilderment, as if someone had just asked her a question she will never be able to answer.

My mother says, in that hushed, dark voice which is new to her, "When I looked at Celia in the mortuary, lying there, with that yellowing hair, I thought . . . did you notice it? I had seen her six days before. And now suddenly she looked so old and I thought . . . how has she become so withered? And I thought: It is not her suicide. It is Mama's. This is Mama, lying there. . . ."

When we walk back into the living room we do not close the door. My mother puts her finger to her lips and shakes her head, listening for the sound of Gertrude's breathing. "So okay," she says at last, "sleeping again."

She walks over to the coffee table and lights a match, blows it out, waves her hand in the air. "Mama and Gertrude were cut from the same cloth. That we have always known. What Celia and I never wanted to be, Gertrude became. The man she married, could you say he was like Papa? Maybe not, maybe not. But still, I tell you, the way he treated Gertrude was like Papa."

She falls silent and goes far from me, knocks up against some pattern she is not willing to speak about, gets entangled and loses herself. But I know perfectly well that in this moment she engages the full meaning of the fact that it was Celia, and not Gertrude, who followed out the tragedy of their mother. Celia, whose whole life was a running away, an extravagant refusal.

"Ach, sisters," she sighs, shaking her head. "Sisters, sisters."

It is at this moment that Larissa opens the door and looks into the room. Tiptoeing, her finger to her lips, she eases herself cautiously into the gray chair.

My mother lifts her head and we see her looking around, vaguely, disquietingly. "Where was I? Where was I?" she says.

"You were telling me about Gertrude and your mother."

"Yes," she says, and her voice changes, "my mother." But now she finds a new timbre, an emotional range never sounded by her before. For a moment, I hear helplessness and sorrow in this voice. There is a sense of unbearable despair that lives forbidden beneath her will to fight.

"My sisters you can only understand if you know my mother's life. And my life, too, you can only understand if you know my mother."

For a single instant she stands quietly, facing her own words. But I can feel that her will is gathering. In the next second she is full of animation again, driving herself so swiftly from one mood to another I am compelled to follow her, swept along in her passage.

She is pointing her index finger, the corners of her mouth turn down. "Yes," she declaims, "now in my life we have come to the fighting time. That's what I've been waiting to tell you. The time I decided to join the Communist Party. I ran for alderman in the borough election in the Bronx. It was . . . what? 1928 or 1929. Two or three years after I married Paul Kusnitz."

She looks around her, her cheeks flushed, her white hair almost transparent. And suddenly, she is standing outside of time. This, I imagine, is what she was like when she climbed up on a soapbox in the Bronx. There is that quality, a fervor, a capacity for vision, which makes you want to listen to whatever she has to say. Does it matter that the dream failed to come true so long ago? The wonder is, simply, she is still a dreamer.

She, a dreamer?

The Fourth Story My Mother Tells

I Fight for My Mother (1928–1932)

My mother at this time was in the state hospital in Binghamton, New York. I used to visit her once a month. She, as you know, had attempted suicide again. My father had committed her. And this, I tell you, is the story of the first victory I won. If you understand this story you understand my life. And why? Because this time my mother was in there for good. My father was her guardian, that's how it was. He certainly didn't want her home again. Over her life he had complete power. He didn't love her. Did I say love? He never even liked her. From the moment we put down our feet in America with his two fists he began to destroy her. Then, he tried to run from her. Now, without paying, he saw a way to be rid of her for good.

Binghamton Hospital was such a place, if you had an enemy, still you wouldn't put him there. No, I tell you, if this enemy was so bad milk would curdle because he came near to it, still you wouldn't put him there. I would not put even my father there.

To this day I see the place before my eyes. Those iron beds. The bare floor. On the walls, a gray color, peeling away. It was filled with forlorn, bedraggled old people. Everywhere was a feeling of despair. Poverty we knew, who could complain? But this was something more, it was worse. For everyone it was terrible. But for my mother it was Gehenna, a living hell. She was completely alone. There was nobody who spoke Yiddish or Russian. Every time I came there she said, "I'm going to die here. Rochele, I'm going to die."

They used to give her injections. These needles terrified her. How could she understand what they were for? Naturally, no one explained anything to her. How could they? She didn't understand English. Later, I made inquiries. I found out she was diabetic. I explained to her why they were giving the injections, but she was still afraid. Each time I came, she grabbed my hand and squeezed it: "Rochele, take me out of here."

When I came away, after a visit, I was in such a state. I didn't know what to do. At the hospital, I used to ask them if we could bring her maybe to New York City. There she could be closer to me. I could visit her every week. But they said, "She cannot be moved." Always the same thing. "You are not her guardian. You're her daughter. Only your father can give the permission for her to change to another place."

I wrote to my father, I asked him if Mama could be transferred to another hospital. Always I received the same reply: "When she gets better she will be released. Until then, what can be done?"

So, every month I went there and every month she was getting worse. She cried all the time. She had been a woman with a nice shape, but now she was so thin you thought maybe they were starving her in this place. No one combed her hair. No one dressed her. She wore one of those institutional gowns, all wrinkled.

"Rochele, I'm going to die here," was all she could say to me.

This was my mother. My mother, you understand? Maybe I sent her back to live with my father. Maybe I left her and went away into my life. But now? Could I leave her now like this, in such a place, desperate?

Finally, I couldn't live with it anymore. It was eating up my life. One time, after my visit, I was in the station. The train was coming. I was on my feet, walking to get on there. But suddenly I was running, away from the train, back to the hospital. I stormed in there, asking for the head psychiatrist.

"It's after visiting hours," the nurse said to me. But believe me,

I gave her such a look, she turned right around and took me to the doctor.

"This is no place for her," I told him. He asked me to sit down. "Sit?" I said. "I should sit here while my mother is in torment?" He gives me a look. Two months before, this look maybe would get me to sit down. But now? Nothing could stop me. "Doctor," I said, "what do I know about medicine? I admit, I know nothing. Do I know what your diagnosis is? This, too, I don't know. But, Doctor, I am here to tell you, you yourself don't know if this woman is sick. You're holding her here because my father wants it that way."

"Sick?" he says. "You can see for yourself. She won't eat. She's terribly confused. The nurses talk to her. The other patients talk to her. She just doesn't respond."

Could I believe what my ears were hearing? "Doesn't respond?" Was there something wrong in this man? "Of course she doesn't respond. She can't speak English. Naturally she won't eat the food. This food is not the food she's used to. Everything here is strange to her. These aren't her people. This is what you are calling insane?"

He didn't say anything. But I remember, he wasn't looking at me. He was looking down, at the desk. So I said, "To you any foreign person would be peculiar, wouldn't they? You think she's insane because you are not used to people like her."

But now, of course, I am beginning to shake. This man, I think to myself, is a doctor. And who am I to be talking to a doctor like this? But still, I notice that my mouth is talking. I begin to reason with him: "What would you lose if I took her home? I'm married. To an engineer. And we are willing to have her live with us."

Here he suddenly looked up. He seemed astonished. "She can't stay in a normal environment," he said. "She's insane. Suppose she killed somebody?"

My mother kill somebody? My mother? She, the most gentle creature in the world? Now my voice went up. It got louder: "Nobody said she was violent. Nobody. How could anyone say such a thing about her? The only person she tried to kill was herself."

But he insisted, "She could endanger your life. You can't take her home. Your father is her guardian. He is the only person who can remove her. And he wants her here."

~ ~

Now, I ask you, what would you do in my place? I had reached the point where I couldn't live with this situation. I couldn't stand the injustice in it. That selfish old man oppressing this woman so he wouldn't have to take responsibility for her.

But what could I do? What could anyone do? Even in America my father had the law on his side. This bothered me. We had expected so much from America. I couldn't believe this old woman would be left to suffer like that. At night I would wake up shaking my pillow, squeezing and shaking it.

Then I remembered we knew a lawyer in Binghamton whose name was Chernin. He was a distant cousin. I looked up his name in the telephone book. The next time I went to visit my mother, I called this man. "You don't know me," I said. "My name is Rose Chernin. But my father always told me that Chernin, spelled like this, is from the same family."

The man was happy to speak to me. After all, we were kinsmen. I went to see him and told him our story. "A Jewish man," he says, "treating a wife like this?"

He wanted to meet my mother, so right away I took him to the hospital. He was a cheerful man. I remember he was talking, telling his stories as we walked through the gate. But in the hospital he took one look and, let me tell you, he reached out, he grabbed my wrist. Good, I thought to myself; now he sees, he'll help us.

My mother came over. "Let me go away with you, Rochele," she said. "Take me away from here." She turned to this man. "Tell her," she said to him in Yiddish, "tell her I'll die here."

Well, I don't have to make a long story out of it. The next time I went to speak with this man he says to me, "If your husband is willing to become her guardian I think it will be possible to get her out of here."

Could I tell you how I felt? I was going to bring Mama home. I brought her a velvet dress. It was made for her specially by a woman I knew, a seamstress who was working in the ILGWU, Sonia Bloom, the sister of the famous painter. She was living downstairs from us and when I told her, "Sonia, I'm bringing Mama home," she went off and ripped down some curtains. She made a beautiful dress for Mama. We went out and bought black shoes, a little purse for her, some earrings.

The nurse brought Mama out, her hair was combed, she was wearing the velvet dress. "Mama," I said to her, "I'm taking you home. You're going home with me, Mama."

She put her hand up to her cheek. Her voice was thin. "Home," she said. "For a vacation?"

"For good, Mama," I said, throwing my arms around her. "You'll never come back here again."

~ ~

So there you have it. This was the first battle I won against injustice. It made on me a deep impression. I had a sense now of what was possible. An ignorant woman could oppose a doctor. She would win against an educated man. A woman could stand up against an institution.

I was not a Communist at this time. I still couldn't commit myself to anything. I read Marxism with your father, I went out to the Russian Club, we supported the strikes of the workers, but something held me back.

Already in the shtetl we were thinking about this country. There we will get an education, when Papa sends for us we will go to America, there we won't be poor anymore.

But now I was hearing about things; I was learning about the exploitation of the workers and we heard about the way Negroes were living in the South. If a Negro man looked at a white women he would be lynched. We heard stories about the Ku Klux Klan and these bothered me, they really bothered me. All this reminded me of the pogrom; this we were used to for the Jews in Russia. But here in America?

Mama stayed with us about a year. I can't say it was an ideal situation. Nina had been born the year before and the apartment was crowded. We lived on the sixth floor in the Bronx and it was hard for Mama to climb the stairs. She had no interest in life. She wasn't interested in the baby. I thought Mama would be happy living in our home. But she only wanted to cook and bake. We had enough baked goods to feed the entire neighborhood. She cooked so much that Paul Kusnitz, who was a slender man, had to eat for five.

He used to say to her, "Bake. Bake. You know how I am, Mama. Always hungry."

She was so proud of him, proud that he was an engineer, proud that he was a Kusnitz. In her eyes the Kusnitz family was very high up. They owned the butcher shop in Waterbury.

But she wasn't well. The fear bothered her, the terrible fear she'll be sent back to the hospital. Nothing I said could reassure her. She slept maybe two hours a night, she worried all the time. Later, much later, when Celia came back to live in America, she had the same symptoms as Mama. All night you could hear her, wandering around in the house. Sometimes I'd wake up for Nina and there I'd find her, my mother, walking around the apartment. "They're coming for me, Rochele," she'd say. "I hear them knocking."

"Don't you worry, Mama," I'd tell her. "No one will ever take you away again."

But it was hard for me. It was like having two children in the house. I would get irritated at her and I couldn't help her. Nothing would make her stop worrying. Even your father, he even didn't know how to reassure her.

And yet, you know how it is. After a while she seemed to get better. She went shopping, she bought flour and yeast and sugar. She began to sing a little as she went about the house and one day she said to me she would like to take a job. She felt it was too crowded in our apartment. She maybe knew it was hard for me with her there. She told us she met a woman in the grocery who needed a housekeeper. She wanted Mama to come and live with her and take care of her two children.

But here I'll tell you something. Before this, Mama had another opportunity. She used to shop at a butcher who was a widower. And (would you believe it?) this man wanted to marry her. When I heard this I thought the millennium had come. I said to her, "Marry him. Divorce Papa."

But she said, "You don't divorce. You marry and that's it. You make your bed, you lie in it."

So, naturally, we didn't expect much to come of her job. But a strange thing happened. Every time I saw the woman who hired her, she would say to me, "Your mother is an angel sent from heaven."

Each time Mama came home to us she seemed better and better. And each time I met the woman she said, "An angel from heaven."

But one day Mama came home and said she got a letter from Papa. He had moved to California. And we were already thinking: Oh no, not that. Because we could see what was coming. But she said, yes, she is going to California because Papa wants her and Lillian needs her. We began to reason with her: "Don't go. Stay here. You have a job. It's nice for you. Why should you go? We won't bother you about the butcher anymore."

But Papa wrote to her again and she couldn't resist. When Papa wanted her, she would go. She was better, she was well again, she had to decide for herself. You can do only so much for a person. Only so much. I fought for my mother when she was helpless, when she didn't know how to help herself. But now it was up to her.

So I let her go. I didn't hold her back. Maybe I should have tried harder, maybe I should have insisted she come back to live with us. But that's how it was. And maybe I even wanted it that way. Should I lie to you?

~ ~

By then it was 1931 or 1932, the beginning of the Great Depression. Millions of workers were unemployed. There was no social security, no unemployment insurance. Hoovervilles sprang up on every vacant lot and city dump. They were houses made of old boxes, burlap bags, rags, and refuse that littered the dumps. The people living in these hovels ate from rotting foods rejected by markets. They lived on garbage thrown out by hotels. In every neighborhood, you saw soup kitchens, and on every street corner people selling apples.

There was a tremendous amount of migration during that time. As soon as you left the cities you saw people begging rides, hopping freight trains or traveling in flivvers — old junk cars that were patched together. People kept on the move, looking for work, looking for a better place to live. There were so many millions of people unemployed. If you went to a factory you could see fifteen, twenty, thirty people waiting there, every day, all day long, hoping that somebody would get hurt, or fired, or die. They stood at the docks, on street corners, waiting. The whole world, waiting.

Everywhere was this same dread and worry: What will happen? They were hungry people, talking, waiting. There was fear — the fear of losing a job, of losing an apartment, of not being able to feed the family. We all felt it. There seemed to be no hope.

But then, one day, the Communist Party called a mass demonstration in Union Square. One hundred thousand men and women came out. William Foster was the main speaker. Mounted police surrounded the crowd. The slogans we carried read: JOBS OR WAGES. This crowd was very powerful. When Foster spoke we would cry out with one voice. JOBS OR WAGES. JOBS OR WAGES. If someone moved everyone moved with them. We were pressed together shoulder to shoulder.

But then something happened I will never forget. The police rode into the crowd and scattered the people. In America, police on horseback rode into the crowd.

Foster was the general secretary of the Communist Party. He said: ORGANIZE. March on the streets, demand food, demand unemployment insurance, demand social security, demand wages. ORGANIZE.

That is how I remember it. His words showed us the way out. I felt the justice of what he said. We could not wait for someone to give to us what we needed. We, the workers, had to make demands. Then I looked up and I could see those horses coming. It was a nightmare. And we were paralyzed. They were riding straight toward us, riding us down. Suddenly someone screamed. It was, how can I tell you? Never in my life, before or since, have I heard anything like that shriek. I heard, in that cry . . . to me it seemed we were standing in a village and the cossacks were riding down. You could go so far back in Jewish history and always you would find that cry. Always, in the history of every people. And then people were running all around me, racing for the subway, screaming, crowding together. And I ran with them, and I was thinking, this, this is the answer they give to the demands of the people. I will never forget it. I stood there, looking out at the crowd. My fear was gone. I felt angry, I felt exhilarated, and I felt purposeful. That was the day I joined the Communist Party.

Now I was ready; I was developing as a socialist thinker, I had fought for my mother and now I was ready to start fighting for the people.

That Celia turned out a different way, that Gertrude, with her heart of gold, became still another kind of person, this, in all my life, I never understood. To me, to become what I became was inevitable. From that family, in those times, who could become some other kind of person?

We were poor. Your father was always worried about what would happen if he lost the job. He talked and thought about it constantly. This worry began to characterize his life. I hated the system for doing this to him. We lived in a small apartment, six floors up. I was a mother, I was active in various political organizations, and your father earned the money to support us. He read and studied Marxism, he belonged to a study club and at night he taught a class in Marxist theory. After dinner, you could see him there, at the kitchen table, the sleeves rolled up. He and another man would be playing chess. Sometimes, when I was going out the door, I'd turn back. There he'd be, a man with such a gentle look on his face. Imagine, I'd think to myself, this is Paul Kusnitz. This man is my husband.

Always, we respected each other. I was proud of his education. I was proud of his understanding. And he admired me for the way I could speak to people and organize. In our home there was, between the husband and wife, something never known in our family before.

This man was to me everything my father had never been to my mother. This man was to Nina all that my father had not been to us. It outraged me to see the way this man was forced to worry what would happen if he lost the job. We saw this happening around us and for everyone the dread was growing.

The things we take for granted now, part of the American way of life, these were revolutionary ideas when we began to demand them in the thirties. We wanted unemployment insurance; we wanted home relief, hot meals for children in schools, and housing for the destitute people living in the city dumps.

In that time, who heard of the eight-hour day? If a man would be hurt on the job, you think the employer would pay a cent to him? Why should he care? There was always another poor man to take his place. Even the idea of a union was in this time a new concept in the world. No one expected decent wages. The others, with the privilege, were born up there. But we were on the bottom. To us, the idea that we had the right to strike was something hard even to imagine.

So what could be done about all this? How could a person, a woman not even five feet tall, change the world?

I'll tell you. It's a good story, because in those days we began to organize. We formed Unemployed Councils. They were spontaneous peoples' organizations and I want you to know about them because I helped to organize them from the first days. In this activity I was already involved before I joined the Communist Party.

We would open an office in the middle of a neighborhood. We'd come in during the morning, make coffee, people would bring doughnuts and we would talk. Suddenly another person would come in and we'd say, "Hi, who are you?"

"I was just laid off."

And you should have heard the shout: "Hooray! Another one laid off. Wonderful."

He would look at us as though we were crazy. Why should we celebrate that he was laid off? For him it meant no wages, no rent, no place to sleep, nothing to eat. So why were we excited? We said, "We're glad you're here. We'll have one more person to distribute leaflets."

This was the way we changed the terrible thing that was happening to this man, and to all of us, into productive action. We got into control of our lives. We were no longer victims.

It's so simple. I used to wonder why other people didn't see it, too. You cannot fail. Basically, failure is impossible; already, just in being together, you have changed the personal tragedy, this despair, this hopelessness, into a collective endeavor.

Our main task was to try to get a congressman to introduce a bill for unemployment insurance. We circulated a petition, house to house, in the tenements of the Bronx.

A typical encounter would go like this: I and another person would enter the building and knock on the first door we came to. Someone, usually a man, would open the door. Just a crack at first. Then, when he saw we were not the landlord, he'd open it wider. I'd say, "We're here circulating a petition asking a congressman to introduce a bill in Congress. We want unemployment insurance and we think we can get the government to give it to us. Is there anybody unemployed in this family?"

"Are you kidding? Everybody is unemployed in this family." Or they'd say, "Most of us are unemployed, one is working but he expects to be laid off by the end of the week."

We told them, "We, too, are unemployed workers and we want Congress to pass a bill giving us either jobs or wages."

So they'd say, not believing, "You're asking the government to give us money without working?" People just couldn't believe we were asking for this.

And we'd answer, "Yes, we're asking the government to give us jobs. If they can't give us jobs, they have to support us."

"But you're asking for socialism."

"We're asking for jobs or money."

We organized around our basic needs. We could speak very easily to people because we also were working people. I always found it strange when people didn't join us. I used to think about this because to me organization seemed so essential. You wonder, maybe, why I became a Communist. But I used to wonder why everyone did not. Basically, I felt that those who failed to join us had no confidence in themselves or in the fact that we could change the system. They are the ones who say, "We're just poor people. What can we do?" We would hear this when we went about knocking on the doors.

I, on the other hand, when I talked to people, could convince them to struggle against their conditions. I believed in this struggle. That is all it takes to be an organizer. Belief in our power.

Take an example: We felt the one thing the system feared was angry women. We wanted milk for the children. So, we would get twenty or thirty women together. We'd go out early in the morning. We would come into the borough hall. We would demand to speak to an alderman. Each one of us came with a child in the carriage. Nina was three or four years old; she always came with me.

Who could forget it, a sight like this? There was a woman in a red sweater, rolled up at the sleeves. Another one with a kerchief on the head. The faces with a look of determination. And the children, this one in a blue cap the grandma knitted. Nina had a little open face with merry eyes. And we would go stepping together, all the women on the left foot, then all on the right. Singing, chanting: "We want milk. Milk for the children."

We would go about the streets advertising the neighborhood councils. We'd ask people to come and told them to bring whatever they could spare. There was always something to eat in the councils. People would drop in, we'd get them to work on a pamphlet, we would involve them in a conversation. Coming off the street in those days, out of that despair, you can imagine the impact the council made upon them.

The women were organized to monitor the prices of food all the time. If an item became too expensive in a particular store, we immediately went on strike. Again, we came with the children in the carriage. We picketed with the sign: DON'T PATRONIZE THIS GRO-CERY. THEY ARE CHARGING TOO MUCH FOR BREAD.

These strikes were very successful. Nobody would cross our picket lines.

The same things were happening in Brooklyn, in Manhattan, in Harlem. In Harlem the starvation was legion and soup kitchens couldn't supply the people with enough food. We used to move whatever we could from the council to Harlem.

This struggle of people against their conditions, that is where you find the meaning in life. In the worst situations, you are together with people. If there were five apples, we cut them ten ways and every-body ate. If somebody had a quarter, he went down to the corner and bought some bread and brought it back into the council.

Life changes when you are together in this way, when you are united. You lose the fear of being alone. You cannot solve these problems when you are alone. They become overwhelming. When you are standing, one to one, with an employer, he has all the power and you have none. But together, we felt our strength, and we could laugh. Someone who knew how to sing would start singing. Others would know how to dance. There we were, unemployed people, but we were dancing.

In those years I was happy. Happy, you say? With the unemploy-ment, the evictions, the high prices of food? But that's how it was. And why? In those years I became what I have been all my life since then. And from this maybe comes happiness, what else?

If you're an organizer and you see how successfully people are coming together you feel fulfilled. We were very successful in our activities. We kept prices down, we kept pressure on the congressmen, we were making people conscious of their identity as workers, and we were winning rent strikes.

You know how people lived in that time, in the tenements of the Bronx. There were brick buildings, most of them without elevators, old houses with dark staircases and narrow corridors. There were people in the basement apartments, people crowded into small spaces, living together, sometimes without a bedroom, sharing kitchens and toilets, and afraid to lose the little space they had.

But these places, which no one would call exactly a castle, were better than the street. If a man would lose the job, a week later you'd see his whole family sitting out on the street. So we decided to ask for a reduction. An entire apartment house or a whole tenement would refuse to pay the landlord until the rents were reduced for everyone in the building.

By that time the Unemployed Councils were well known: our workers were everywhere, leading demonstrations, circulating petitions, speaking on street corners. So we would go into a building, introduce ourselves, and ask the people to organize. We said, "As long as we strike we certainly don't pay rent. Let's say we're striking for three months. That rent will never be paid."

The people listened, the idea appealed to them. We promised that we would fight the evictions and help take care of the people who were thrown out. In those days you would walk down the street and see whole families with their children sitting on the sidewalk surrounded by furniture.

When an entire building was organized and willing to participate in a strike, we formed negotiating committees for the tenants, put up large signs in every window facing the street, and picketed the house. The signs read: RENT STRIKE. DON'T RENT APARTMENTS IN THIS BUILDING.

The landlord, of course, would rather die than give in to the tenants' demands. So the strike began. We knew that one day he would give some eviction notices. But he could never evict everyone. It cost too much.

On the day of the eviction we would tell all the men to leave the building. We knew that the police were rough and would beat them up. It was the women who remained in the apartments, in order to resist. We went out onto the fire escapes and spoke through bull-horns to the crowd that gathered below.

In the Bronx you could get two hundred people together if you just looked up at the sky. As soon as the police came to begin the eviction, we roped off the street and people gathered. The police put machine guns on the roofs, they pointed them down at the people in the street.

We, meanwhile, were standing out on the balcony. I would address the crowd gathered in the street below: "People, fellow workers. We are the wives of unemployed men and the police are evicting us. Today *we* are being evicted. Tomorrow it will be *you*. So stand by and watch. What is happening to us will happen to you. We have no jobs. We can't afford food. Our rents are too high. The marshal has brought the police to carry out our furniture. Are you going to let it happen?"

Or sometimes we would address the workers who had been brought to take the furniture: "We are talking to you, you men who have come here to throw out the furniture of unemployed workers. Who are you? You, too, are unemployed men who have had to take this job in order to eat. We don't blame you. You are one of us. We represent the Unemployed Council and last night we made a collection among the unemployed. We have enough money to pay you off. How much are you going to get for evicting an unemployed worker? Five dollars? Six dollars? We have the money for you. Come up here without the police and without the marshal and we will pay you off. Look at the marshal standing there. Is he working? Let him do the work."

And so we would harangue. We could see the men hesitating. We would continue: "We women are standing here with the furniture that is to be evicted. The water is hot in our kettles. The doors are locked. We're not letting you in."

Often, the hired men would come up anyway. Our doors were locked but they would break them in. We were behind those doors, with our kettles. They would grab a piece of furniture on one side and we would grab it on the other. And both would start pulling. Meanwhile we would say: "Here, here is the money. Leave the furniture."

Some would take the money and go. Sometimes we poured the hot water on the men. Sometimes they would hit us. And then we would run out onto the fire escape, grab the bullhorn, and shout to the crowd: "They're hitting us. They're big men and they're hitting us. But we're not going to let them move the furniture. They can't overcome us. We shall win."

Sometimes, they'd get so disgusted with all this fighting and hollering they'd take the furniture from the apartment but leave it on the landing. That was a victory. We'd stay there and wait for the husbands to return and then we'd put the furniture back into the apartment. We'd put a new lock on the door and the landlord would have to get a new eviction notice. He'd call the marshal and the whole thing would start all over again.

Our fight was successful. The rents came down, the evicted families returned to their apartments, the landlord would stop fighting us. Sometimes we failed and the furniture was carried into the street. Immediately we would cover it with a tarpaulin so it wouldn't get spoiled, and then we'd hold a mass meeting on the furniture, using it as a platform. We were only waiting for the police to leave. As soon as they were gone, the people standing around would pick up the furniture and carry it right back into the building. We'd break the lock, put back the furniture, install a new lock, and the landlord would have to go through the whole procedure another time.

Within two years we had rent control in the Bronx. That's the way it was in those days.

— —

At that time I was running for alderman in a borough election in the Bronx. The idea was to establish the right of Communists to file themselves as official candidates. We knew we couldn't win the election, but if you were running you had to conduct a campaign. It was an opportunity to raise the issues concerning the people.

That was when I made my first street-corner speech. You'd bring a box or a little ladder with you, someone would distribute pamphlets, and you'd introduce yourself as the Communist Party alderman candidate. Hundreds of people would gather.

When I began to speak, I was very scared. Every time I got up to open my mouth I'd feel the fear. But I was a Communist, I felt that a Communist shouldn't be afraid. Rose, I'd say to myself, with this fear you could have spent your life in Waterbury. I'd put down my box, I'd get up there, and let me tell you, I would be shaking.

The crowd used to heckle. It was not a hostile crowd but it liked to taunt. I felt, on the one hand, it was my obligation to instruct the people and raise their understanding. These were my people. Between us, there was no difference, only a difference of understanding. But, on the other hand, who wants to stand there and have questions fired at you?

"What do you think of the Soviet Union?" someone asked.

"They don't have unemployment there."

"How do you know?"

"I read it in the paper."

"What paper do you read?"

"I read the *Daily Worker*."

"You can't believe a word you read in the *Daily Worker*."

"And I say you can't believe a word you read in the *Times*."

When I came home, at night, I would say to your father, "I just don't know why I joined the Communist Party." I was doing something so difficult. I was scared to death. Your father would put everything aside and sit down and talk to me. He always encouraged me, he supported me. We discussed together the questions that were raised by the people in the crowd and we looked for answers.

Your father was not yet a Communist, but he surely was a sympathizer, and he was much stronger theoretically than I was. I felt, during those early days as a Communist, my strength lay in my ability to organize. But I had doubts about my knowledge of Marxist theory. Always when I got up on a street corner, I was afraid someone will ask me about the theory.

I heard a speaker at that time who was a master of the street situation. He was addressing an open-air meeting; he had a thick Irish brogue and he would stand there talking, easy, like he was speaking to his cronies. Somebody from the crowd called out, "Mr. Quill, are you a Communist?"

And I'll never forget his answer. "If I thought that you knew the difference between Communism and rheumatism I would tell you."

I did a lot of footwork at the time. Wherever there was a strike I was there as a candidate, representing the Communist Party.

In the Bronx, at that time, we had a Communist cooperative. It was the first integrated building in New York. There were many Jews there, of course, and many black people moved in, too. And their children (I am the witness to it) talked better Yiddish (and still do) than all the other kids there.

It was a real cooperative. People put their money together, borrowed from the bank, rebuilt the building, and lived together. Your father and I wanted to join them, but we didn't have enough money for the investment. They had everything there — a shopping center, a nursery. They organized summer camps for the children and you will come across many important people, to this day, who could tell you about this cooperative, if they wanted to admit their beginnings.

There was a wonderful mood in that cooperative. Something you just wouldn't see anymore in the world. There, it was a common thing for the children to be named Leon Trotsky Blume or Vladimir Lenin Jones. You'd be walking past the building and you'd hear a mother shout, from the fifth floor, "Leon Trotsky, come right up here, if you don't want to get a smack. You can't fool me, Leon Trotsky, I know you wet your pants."

The cooperative was an enclave, a little corner of socialism right in the middle of New York. All this was part of the International Workers Order, which the Communist Party had organized; the IWO was very powerful, it had local groups all over the city, with musical performances and Yiddish folksinging, there were theater groups, schools for teaching children about political events, there were literary groups and even a mandolin ensemble. The cooperative in the Bronx was part of this movement and it had its own educational events, clubs for men and women, lectures, motion pictures. It was a center of culture, and the workers who lived in it, I tell you, were proud of what they were.

These were the early years of our movement and there was always an excitement. The Party at this time was organizing the Young Pioneers and you could see these children all over the coop, running around with their red scarves around the neck. As your sister grew older, she became part of all this; her entire life she lived in the movement. When I joined the party and began to organize full time, I always took her with me. I felt I had something to give to this little girl, an understanding to pass on to her. Children were very important in our movement; who else would carry on our struggle? You felt proud to be a mother who had contributed also her child to building the future.

Nina was very receptive to all this. She was a good-natured child, very easy to get along with. At night, when I was preparing dinner, she'd stand up on the chair in the kitchen and make speeches for alderman in the Bronx. We couldn't get her to take off the red scarf when she went to sleep at night. So of course we used to worry. "What if she strangles herself with the scarf?" I'd say to Paul. He'd go in there, very quietly; he'd take off the scarf and lay it on the pillow. Then, in the morning, she'd ask him, with her big eyes, "Papa, how did the scarf get off? Who put it on the pillow?" And he, with that twinkle in his eyes, would always say to her, "Ninochka, my apple, better you should ask the scarf."

She was your father's child, with the same twinkling eyes. But if I didn't want to take her with me to a demonstration she would just howl! Of course, we knew she didn't want to be left alone without her mother. But we would joke. "Look at this little one," we'd say, "howling because she can't go out to demonstrate for the people."

We knew, when she grows up, she will be joining the Young Communist League. She will be going down to write for the *Daily Worker.* That was the great dream we had for her and in fact all this happened, exactly the way we dreamed. She was very proud to be a Communist when she was in high school and this pride began when she was a little girl, holding my hand when we walked in the coop in the East Bronx. This was the golden time of our movement. Always I regretted that you, my daughter, could not participate in it.

~ ~

The alderman election was held in 1932 and, of course, I lost. We never expected to win but the campaign itself was important. We established our right to file as official candidates in an election. We raised the issues of the workers. All over New York people knew the work the Communist Party was doing for the poor, for the Negroes, for the unemployed.

If I heard someone talk about the Communist Party, I knew also they were talking about me.

But now, after the campaign was over, I felt exhausted. I had a terrible case of laryngitis. Right after the election I went to California with Nina, for a rest and to visit my family.

There everything was the same. But now it was a terrible shock to me. I had forgotten about it. Here was my life. Such purpose it had. In this small life of a person, was something so big, maybe already the future of the world.

But here, with my family, everything was the same! My father was as bad tempered as ever, just as cruel to my mother. My sister Lillian, who was sixteen, seemed a very unhappy person. She didn't talk to anybody. She sat in a rocking chair, listened and didn't say a word. Gertrude was married and was in training as a nurse. My brother, Milton, was a graduate student in college. Celia was working with her husband Harry in their delicatessen store. I admit, already it didn't seem a life for Celia, but who could know then what was hidden in the future?

I had come from New York, from the campaign, the strikes, the council, from all our activity. And there was Celia, sitting in the delicatessen store, selling salami.

The minute I came to Los Angeles I got in touch with the Party. I told them I was staying for a month. Right away they wanted me to begin organizing.

Then, I heard from your father; he was working for the city of New York, on the Eighth Avenue Subway. The work was completed and all the engineers were laid off. So, finally it had happened. Everything we feared. Now, what would happen?

In New York the only jobs available for the engineers were in those cubbyholes in the subway, exchanging dimes for nickels. Paul couldn't accept the job; none of the engineers would accept it, they agreed.

He was the sort of man who didn't like to show he was upset. But this time he couldn't hide it. We talked many times, from Los Angeles to New York, and one time he said there was maybe the possibility of finding work, as an engineer, in the Soviet Union. He had been down to Amtorg, the American Trading Company, and he heard they were starting to build a subway in Moscow.

Finally, he came to me in Los Angeles. We took an apartment

together and tried to find work. And meanwhile, we were waiting to hear about the Soviet Union.

In my usual fashion, I told myself it could never happen. We had a saying in the shtetl, it was in Russian, but the Jews learned it from the peasants. *"Da nashevo berega, dabro nie daplievot."* It means, "Nothing good ever swims to our shores." Your father of course didn't believe in this saying. Always, in his life, he was a very optimistic man. "You, a Don Quixote," I would say to him when we quarreled. "Are you living at least in the real world?" We tried not to think about the Soviet Union. Better, I thought, we should just forget there is such a thing as the subway in Moscow. Such happiness, in this life, is not for me.

We had, at the time, about two hundred dollars in savings. Food was very cheap. The government was giving away beans and canned milk for children. You could live on three or four dollars a week. Everything was cheaper than in New York, especially the fruits and vegetables. The Kusnitz family was still in the meat business and most of them had already moved to California. We lived on our savings and we waited.

I certainly did not take a month's rest. My voice got better and I immediately became active. There were Unemployed Councils in Los Angeles, too, there were strikes and there was talk of revolution. Everywhere you heard people speaking about the revolution.

Then, one day, we received notice that jobs were open in the Soviet Union. In New York a group of engineers was forming. We were going to Moscow!

We went to say good-bye to my mother and we told her that we're leaving for the Soviet Union. She said, "Where will you live?"

"We're going to live in Moscow, Mama. Paul is going to build a subway."

"In Moscow!" she says. "You can't live in Moscow!"

"Mama," I said to her, "what do you mean?"

"No Jews are allowed to live in Moscow."

The world hadn't changed for her. For her, it was all exactly the way she had left it twenty years before. I said, "Mama, there was a revolution. And now we're going to live in Moscow and work on the subway."

She had no idea what the revolution was. I explained to her, "There is no czar, Mama."

"It can't be. No more czar? What happened to him?"

"The czar was put to death by the people."

She looked shocked. "The czar?" she said.

"Mama, it was a revolution for the people."

But she shook her head; she couldn't believe it. "The czar?" she repeated. "What a terrible thing."

Wasn't I Once Also a Daughter?

Suddenly we are dancing. How this came about we cannot say. Perhaps I was on my way back to the kitchen when Larissa intercepted me. We are whirling about on a treacherous obstacle course, between the red chair and the coffee table, out onto the polished floor, slipping and gliding together. I leap over the coffee table and throw myself on the couch. Larissa races after me. "You can't live in Moscow. No Jews could live in Moscow," she hoots, understanding something she could not have grasped even a week ago.

But my mother cannot get used to seeing us like this; our playfulness still takes her by surprise. "Yes, yes this is what she's like, Grandma," Larissa calls out, beginning to sound just like my mother. "Here we have the true, hidden nature of your daughter."

Puzzled, my mother shakes her head. She has not returned yet out of the story and now she falls to marveling about the way her mother did not allow the world to change.

"Mama," I shout over to her, putting my arm around Larissa, who is growing younger, her golden eyes deepening into the stories. "Just think of it, Mama. That old woman, living here in Los Angeles, dressing herself on the warmest summer day in three sweaters beneath her coat. For her the shtetl still existed. She believed her father was alive there, that Jews could still not live in Moscow, that the czar had not been deposed. That old woman, I tell you, carried a world around in her, still living, the rest of us have lost."

" 'So who's crazy,' Aunt Gertrude might say," adds Larissa, in her new Yiddish style, "who's crazy?"

But my aunt has not wanted to keep us company today. She has refused telephone calls and now, for hours, has been coughing and turning in the back of the house.

My mother, too, shows signs of strain. "You," she says to me, "from every scrap you make a blanket. This is what you understand from the story? From the ruin of that woman's life you see something to make you proud?"

I get to my feet. I am aware of that peculiar quickening in my chest that comes before anger. "Yes, sure, I see something here to make me proud."

But then, for an instant, I am standing outside myself. We see the world differently. What of that? We're not enemies. We're only, of necessity, a mother and daughter.

"I know there was poverty in the shtetl, Mama." My voice speaks these words calmly as if they were facts. "I know that I can't easily explain the nostalgia I feel for that vanished world."

She is sitting forward in her chair, her eyes narrowing. But now she tilts her head to the side, listening the way I have seen birds listen to what the world around them is saying.

And I know that between us the time has finally come. I will tell her, simply, the way the world looks to me. And she will listen.

"What we — my generation — long for, grew up in the shtetl in spite of hunger and dust; a sacred dimension to daily life, which held its own alongside the terror and violence."

For a moment, she says nothing. I have the curious sensation that I have spoken in some strange tongue that is incomprehensible to her.

But then, clearing her throat, she says, "This is a different shtetl than the one I knew. Or maybe," she whispers, and a look of great weariness comes into her eyes, "maybe I have forgotten."

~ ~

The first smell of almond and vanilla comes into the living room. My mother has crouched down in front of the oven, worrying about whether the cake will rise. This profound doubt used to infuriate me when I was learning to bake, this lack of faith, this certainty nothing left to itself could turn out right. "It's maybe not hot enough in there," she says to Larissa, who is standing in the doorway, her hands on her hips. But Larissa answers, after a moment, "It's hot enough."

My mother, reassured that everything is in good hands, comes back into the living room. She whispers to me, "A shame if that brilliant girl should spend her life baking."

Shall I tell her there is no need to worry any longer, that we no longer need to protect this child from her grandmother's fate?

"Remember," she says to me, "when I did not want you to learn typing? I worried," she says, "what if she becomes a secretary through this? You became the fastest typist in your school. Advanced typing already in junior high school. And so of course one day the principal calls you in to suggest secretarial school. When I heard this I went storming down to the school. "What do you mean, giving such advice to this girl?" I asked. "She has straight A's, doesn't she? She's the brightest girl in her class. This girl is going to college. How can you, a woman, advise her to sacrifice this? Don't you know how hard it is already for a girl to make the right choices? Shame on you. You should be ashamed."

She stares around her with a look of triumph; her eyes fiery, as she renews once again this ancient battle against the limiting of women.

"Mama, don't worry," I say to her through my tears, trying as always in the presence of this woman to keep watch over the extravagant emotion she awakens in me. "Larissa will be fine. She never knew your mother. What can she know about the breaking of a woman?"

"And what," my mother says, pressing our intimacy further than before, "about her sacrifice?"

This guilt, spoken directly for the first time, changes everything between us. Now, in a single instant, after a lifetime of longing, I have become her confidante. Finally now, because I have opened myself to her, she has brought out this stark, confessional word.

"She was not an easy woman," she says, taking another step toward me. And now there is a hesitation in her face, as if she were listening intently for signs of danger, sniffing the air, looking at me from the corner of her eyes. I do not move; I am praying that she will come closer. I feel a cough of tension scratching at my throat and it takes all my discipline to fight it down again.

"She always worried. She did not live in the same world we were in. In New York she could wake up and be terrified the cossacks were coming. 'Rochele, Rochele,' she would say, clinging to my hands, 'will we live until morning?' You tell it and the heart breaks. But it was not easy to live with."

I find it impossible to talk. One false move and I shall lose her again. But how can I remain silent in the face of this terrible vulnerability? There must be some right word, a gesture, something so perfectly modulated it will be neither too little nor too much.

And finally the silence has become unbearable, I am not deciding any longer, I am talking. I tell her a story about a girl from the shtetl who has come to the United States; and somehow she has managed to make her way to college. But now, although she works day and night to support herself, she is starving. And so one day she eats up her niece's porridge, she steals food from the child in order to survive.

At first, my mother looks warily at me. Then, frowning, she says, "Who wrote this story? Do I know her?"

"Anzia Yezierska," I tell her, not certain she will approve.

"Ah," she says, "that one." And the tone implies: Well, she may not have been one of us, but she did not belong to the enemy either.

Now we exchange that long, difficult look it has taken me almost forty years to understand. There is that piercing quality in her gaze which makes you feel you have been seen more deeply, more knowingly than ever before in your life, but not by a seer who is untroubled by this gift. And soon you come to realize that in this gaze is also a look of insecurity, an asking for approval that, even when given, will not be believed. It is the sort of look women exchange between their words, determining the outcome of their relations, fatefully, silently. And meanwhile, the conversation, despite its futility, races on at even greater intensity, trying to overcome the judgment that has been passed in silence.

But this time, she is going to push herself further. "This story," she says, "I understand. It is easier when you hear it about someone else's life. It seems . . . even, forgivable. One sees the social meanings; this tragedy of woman, always needing to sacrifice someone else in order to go after her own life."

"Mama," something in me cries out. But I am stunned to silence by the fact that she has not closed me out of her despair. And now, raising her fists to her temples, she hammers upon them in a sudden excess of grief. She says, echoing me: "Mama." She says it once, softly. Then there is that closing down in her face, a look of rage that her secrets have been exposed, a flash of accusation, of warning. Our intimacy is gone.

But in the silence that pushes itself between us there is a new sensation. She has given me this moment of truth.

Larissa enters the room with a perfect oval of cake, a light yellow slightly browning, steam rising from it, her face flushed with an effort not to show her pride. We see her for a moment beneath the hall light as she passes farther into darkness and knocks softly on the bedroom door. "Tante Gertrude," she calls out, "I have a surprise for you."

~ ~

After dinner, the youngest sister, Aunt Lillian, arrives breathless, in a rush of anxiety and grief. My mother tells her to be strong, to remember what a brave woman she is. But my aunt hears nothing. She looks nervously around, her eyes darting rapidly from my mother to me. Now she catches sight of Larissa, who is standing near the door with an empty tray in her hands. Lillian rushes over to her. Immediately, Larissa reports in a clear voice, "She's resting now, she ate dinner, she ate a large piece of cake, she's taking her medicine, she's not smoking."

Temporarily reassured, Lillian takes off her sweater and scarf. She sets down her red purse and straightens her hair in the mirror. But then, moving rapidly, with that nervous animation so characteristic of her, she rushes off into the bedroom. At the door she stops, and calls behind her, tossing her words back, "She's trying to starve herself to death. That's how it is. She just can't get over what 'that one' did to her."

"That one?" I say to my mother. But I already know. She's talking about Gertrude's daughter, my cousin Vida.

My family keeps its secrets. And I as a small girl learned how to listen in silence. If I keep watch for the sudden movement of a hand, or an expression in passage across a face, I shall find out soon enough what Vida has done to her mother.

Lillian comes back into the room, her eyes roving from one to the other of us, trying to determine where the greatest sympathy will be found. Moved, as always, by this lost, unhappy woman, I hold out my hand to her. She accepts me. There are times when I feel that she, who finds it so difficult to trust, distinctly trusts me. She sits down next to me on the couch. She does not want to cry; she takes out a handkerchief from the sleeve of her sweater and presses it hard into the corner of her eye. She is afraid my mother will not approve of this weeping.

"Why wasn't I stronger all my life?" she says.

"You'll *be,*" my mother answers, admonishing.

Lillian is filled with despair. Her hands rise to her temples, she presses her fists against the sides of her face. "Too late," she cries out, "too late," and my mother intones, "You'll be strong. You have to be."

Larissa watches them as if she were studying an unfamiliar species. Her eyes, with their precocious intensity, seem to be recording everything, gathering in material. But there is nothing cold, unfeeling in this gaze; its detachment hides a hunger for understanding. Her reserve is an illusion.

Lillian paces the room. She is a short, plump woman, with dyed hair, childlike in her undisguised vulnerability. Her heavy breasts, bound securely beneath a tight dress, rise and fall with feeling.

"I remember when Mama arrived in Los Angeles," she suddenly bursts out, with a tone of such passionate outrage we all look over at her and wait, shrinking inwardly from what is to follow. "I saw a short, shabbily dressed, stout, chubby little woman who threw herself at me and yelled in Yiddish, 'I'm your mother.' I drew back. I hated her. I felt that she had usurped Gertrude's place. I don't remember her from Waterbury. I don't remember her from Canonsville. I heard talk, and it was frightening; I heard that my mother was in a mental hospital. But I never had the kind of mothering from her that they did. She gave all her mothering to them. She had nothing to give me. By the time I came along, it was all used up. Whatever I got had come to me from Gertrude."

"Lillian, Lillian," my mother cries out, impatient with this flood of words. "Lillian," she repeats, "remember. You're a nurse."

"What's that got to do with anything?" Lillian shouts back.

"You know what life's all about," her older sister answers.

And Lillian, gesturing with a Kleenex in her hand, shouts over her head, "Don't tell me. Death is not part of life."

Larissa glances at me. She manages to have absolutely no expression on her face; if I think she is about to burst out laughing that is my problem.

My mother has managed to bring Lillian around. "We're strong women," Lillian admits, looking at no one in particular. "Why should I deny it?"

Larissa is gracious. She accepts the burden of love I feel for these women I loved so passionately as a child, these sisters of my mother whom she scarcely knows, having been raised in another city, during a time when I rarely visited the family, feeling that I needed this distance from them in order to become what I then called my "self."

"Become your SELF?" my mother would shout over the telephone. "Why should you need to become what you already are?"

Larissa offers Aunt Lillian a plate of cookies, the sesame seeds sliding about nervously as my aunt hesitates, her fingers uncertain, before selecting a plump almond cookie with a golden edge.

Gertrude enters the room. She is wearing a beautiful satin robe, which makes her look older and even more emaciated. She walks slowly, carrying Larissa's cake. She is not smiling, but something like joy rides so recklessly over her features I feel, for the first time, just how deeply she has been wounded.

Lillian is on her feet, hovering over her; she straightens a yellowing lock of her sister's hair, touching her forehead; and now she admires to excess the satin gown which, we all know, was handed down to Gertrude by her daughter.

Then, as Gertrude settles herself painfully into the rocking chair, Lillian comes to sit next to me. "That one," she says, not quite under her breath, speaking as if Gertrude were not present, "that Vida," she repeats, her voice grown somber with judgment, "that one is responsible."

Once, when I was visiting at Gertrude's home, I saw her husband eating and drinking alone at the table, lifting a huge bottle of distilled water to his lips and guzzling audibly, while my aunt stood in the doorway, her hands clasped nervously, waiting to bring him his next course. Aunt Gertrude's daughter, we always said, took after her father.

Gertrude leaves her cup of tea growing cold on the table beside her. She fields Lillian's questions with bland reassurances. Yes, she is feeling well; yes, she has good appetite; yes, she has managed to sleep a bit. But I imagine she has been lying awake, searching through her life, trying to understand what has happened between her and her daughter.

But what is it Vida has actually done? Whatever it is it must have hurt deeply. If you look at Gertrude knowing something has gone wrong, you might even think she was dying of a broken heart.

My cousin Vida ("the wild one," my family said) went off when I was thirteen years old and she was a girl of eighteen, to begin her career as a dancer on Broadway. I liked the stories I heard about her love affairs; how she almost married a Spanish bullfighter, how she almost became a Catholic. I was disappointed when I came home from college one summer and found her settled, married to a police officer and living in the San Fernando Valley.

She no longer looked the way she had when she ran off; the gypsy quality was gone, she'd grown stout and wore long tent dresses which made her look, I thought, like a tea cozy. She had by then acquired the habit of following her mother around Los Angeles, appearing suddenly at a dinner to which she had not been invited.

"You can never see Gertrude alone anymore," Aunt Lillian protested to my mother one night before dinner. "What if the three of us want to talk by ourselves?"

"Sibling rivalry," my mother said to me beneath her breath, as I watched everything.

My cousin would squeeze herself in next to Gertrude at the table; she would draw up a chair that was larger than the others, elbow Lillian out of the way, and sit with her straight back and wonderful black eyes, leaning forward to eat from her mother's plate.

But what has Vida done? What is it, what could it be? Suddenly, a fever of curiosity comes over me. As a child I had more patience. I would wait for days, reading the silences, weighing the sighs. I look at Larissa. She has a serene, contented look on her face, as if she'd been nibbling away at forbidden fruit and doesn't even know it's forbidden.

I lean over and put my arm around Aunt Lil. "Maybe," I say to her, as Gertrude and Larissa talk together across the room, "Vida felt abandoned by Gertrude."

I want her to think I know exactly what's gone on, but my little stratagem is working better than it should. Lillian is freezing into one of her silences. "Think," I say, "how she must have felt when Gertrude decided to take on another position in the Peace Corps."

Now, I am trying to keep my tongue from uttering these things. But my tongue has its own intentions. "You know what I mean," it chatters on, as if it knew what all this furor was about. "Haven't we all felt the same way?"

It is getting worse and worse; there is no knowing whom the tongue is about to include in this impossible topic of resentment and bitterness. But now my mother comes to my rescue. "Stop glaring, Lillian," she says. "Kim is merely trying to understand."

"No," says Lillian, forgetting to whisper, her voice rising. "First comes understanding, then forgiveness. But I say, to do this to a mother, who would have thought a daughter capable."

"Lillian, Lillian," my mother sighs, looking anxiously at Gertrude.

Gertrude, raising her eyebrows, tilts back her head, as if she were considering the possibility that Lillian has spoken nothing more than the truth.

But the larger truth, which I was unable to speak to Lillian, is almost audible in the room. The real gift Gertrude had from her mother, which made it possible for Vida to break her heart, was Gertrude's capacity for loving.

"Can you imagine," Lillian leans over to whisper, "how terrible it must have been for her? It broke her heart, I'm telling you, it broke her."

Inadvertently, I hold my breath. She'll tell me now because she thinks I know what happened between Vida and Gertrude.

"Imagine," says my aunt. "She telephones to her bank to arrange for the transfer of funds. 'But Gertrude,' they say to her, 'Vida's withdrawn it.' "

I shake my head, my eyes betraying no slightest sign that this is my first knowledge.

"Vida used it for herself."

My hands move, I restrain them.

"Who knows how many dollars? Saved, you know how, from that little salary of hers."

Her voice is beginning to rise. "And Gertrude was already ill," she shouts. "She'd already had her heart attack."

As we say good-night to Gertrude and close the door to her room, none of us is pretending now that she will live for long. Helping her into bed my hands draw back from the bones in her shoulders. And then, as we are walking back down the darkened hallway, my mother takes Lillian by the arm. "Don't judge," she says. "Don't judge. Maybe Vida was planning to return it." But Lillian draws her arm away; with her hands on her hips, wagging her head, she says to my mother, "Rose. Don't you deny it, Rose. She made use of it. There's no getting around that. And with her mother on her deathbed."

Larissa will not look up at me; but that is a relief. I would not like to see what is in her eyes now. She's a very passionate girl when she loves, loyal and faithful. She would, I know, be willing to pass judgment on Aunt Gertrude's daughter.

But then she takes my hand and squeezes it, insisting that I look at her. She says nothing, but her eyes tell me she sees. I look closer. Has she already caught the habit of seeing things in patterns? She grabs my arm and leans passionately against me. For a moment we think the same thought, both of us stricken by the fear that one day the same thing will happen between us.

But I am most astonished at my mother. She, refusing to censor, she who is so quick to settle matters of right and wrong? Doesn't she believe Vida withdrew the money?

"Mama," I say to her when we are alone, having walked Aunt Lillian to her car. "Tell me," taking her arm, strolling back beneath the tall brick buildings where there are so few lights on now in the windows. But now all the outrage I have been trying to control makes its way to my lips. "Vida," I say, practically shouting this word, "do you think Vida really did it? Do you think she really used Aunt Gertrude's money?"

In the silence that follows I hear in my own voice this judgment that hopes to separate me out forever from the life choices of my cousin.

But my mother only shakes her head at me. Very gently she puts her hand on my arm. "That girl," she says, in a deeply musing voice, "is not like the rest of us. Why should we judge? She took after her father. From him she picked up the taste for gambling. And from a gambler, what can you expect? They believe themselves; this time they have a system, everything will work out, this time the debts will be payed and for the mother the daughter will be able to buy a beautiful home in her old age."

She stops walking; she stands there, holding my arm against her waist. For a moment she looks up at the sky as if it were there she read her new vision of the world's people. This woman, I think, is softening. "But who," she says finally, "am I to judge or forgive? I'm not God. I'm not a God of vengeance. And wasn't I once," she asks, with only the slightest tremor in her voice, "wasn't I once also a daughter?"

PART TWO

The Almond Giver

She Comes to Visit

I stand with my hands in my pockets, trying not to look excited. What a foolish person I am, I think to myself, as I notice how fast my heart is beating. It is four years since I last saw her. Dry mouth, moist palms, I have all the symptoms of a young woman in love. But I am thirty-eight years old. And now as I glance over at the passengers it is my mother I catch sight of, a small white suitcase in her hand, her red cape folded neatly over her arm, as she comes down the steps from the airplane.

Suddenly, I am overcome by feeling; the years during which I have kept myself from her rise up aching and roaring in my cheeks. This is love I feel, forgetting my embarrassment, pushing past the small crowd of people gathering at the gate, and I run now, opening my arms to her. She is frowning in the light, the recognition dawning as I sweep her against me, rocking her. "Kimmie, Kimmie," she is saying, her hand against my cheek, refusing to let me take the suitcase out of her hand, slipping her arm through mine.

Soon, she will tell me that I have grown taller. "You're so thin," she says and stops walking, although the other passengers press up behind her. "And you know," she muses, her voice full of astonishment, as if what she is about to say had not been said every time she has seen me over the years, "you've grown taller."

"Mama," I say, still trying to get the suitcase away from her through every sort of subterfuge. But she holds on with a mighty grip, refusing to be distracted by my hand slipping over hers, affectionately. "I can manage," she says. "I can manage."

I have parked my car in the red zone but there is no ticket. I drive too fast going to the freeway but she is too excited to notice. "Are you hungry?" she asks. "Are you?" "I could eat," she says, "if you could." "Well," I say, "if you're hungry, why shouldn't we eat?"

For a moment the car stands still and a delirious landscape whirls past outside our window. But she, suddenly changing her mood, says in a loud voice, "It's been too long." And her words have all the solidity of simple, factual statement. Then, hurrying, in case I think she is reproaching me: "I understand," she says. "A writer needs time alone, without distraction, to work on the material."

She is repeating words I have spoken to her, pronouncing everything carefully, in this new language she does not entirely trust. But then, she throws aside this unnatural restraint. A firm hand falls enthusiastically on my shoulder. "Daughter," she says, back on her own ground, "next time I won't wait for you to invite me."

When we are leaving the car I lock her suitcase into the trunk but I take along with me the manuscript on which I have been working. She raises her eyebrows, whispering, as if we were conspirators. "Our book?" she says.

As we walk through Jack London Square she takes it from my hands, folds her arms across it, and carries it against her breast.

"If only Gertrude could have lived to see it. This book, I thought, would give her back everything she lost. Sometimes, maybe, I think those people are lucky, the ones who believe. Wouldn't I like this comfort? My sister looking down, knowing everything. . . ."

The First and Last Chance Bar is a tiny room. The floor slopes at a steep angle and she, determined not to spoil our day, laughs as she takes my arm. "You remember," she says, "the way we read *Call of the Wild* when you were eight years old?"

"Jack London used to come to this place. Now it's only for tourists. But I always promised myself to bring you here one day."

"Never mind," she says, patting me confidingly on the hand. "Am I too proud to be a tourist?"

"Well girls," the bartender says, "what will it be?"

Oh, mister, I think, you don't know what you're asking for.

"Pardon me," she says, "you are talking to two women."

"Well ladies," he answers, "no insult intended," and turns his back to prepare the drinks I order.

She takes a matchbook out of an ashtray, turns it up and down on the bar. Finally: "You're a nice man," she says to his back. "Why shouldn't you be careful what you say?"

But now she thumbs through the manuscript, her face furrowed. I notice that I am as eager still for her judgment as I was when I used to bring my school essays to her for approval, proud and terrified as I set my writing down on the kitchen table with a thump. But I am interrupted in my recollection by the return of the bartender. "You live around here?" he says to me, setting down the frosted glasses of tomato juice and vodka.

"She's a writer," my mother answers. "She lives in Berkeley. And this," she says, lifting up the manuscript, "is a book she's writing about my life."

~ ~

After dinner, she wanders about through my house, strolling along with me as if we were on tour together through some famous villa that does not really interest us now. Her hand passes over the Tiffany lamp, she touches the chain, moves on and stands in front of the grand piano, touching the keys without making a sound. She looks for a moment at the oak mirror, with its ornate brass railing, trying to remember how I acquired all this splendor.

"So how's Peter," she asks absently. "He still sees Larissa every weekend? He still pays child support?"

"He's devoted to her, Mama. You know what he's like."

"So, if he's such a nice man, you couldn't stay married to him?"

Her wandering leads us finally to the French doors, where she twists the handle back and forth several times before it opens onto the deck.

A ship moves out under the Golden Gate Bridge. A late bird

passes over the holly tree below us and my mother sighs. "One day we'll be done with this," she says. "My whole life will be in the story. And then we'll have to start all over again. But this time you will be telling. Everything I don't know about you. It's too bad you sent Larissa away for the summer. These stories are also for Larissa. Who her grandmother is, who her mother is, for a fifteen-year-old girl, what could be more important?"

She bends down and places her purse very carefully next to her feet, fiddling with the clasp. I am wondering if the time will ever come when I can bring myself to tell her about my life.

"You were always a secretive person," she says. "All your life I got the impression, if something matters to you, that's the very thing you don't tell to anyone."

She gets up and strolls around the deck, pulling a few dead leaves from the geraniums. "Tomorrow," she says, "I'll water for you." I stand up and walk along with her. But then suddenly she slaps down her hand on the railing of the deck. "Okay. Enough," she scolds, shaking herself all over. "Back to business."

For a brief, wonderful moment, she frowns into my eyes. "You," she says, knowingly, shaking her finger at me. "You won't say a single word if I don't go back to the story."

And so we sit down in the rattan chair and the blue swing. Again, she bends over and touches the large black purse that always stands next to her. "You see," she says, "I have been making preparations." Very carefully she takes out a pad of yellow paper, folded into thirds and tied with a ribbon. Holding it at a slant, to catch the light from the window behind her, she reads, "It was November, the early winter of 1932. We were on our way to the Soviet Union."

But now she interrupts herself. "Did you know," she asks, "your father did not sleep for a whole week before we left?"

She makes a wide sweep with her arm, gesturing with the yellow pad which will never, I know, be unfolded again. She would never rely upon the unchanging quality of the written word. "Don't think I'm exaggerating," she says. "Not once did he close down his eyes. And why should he? He was going to the place he always had dreamed about, the place he was born, where the great socialist revolution had taken place."

But now she rolls up the yellow pad, shifting over into her storytelling style. "So what were they building in Moscow?" she asks. "They were building the great subway. And how was Paul going to Moscow? As a professional man he was going, as an engineer, to make an important contribution. Now I, too, of course was happy. How else could it be? But for me all this would not be so easy. What did I have to offer? This used to worry me. I talked it over with Paul. 'I am an organizer,' I said. 'And who needs rent strikes and Unemployed Councils in the Soviet Union?' "

There are times when I am sorely tempted to answer these rhetorical questions. But that of course is only my playfulness, and just now it has to wrestle with a growing sense of dread. Coming soon, out of these stories, although she pretends not to be aware of it, is our most serious confrontation. Her voice, however, gives no sign of this: "It was, after all, a big thing that was happening to us. We were, as you know, poor people. For us travel was always out of the question. But now, what happened? We went to Europe in tourist class on the *Aquitania*. It was the same boat that brought my family to America in steerage almost twenty years before. The same boat!

"You see? I was going back to Russia. And in Russia, there was no more czar. The Soviet Union in 1932 was something new in the world. In the whole history of humankind, who had seen such an experiment before?"

Here she breaks off and frowns at me. But I expect this. I have heard the story so many times before and am familiar with all its ritual interruptions.

"You maybe don't see it like this," she says and we are both aware that we stand, once again, at the edge of our interminable quarrel.

But this time she stops herself, willing her own silence. And now, when she speaks, her voice seems to search for a new way, something never tried by her before. It falters, it confesses: "I'll never forget the day," she says. "I came into your room. You remember?"

She expects me to know what she is talking about and, in fact, I know. But she has never mentioned this before.

"You were maybe sixteen years old. 'So what's wrong?' I say to you. Then, I notice you're holding a book. And you're shaking, literally shaking. 'Tell me, what is it?' Nothing, not a word from you.

"Okay, I go out, I shut the door. Later, after dinner I go to see what you were reading. You never mentioned a word, never told me what you were thinking. The Khrushchev report. But I knew. That's when all the trouble began."

For both of us this memory cuts. It reminds me of the time I told her I was no longer a Marxist and she stood with her hands on the ironing board and wept. It reminds me of the way I myself wept, in front of a university bulletin board, looking at the face of a Jewish woman imprisoned in the Soviet Union.

I look at my mother. She is watching me with her hawk's eyes. More than anything in the world I want us to agree, to share a vision, to experience the world identically.

The moment breaks open, it seems to tear from our hands all that we have accomplished so far together. We can't go on, the story ends. To tell her life I would have to be able to listen to these stories about the Soviet Union the way I listened as a child. But now I can only hear them through my disillusion.

For a moment I think she is going to sigh, but she only straightens her shoulders. And then, in the same instant, we are talking.

"Mama, I want you to understand . . ."

"It's not your fault," she answers, simultaneously.

Then her words come more easily. Her conviction carries them, giving them a power they would not have if they were spoken by another person.

"By the time you came into the world a person could take for granted the socialist revolution. But for us the Soviet Union was . . . what should I say? In that underdeveloped country, the impossible was happening. This made you feel that even to a worker, to a poor Jew, even to a woman, the world, history even, the whole future belonged."

She stops, looking at me with an eagerness that breaks my heart. I see that now, for the first time in our life together, she acknowledges, without blaming me, the differences between us. And, in the wonder of this, I find myself as open and innocent as a child. There is a burst of laughter on my lips. And then, from far away, I can hear my father's voice: "So when," it says, "when was truth ever simple?"

She, too, has been freed by my laughter. She claps her hands together, throwing back her head. And now, in one of those wild, spontaneous gestures the very old discover again after a lifetime of restraint, she throws her arms up over her head. "And so," she shouts, beside herself with relief, "the work begins again?"

For a moment, completely revealed, I see the truth of her life in her eyes, in all its severe, problematical beauty, willing the world to fit the architecture of her dream. "It begins, Mama — yes, it begins again."

"So sit back," she smiles, waving at me with her hands. And she tells again this story I heard first when I was three or four years old.

"We were very busy before we left for the Soviet Union. What were we doing? We were buying clothes. We knew the winters were cold in the Soviet Union and of course we heard there were shortages in consumer goods. And so we were traveling there with twenty-two crates of belongings.

"Well, the day comes and we are arriving in the Soviet Union. Can you imagine? Where will you look first? What will you talk about? Your sister, five years old, runs out to the deck. There she whirls herself. She's not singing, she's not shouting, she's not saying a word. With her arms out over her head she's turning herself round and round in a little circle. Your father goes and takes her on his shoulders."

But now my mother stops talking for a minute and then she says, "You will forgive me. This I can't tell you so easy. Your sister dancing. Who could have known it? When she was sixteen years old, this dancing one would be already dead."

She places her palms on her knees, her body rigid with the effort to continue. This interruption is not part of the story I heard so often as a child; it has never happened before.

"Oy," she says, "I tell you . . . it's not easy."

Suddenly, I notice how tiny she is. Her hands could fit into a child's pair of gloves.

"But this is not for now," she insists, arguing with herself. "In its own time it will come. It will come . . ."

And I realize that she is making me a promise. One day we shall relive together the death of my sister. She shivers, pulling herself together. "It is better," she says, "we should think about the years she was with us." For a moment I catch sight of a little girl riding on my father's shoulders. It is my mother's memory, but it comes to me because of our silence. And now she says, "Sometimes, when you tell a story you go back. Even the dead ones come alive again." And then she says, "So, Nina . . . is riding on your father's shoulders." And I realize, from the steady tone in which she speaks, that in our silence, together, we have crossed into the story.

The Fifth Story My Mother Tells

Motherland (1932–1934)

Now began our life in Moscow. But this life, I tell you, was not like anything we lived before. We would walk in Red Square, looking at the walls of the Kremlin. Here was a city where a Jew could hardly even walk before. And so we would marvel, all this which belonged once to the czar was now for the people.

Moscow is an ancient city, very beautiful. People packed the shops, they poured into the Bolshoi, they swarmed in the streets. You could see new modern buildings coming up alongside the onion domes. Everywhere contrasts. Cars in the street, horses drawing carts, men and women wearing Western clothing, people wearing embroidered shirts and leather belts with high boots and fur hats on their head.

Of course I'm not trying to say that you could take the American standard of living and find it in the Soviet Union. Then it was only sixteen years after the revolution. In certain respects life was very difficult in Moscow during those years. The First World War, the defeat of the czar, the revolution and the intervention — all this caused hardship for the people. There were shortages of all kinds. There were scarcely any stores open and those were mainly farm markets that sold only the most necessary produce. Everything was rationed. Even bread was on rationing. In the stores, for the few goods that you could have, there were always lines. If anyone would see a line right away they would get into it. They would stand there, reading the newspaper. You'd come up to someone and you'd ask, "Citizen, what are they giving?" "Who knows, who knows?" "So why are you standing in line?" "Anything they have, I'll take."

We were assigned an apartment with one big room, but the kitchen we shared with two other couples and their children. And of course the toilet down the hall. Housing was very scarce. The first Soviet apartment buildings were just beginning to go up. This apartment was in an old czarist building on the Moskva River. From the room you could see a view over the river. It was winter, very cold. Snow everywhere. This was a beautiful sight. In one corner of the room we hung a curtain to make a little bedroom for Nina. At night there came the footsteps of people walking on the cobbled streets.

The first thing I did after we cleared customs was to arrange a nursery for your sister. In the Soviet Union at this time they already had a very good system of nursery education. Right after the revolution a call was issued for the women to come join the labor forces and build the new society. So of course care had to be taken of the children. They made a complete children's world. The nurseries were in the suburbs. In the summer they took the children away for four weeks to the country. Three hot meals a day were given in the nursery. Whatever shortages there were, the children lacked nothing.

For me, as a mother, you can imagine what a relief this was. In New York at the time only the Bronx coop had a nursery. But a woman with a small child who did not live in the coop would stay at home. What could she do? Even I could only do those things where a small child can accompany you. Of course you can take her on a march to have lower prices for milk. But in the afternoon when she is tired you will have to go back home again. That is how I lived. But here I saw that she was going into a good school, with someone who would take her for a walk even on the coldest days. Everything in the schools was made exactly for the children's size. I, as a small woman, could appreciate this.

Of course I was happy in Moscow. At night we went out to the theaters and clubs. They were all over Moscow, they were set up by the Communist youth. Food was then scarce in the Soviet Union but in these clubs there was always something to eat: for a few kopeks you could have piroshki, baked pastry with meat and onions and eggs. You could have butter brot, open-face sandwiches with ham and cheese. But the most popular thing was the poetry readings. All the great poets would come into the clubs. They wrote about the battles that went on in the revolution. They wrote about what was happening to people on the collective farms. This poetry I liked very much, I always loved poetry. But of course before this I never felt I could understand it.

The trade unions gave free tickets to all the cultural events. The Moscow Art Theater, the greatest theater in the world. The Bolshoi Ballet, where else could you see such dancing?

But even this was not for us the most important thing in the Soviet Union. You must have security in life. In the United States, when your father was working he used to say, "Well I don't know whether I'll be working very long." This was something you didn't hear in the Soviet Union. On the job you had all the conditions a worker seeks. These maybe couldn't be so important to you. An eight-hour day, extra pay for overtime, free health care, four weeks vacation every year. But for us, it was everything, everything we always wanted.

For me, nothing in the Soviet Union could compare to the work I did there. In the beginning I felt I could not offer anything. As soon as I had Nina settled I went to look for a job. I kept asking people, "Is it possible for people like myself to get work?"

They used to say, "What do you mean, is it possible? You want to work?"

"Of course I want to work."

"Well then, all you have to do is look for the kind of work you want."

"But I don't know how to do anything."

"That's impossible. Didn't you ever work before?"

"All I ever did was to work in a store. I don't like store work."

"Well, you know English don't you? Why don't you go to the State Publishing House?"

Naturally, I didn't pay much attention at first. I felt I had no qualifications. But I heard it so many times that one day I went down to the place. I applied for a job.

I was given an interview right away. I explained to the man that in the United States I was an organizer for the Communist Party. I knew some Russian. I told him I was looking for a job. The man thought for a few minutes. He said, "Yes, we have a job for you. We have an assistant editor's job . . ." (He used the words Assistant *Responsible* Editor.) He said, "I think we can offer it to you."

But now I got angry. My voice got loud. I said to him, "I come from the United States. There I'm used to being insulted when I apply for a job. But I surely didn't expect *you* to make fun of me. When you asked me what I could do I told you honestly. My abilities I said are limited. I don't have a trade. I'm a Party member, an organizer, and all I have done is to organize. But I surely didn't expect such treatment from you. Here, in the Soviet Union, to make fun of a woman who applies for a job . . ."

I was beside myself. The man was looking at me. He seemed astonished. Then he said, "Wait just a minute. I wasn't making fun. Why would I do that? I considered very seriously what you said. I considered your abilities. I thought about what we needed. You are a Party member. That's very important. You know English well. That's very important, too. You know Russian and that's essential; I wanted someone who could translate. You have all the requisites. And furthermore, what you don't know we can teach you."

You can imagine how I was listening. From that serious face I could see he had no intention to make fun. My heart began to beat, very fast. He said, *"Tovarich,* I want to tell you something. We have no experience, we, *rabodie,* the working class of the Soviet Union. We have no experience in making a revolution and yet we made a revolution. I think you will agree we did a good job. We learned in the process, and that is how you will learn."

As you know, I am not a soft woman . . . as you know. But that time I began crying and I couldn't stop. I cried all the way back to my apartment.

This job was a very important job. The Russian people admire books, they admire education. Every scrap of paper they could find they used for publishing books. It was such a time in the Soviet Union. Workers being educated in the factories. Special schools and universities for minority peoples. Women studying, peasants on the farm studying, the blind and the handicapped studying. The Russian people would line up in the snow to buy books.

Soon after we arrived in Moscow I was sent to study at the University of Minorities. Suddenly, because I was an American, I found myself a member of a national minority. This school was organized by the trade unions for workers, to study at night. Your father would go home from his work, he would pick up Nina, he would take her home. She of course would have her dinner at the nursery. And I would go to study straight from work. We were studying political science in this school. I read all the classics of Marxism, I studied Engels and Lenin, I read the works of Stalin. We discussed everything. I used to remember, when I was a girl in high school, after my father ran away. My mother would watch me when I would study at the table. She'd bring an apple, she'd put it down next to the books. Then she'd sit down in her chair. This was the redeeming moment of her life. So I would think: if only Mama could see me now, a student, studying political science, at a university, in Moscow.

At night we would walk in the snow after our classes. Arms linked, wearing the fur coat and the *valienki,* the woolen boots. The moon would be shining. And then we would hear, as we approached the Kremlin, the sound of the bells. Every hour at the end of the hour the bells would chime the "Internationale." You'd look down and you'd see the red star from the top of the Kremlin reflected in the snow. I can't tell you how we felt. Here we were being educated, free of charge. We had a job. How can I describe it? The sense of purpose I felt. We stopped, all of us, students from different countries; we stood there together, we felt tremendous strength. The "Internationale" was being chimed from the Kremlin and it seemed to us that the whole world must realize how terribly strong the working class is.

I loved my work in the publishing house. It made me feel so important. I would just walk on air. Everybody then would go to the job an hour early. No one was forced to do this but people went.

Then you would come into your place of work, you'd see the buffet. That was the first thing you noticed. The book kiosk and the buffet. People would be there, eating, drinking tea. You'd take off the coat, you'd go into the gymnasium, the director of athletics would be waiting to put you through your paces. We did stretching exercises, all together. And then we'd go off to do our hour of social work. That is why we had come early. Everyone contributed something extra to the collective. My job at the time was to teach English. And so now, in addition to my work that I was doing as Assistant Responsible Editor, in addition to being a student, I was also a teacher.

Then something happened. After six months on the job I was elected chairman of my trade-union department. I was always a good worker. I learned fast, I was very willing. For me, serving the people was a thing for itself.

~ ~

Our main meal was taken every day in the publishing house. All over the Soviet Union in that time you ate dinner wherever you worked. Every worker got a monthly card and paid a minimum for that dinner. At the same time you also got your ration of bread. In my case, a woman with a husband and one child, that was two pounds a day. You know of course the Russians like to eat. And those meals would throw a soldier. Maybe you'd get a bowl of borscht. Well not even a bowl. A tureen. And there would be in the borscht a hunk of meat. Then, they'd place the two pounds of bread beside you, wrapped up. After that, you'd get your main dish. It would be either fish or meat. Most of the time it was fish, because there was a shortage of meat. Then a salad of cold beets, carrots, potatoes all mixed up, and a little bit of vinegar on it. And then we'd get, for dessert, tea and compote, stewed fruit, wonderful pastries.

This meal was served in a large dining room. The tables were set with white cloths, there were cloth napkins. Music would be playing and we had an hour and a half for dinner. But by the time you finished that meal you didn't want to go back to work. I decided not to eat all of this food. But if I left a little bit on my plate the waitress used to come over. She'd say, "Comrade, you don't like our food, do you?" I used to say, "I'm a little woman, how can I eat all this food?" But she'd look at me, she'd nod her head, with the bright red kerchief. "Comrade," she'd say, "you Americans just don't like our food." What could I do? I ate up the food.

At this time Lenin's widow, Krupskaya, was a member of the board of education. In the publishing house one of my chores was to bring in the books for review. So, one day I went up before the board. That was nothing unusual. I was called up to report on my manuscript. I walked forward and then suddenly there was a tremendous sight. What did I see? Krupskaya, herself. She was a tall woman, very imposing. She was sitting at a broad table and in back of her was a life-size statue of Lenin. She was leaning back with one hand resting against her chin. I saw this whole scene as a magnificent study. Krupskaya, looking at me. Lenin, behind her, one arm raised up, like someone who is talking. And I thought, Leninism is alive; it is here speaking through Krupskaya.

All over the Soviet Union at that time there was celebrated International Women's Day. This celebration, as you know, was founded in the Soviet Union. On that day all the women would receive a half day's holiday from work.

When we came into the office in the morning every woman had a little bouquet of flowers on her desk, placed there by the men workers. My job, as chairman of the trade-union department, was to make certain all the women took this holiday.

Most of the time we would go on this afternoon to have lunch together. And then we would go, thousands of women, into the great trade-union hall. That was the other place I saw Krupskaya. Generally, it was she who spoke to us.

We, as you can imagine, felt very important. And then, like women all over the world, we would go into the shops, looking for some candy, a nice gift we could bring home for the husband. On the evening of Women's Day the few teahouses in Moscow would fill up. Ice cream was one thing they were never short of. The women would be sitting there, eating cakes and ice cream, drinking their tea. And then, at every table, you would hear the same conversation. Everyone calling out in those high Russian voices, discussing Krupskaya.

I remember another women's conference. But in this one all the women came from the collective farms. They came to Moscow and there were maybe three thousand women delegates. Their general age was about twenty-five. We, from the publishing house, came early; we talked to the women. And finally the conference was brought to order. But now we have a surprise. Who is the chairman at this conference? A woman fifty-five, sixty years old, gray-haired, very matronly. She greeted the delegates and she said, "I realize how surprised your faces look, that here at a meeting of young women

I am the one chosen to be chairman. Well, don't look so surprised,"
she says. "I am a young woman. I am only seventeen years old." So
of course everybody howled. "Yes," she says, "I'm the youngest of
you all." And everyone just roared. "And," she says, "I'll tell you
why. Before the revolution I, the wife of a peasant, had five children.
I was illiterate. I worked not only in the house, with the cooking and
the cleaning, but I worked also in the fields. Six days a week. From
dawn until midnight. On Sunday my husband would go out and get
drunk and beat the life out of me. This was until 1917, until the
revolution. Do you call that living? Then came the revolution. Our
farm became a collective, it was organized. I was sent to school and
became literate. And now I am the chairman of the collective farm.
My husband works for me. I don't have to tell you. He doesn't beat
me anymore. So I count my living age as a socialist from the days
of the revolution. With me are five more delegates my age."

Well, I tell you. I think you almost would be able to hear the
applause and the shouting. Of course this meant a great deal to me.
Who ever forgets the fate of her mother? Afterwards we all rushed
together, everyone talking about the women's question. But I, what
was I thinking? This, I thought, could have been the life of my
mother.

In Moscow during those days the most important project was the
building of the subway. The city was growing. People were coming
from all parts of the country.

There were huge signs all over Moscow: WE ARE BUILDING SO-
CIALISM FOR THE ENTIRE WORLD. And there were other signs.
WHO IS BUILDING THE MOST MODERN SUBWAY IN THE WORLD?
WHO ELSE? THE KOMSOMOL. All over Moscow you could see that
sign. THE KOMSOMOL IS BUILDING THE MOSCOW SUBWAY. But of
course everyone participated. The children, all the people on the
street. Everyone would be gathering scrap metal for the subway.
Nothing was wasted. And so you'd walk by, you'd see them working.
They would be singing all the revolutionary songs. But one thing
they did not do. They did not call women to work on the subway.

Now this was the only protest I witnessed in the Soviet Union. The
young women from the Komsomol, the students and the young
workers, lined up in front of the metro. There they stood, with
linked arms. And they shouted: "Why aren't women being called to

the work?" So the men workers would answer: "What would you do? You're women. This is heavy work. We're digging the tunnel." But now the women would call back, shouting in chorus: "Try us. Try us out. What a man can do a woman can do also." Finally, a head of the trade union came out. It was decided that women would work on the metro. After that, you'd come along and you'd see them all along the street, young women and young men working together, in their overalls, with their shovels and hammers, digging the frozen earth.

Of course the American engineers were very impressed with all this. It was beginning to have an effect on them. In the first days they had great difficulties in the Soviet Union. Not many of them were radicals. They came only because they were laid off in New York. Here they could get work, but they weren't interested in building socialism.

In the Soviet Union at this time some of the women engineers were in charge of the subway project. The men had to take orders from women and they weren't used to it. This was especially true of one engineer. He was a man named Morgan. Him, the Soviets brought over as a very highly paid specialist. At the first meeting with the American engineers he said, "I don't know why I came here at all. I must have been crazy. They'll never build a subway here. It can't be done. First of all, they're using women engineers. Second of all, the earth is frozen forty feet below. How are we going to build a tunnel? They don't even have any tools. They're going to use wheelbarrows to carry the earth."

The more radical engineers, your father among them, argued. "They'll find a way," they said. "They have to."

Did this convince Morgan? It did not. "I have to laugh at you radicals," he said. "You believe willpower is going to overcome a physical impossibility?"

So the work began. The first task was to dig the underground tunnel. And of course secretly you are wondering. Will they be able to do it? But now special equipment was brought in to cut through the frozen earth. And alongside the machines all the young people in Moscow are working. From early in the morning they are working, lifting the hammer, striking into the earth. And now, what do you think happened? The men from the group of American engineers went out to work on the tunnel. They went, all of them, as laborers. Including Morgan. If they didn't come in with enthusiasm, soon they picked it up. Even a stone could not resist it. Now, they were working alongside the women, taking orders from the women, working with the laborers, digging the frozen earth.

Every time they finished a stretch of tunnel there was a *smitchka*, a celebration. You'd hear, on the street, in the newspaper, on the radio: "The subway moves forward. The tunnel is advancing." They'd announce the distance covered and the streets where the *smitchka* would take place. Sometimes, it would be late at night. You'd hear a shout, a bottle of vodka was opened. There was always an accordion. Someone brought out the black bread, the dancing began, and no more work would be done that night!

Finally, the day arrived when the first line of the subway was completed. All the people in Moscow were invited to inspect the station. There were escalators going down into the earth. I walked in there. I saw the row of lights falling away, down into that frozen earth.

The stations on the first Moscow subway were very beautiful. Each station a different color of marble. Each dedicated to some hero, to a writer, to some person close to the people.

Your father worked on the most beautiful station. They were building the stations in heavy columns of concrete. But he wanted this station to be different. He suggested they should do it in stainless steel. He argued for it and he, as you know, was not a fighter. But this he wanted. He overcame a tremendous resistance. Anybody who would walk into the Mayakovski station would agree. This station is the most beautiful station in Moscow, even if I do say so myself.

Your father loved the Soviet Union the way not so many foreigners would be able to love. He was the happiest person in Moscow while he lived there. He had no desire to return to the United States. He wanted to become a Soviet citizen. It was his life's desire. In his office there was a whole series of chessboards that stood open all the time. When the men took a break they'd go over there, they'd stand for a few minutes, they'd light up a cigarette. Then they'd make a few moves and go back to the desk. They organized teams and they traveled all over the country playing chess. Your father traveled with them. He became an outstanding chess player when he was in the Soviet Union.

I, too, left Moscow for a short period. I went on a *komanderofka,* a command performance as we used to say. I was sent to Leningrad, to the State Publishing House there. I was in charge of a book with phonetics and the only shop that could do this kind of work was in Leningrad. There was very little housing in Leningrad at the time. I was put in a room with another woman, an English editor, in the same hotel. She was there too from another publishing house. It was winter, it was dark most of the time. You get up in the morning, the stars are out. You go to work, the lights are on in the street. About four o'clock in the afternoon a bit of light in the sky and then dark again. I of course did not know anyone in Leningrad so usually I would go to work, come home from work, listen to the radio, and go to sleep. There was showing in Leningrad at the time a film about the peasant leader who defeated the Germans when they invaded the Ukraine. Whatever else we did, on the free day we'd go to see that film. The weather of course was below zero. I don't have to tell you. But we took walks together. Leningrad was even more beautiful than Moscow. It was built by Peter the Great, a showplace with the wide boulevards, the river, the many bridges, the large palaces, and of course the Hermitage. This collection of paintings had belonged to the czar, but now it was on public exhibit, and everyone came.

You would see groups of schoolchildren, you would see groups of farmers, groups of workers, groups of women, everyone in the working clothes and heavy boots, tramping through the rooms. The Hermitage was always packed with people. Everyone was pushing forward to look, to talk, to ask questions. You could hear them saying "our paintings," the way in Moscow they would say "our subway," "our revolution." Where else in the world could you see a sight like this?

The mayor of Leningrad in that time was an outstanding Soviet leader. He was a wonderful people's man. Kirov was loved in Leningrad the way Stalin in Moscow was never loved. He, too, of course fought in the revolution. But he was not like the usual politician in any country. He refused to live in the official residence for the mayor of Leningrad. He lived, like the workers, in a housing project. He never believed in guards. He would sit on benches in the park for people to come and speak with him. He made his own mood in Leningrad while he was the mayor. There were signs everywhere, always in neon, signed by Kirov.

IF NOT IN LENINGRAD, WHERE ELSE?
OUR LENINGRAD IS THE GREATEST CITY IN THE WORLD
LENINGRAD WILL BE THE MODEL OF SOCIALISM
WHERE ELSE IF NOT IN THE CITY OF LENIN?

Then what happened? Kirov went to Moscow for the Seventeenth Congress of the Communist Party. He fought to have bread come off rationing. It was, of course, a symbolic issue. If bread would be off rationing then other things would come off. The economic policy would be shifted. This was the big issue in the Soviet Union during the thirties. Until that time, the major emphasis was on the production of goods for heavy industry, for the military, for the large-scale projects to build socialism. But there was now another movement, and Kirov was the leading man in it. He was in favor of whatever would benefit the people, in their daily lives. And he was beginning to be successful. While he was in Moscow, at the congress, it was announced in the papers that bread would be taken off rationing. Stalin came on the radio. "Life will become much easier and much better," he said. "We'll not only have our good healthy black bread. We'll have white bread, like our own Siberian snow."

There was such a mood in Leningrad when we heard this! We had the impression, and we spoke about it, the way people do; life was going to become easier and better for everyone. Kirov of course was the hero of the hour. The next day bread was in the stores and it was no longer rationed. The stores opened up as if by magic. Bakeries opened. You never saw such crowds. There was such a joy. There were all kinds of bread and rolls, white bread and sweet pastries. Within five minutes nothing was left. Kirov had succeeded.

Then, he returned to Leningrad and what happened? He was sitting on the bench in the housing project. He was talking to the workers and suddenly he was assassinated. He was shot down in the snow.

Who killed him? Did we know? Do I know to this day? We had been celebrating his victory and now suddenly he was dead. We heard the news on the radios and the people just flocked into the street. I'll never forget that scene. Thousands of people just walking in the street, weeping, mourning. We walked there in the freezing cold for hours and hours, arm in arm, until morning. The Russian people are very emotional. In the morning the casket carrying Kirov came by. It was going to the railroad station, to be taken to Moscow, to be buried in the walls of the Kremlin. We walked behind the casket to the station.

After the assassination there was a change. You had the feeling there was an enemy, someone who had taken the life of one of the great leaders. We never knew who this enemy was. But we felt, in the terms that the people use, it was someone who didn't want the people to rejoice, to take pleasure in an easier life.

There was fear. People were worried, maybe there would be a search for the assassins, maybe there would be arrests. It was vague, people didn't speak of it much. But something changed. You could imagine maybe it would not get better after all. Who could be certain? I remember, the harvest was large that year. Bread had been taken off rationing. Maybe I was just afraid?

I returned to Moscow. I was so happy to see your father and sister. I had come home after a long absence. It was easy to brush away these impressions. Maybe, I told myself, maybe they were just fears.

Our life in Moscow had become very familiar to us by that time. On the free day we would either stay home reading, talking, or we would get dressed up in the warm coats and go skating at the Park of Culture and Rest. We'd take Nina, dress her up, bring her skates, and we'd go out for the long walk across Moscow. There was a little village in the park which was called a Children's Village. There you would leave your child. You got a ticket for her. It had her name, the date, and the time she was left there. They would feed her, put her down outside for a nap in a thick coat, and then they would take her out on the ice with the other children. They used to cover up the children with fur blankets. When you came back they would have these bright red cheeks like an apple.

Meanwhile, where we skated, there was music playing, all the popular songs. These were always very sentimental, very sad. Later in the day they would play classical music, for the best skaters to dance to. Your father, of course, was among them. He used to twirl and leap and women would go after him as if he was the only man there.

Once I came back to pick up Nina from the Children's Village. The teacher there said to me, "We teach the children here different than you do in America. Here they begin, the way children do, fighting for the toys. We don't scold them. We stop the fighting. We talk to them about it. If one grabs a ball and says 'Mine,' if the other grabs it back and says, 'No, mine,' we take the ball from them. We say, 'It is our ball. Ours.' Then we show them how to play together. But today Nina saw you coming. She came running over to me. She said, 'Comrade teacher, I have to go now. Here comes our mother.' "

From the very beginning Nina had no difficulty adjusting to the Soviet Union. She didn't know Russian, but her first teacher knew a few words of English and began right away to teach her. Within six weeks she was perfectly fluent. Then she became a translator for your father, who was a small boy when he came to America. In his family they spoke only Yiddish. If someone would knock at the door to our apartment, Nina would fly to answer it. And she would say in perfect pure Russian, "Welcome comrade. Please come in."

Our visitor would look down at this pretty little girl and say, "*Zdrasvoytye.* Where's your Papa?"

"Oh," she would say, "he's over there. You are welcome to come in. But you'd better speak to me and I'll tell Papa what you want. He doesn't know how to speak yet."

Then she'd run over to your father. "Papa," she'd shout, "Alexander Duberovitch is here to see you. But don't worry. I can talk for you."

She had been a very shy little girl when we were in New York. But now a new character came out in her.

She loved it in Moscow. She wanted to look exactly like the other Russian girls. She would get dressed up in a red sweater. She had her hair cut short, the way the children were wearing it then. With her bright eyes and those red cheeks from the cold weather people would just stop to look at her on the streets. One day an artist, a French Humanist, as people called themselves then, came to the apartment where we were living. He took one look at her in this outfit and her red Komsomol scarf and he said, "I must make this painting." Wherever I have lived I have put up this painting in the living room.

The Russians love children. I'll give you an example. One day we were walking along the Kremlin wall. There was a guard standing, in his full military uniform, outside the Kremlin. He takes a look at this cute little girl and he says, "Hello comrade. What's your name?"

She tells him and then she points to the Kremlin. "Who lives there?" she says.

"Stalin lives there," he answers, crouching down next to her. "You want to visit Stalin?"

"Where is he?" she asks. The guard stands up and points to a window. "Come on," he says, "I'll take you to visit Stalin."

"With Mama and Papa?"

"No." He shakes his head. "You come alone."

But now she took your father by the leg. She wasn't ready for that yet. But when you think about it, she would have gone right into history. When we were walking away we looked back and what do you know? There was a man standing in that window.

When I think of Moscow I remember always the winter, I remember the snow.

Did I say this? Here is a memory from the summer. During our first year in Moscow we were selected for a special vacation. The best workers on the subway project were chosen to go down the Volga River on a boat. And I, from among the workers at the publishing house, was also selected.

Naturally, we were very excited. The boat was beautiful, it carried a full orchestra, the food was excellent, and we traveled in luxury. In another context I would not have been able to enjoy it. I would be wondering who had been exploited. But in the Soviet Union this boat was for the workers. It carried two large signs. They said UDARNIKI. It means "Excellent workers — Those who have achieved the quota in production."

Whenever our boat was sighted from the shore a reception would be held for us. People would come to meet us in their national costumes. They'd come with their accordions. We'd make speeches, they'd make speeches. They'd come over to take our hands. It was summer; they'd take us to a table that was spread out near the river.

There you would see everything that was good in the world. Cheeses and yogurt. You would see cherries from the tree. Huge loaves of bread, jugs of fresh milk. Across the field were the farm animals. If the wind would be blowing to the river you could smell these animals. You could smell hay, onions growing. It would begin to get dark, someone would make a fire, the dancing would start. Then your father would come to life. He would grab the best-looking girl, everyone would begin to clap hands, a large circle would form, and Paul would begin to dance.

People always loved your father. But there, whenever we stopped along the Volga, he was more than ever the most popular man. His Russian was by no means perfect. Yet, he would sit there, telling his stories, playing with the children. The children flocked around him; he would twirl them high up in the air. He would throw them up and catch them. Maybe he was missing Nina. She was in her summer camp. Paul would put the children down to sit on his lap, they would play with his mustache. I thought I was happy, but when I looked at your father I said to myself, There is happiness.

You would look up and see a sky full of stars. The water was lapping. Far away, along the river, fires along the banks. There is a legend on the Volga, the story of Stenka Razin, a leader of the peasants, long ago. Every place we stopped they sang this song.

We would sit there, leaning against one another, drunk from all the vodka, in that huge Russian night. And then, in the morning, we would travel on. The man in charge of physical culture would go through the boat singing:

> Get up, get up you workers
> It's time to organize
> You need a healthy body
> To fight the parasites!

At each republic we got the same reception. Each time I'd think: Is it possible? I thought my heart was getting bigger.

When we came to the Caucasian republic I met a wonderful old man. I said to Paul, "You can take any of these young women and go anywhere you want. Take them. I'll take this old man."

He was a tall, healthy man with ruddy cheeks. He had a long gray beard. It was the kind of face that is always laughing. His eyes would be dancing with fun. "Here is your American man," he said, "two drinks and he's stretched out."

"And you?" I said to him.

"Me? I was seventy years old ten years ago."

I will never forget him. You looked at him, you saw life.

"Are you retired?" I said.

"Retired? What does retired mean? I have to work. They couldn't manage without me. The young people go to Moscow. What can they learn in college? Let them show me a cow, I'll raise it better than any agronomist. Look at our fields. Look at our tomatoes. Look at our corn."

He wanted to show me the whole farm.

"What a life," he said. "Imagine. No enemy to be afraid of. The soldiers come home. They get drunk with the best of us. With their girls. With our girls. And the cows give more milk than ever. Socialist cows."

"Sure," I said, "they give more milk. You feed them better."

"No," he said. "They're socialist cows. They understand."

We were a hundred people on that boat. Now we all went to work in the fields. When it grew dark they made a fire in the field and sang for us. The baskets were spread out all around us, filled with vegetables.

Can I tell you how I felt? More than happiness. If there would be religion for me, this would be it. Right there, with the people. All this I have seen. With my own two eyes I have seen it. If you know this is possible, why would you stop in the struggle before every working woman and man in the world could have the same thing? Why would I stop being a Communist? What for?

But there is something more I want to tell you. A story you will remember. This one you loved when you were a little girl. This is how it goes:

"May First in the Soviet Union is a very important day."

You remember?

"In the socialist countries it is a national holiday."

You wanted me to tell this story to you again and again. If I changed one word in the story, what a rage you would be in.

"The whole city," I would say, "would be decorated. Buildings painted with fresh paint, flags hanging from the buildings, and slogans all over the street."

That is how I would tell it to you. But now in all this talking I find myself carried back. I remember. A sense of people hurrying, preparing for the event. In all the large streets music is playing through the loudspeakers. The stores are filled with people shopping.

Then comes the dawn. You are in a holiday mood. You walk out into the street. Not a trolley or bus; if you want to get somewhere you would have to walk. You take a few steps. You are part of a group. You walk farther, you are part of a crowd.

On the way you keep meeting people. You stop and say to them, "Where are you from?"

Immediately, a chorus of replies: "We're from France, We're from England, We're from Italy, We're from Spain."

And then you get the feeling, the overwhelming feeling: *Bougemoi,* my god, the whole world is part of socialism. Everyone is here.

You come to Red Square. It is decorated in flowers and flags. On one side special seats for the workers and the engineers building the subway.

Then, at the side of the Mausoleum comes a horseman on a white horse. He is a tall man, with a mustache, wearing a white dress uniform, he is holding his saber high up in the air. He shouts out, "Hail May First!" and rides across Red Square. Then all of a sudden we see, way up on top of the Mausoleum, all the leaders of the Soviet Union. Stalin is there, the members of the Politburo are there, the generals, the foreign dignitaries are there. They are standing in salute.

The people respond with a tremendous cry. "HAIL THE SOVIET UNION!" Then the military contingents begin to march. Everyone shouts again. "HAIL THE RED ARMY!" Then, directly behind them, come the children. They begin to sing. To this day, I can hear those high pure voices singing the "Internationale."

After them come the workers from the factories, the people from all over Moscow, all with their banners, their slogans, their pledges, their flowers, their flags. And suddenly it seems there is only one person marching. There is only one goal. And you are that person.

Then your head clears. You hear the "Internationale" playing over the loudspeakers. You feel so happy to be there. You think: I might have missed this. I might have missed it. There are so many millions of people who don't know this exists. There are so many millions who don't realize how important this is. But I am here. I'm part of it. My child is part of it too. This I can tell to my children and to my grandchildren and to their children after them. I will say, "You, too, will participate."

After the parade we went back to the hotel for dinner. I looked over the room and there I saw all the world's people, the whole of humanity was there. Every color. Each more beautiful than the next one. From the darkest black to the fairest white, to the most beautiful smooth brown, to the loveliest yellow. All the faces shining. All standing up, raising their glasses of champagne.

TO A WORLD OF PEACE AND FREEDOM FOR ALL.

In that instant I knew it would happen. A new world would come. And I, a small person standing there, I would help to make it happen.

In that moment you don't want anything from anyone who is present. No matter what they have to give you, you don't want it. You want to give that little bit of which you are capable. You want to open up your heart, empty it out. Whatever strength or ability you have — all, all would be given to this wonderful world humanity is creating!

A Walk in the Woods

She says, "It's a good thing Larissa is in summer camp. What would she think of us, sitting up so late talking?"

"You forget she's stayed up late with us before?"

"It's a funny thing. All night I never noticed how cold it got."

"Are you cold? Shall I get you a sweater? You want to lie down for a bit?"

"Cold? Me? What are you talking about?"

A few hours later, in the coffee shop, I watch her drink her cappuccino. "It's better in Italy," she says, confidentially, leaning towards me so that she won't hurt anyone's feelings. And then she falls silent.

In the car, she puts her head against my shoulder. Tired? I want to ask. But I know better. And then, just once, at the very edge of the woods, she whispers to me, "If only Larissa could have been there to hear it. With this she could have understood everything. My whole life."

Since then we have been silent. My mother is gathering small pine cones. We cross a wooden bridge and look down at the water. The mud hens come toward us, dragging a ripple of light across the water. Never in my life have I brought anyone to this place. I have come here for its silence, early in the morning. And she, for the first time in our life together knowing exactly what I need, enters with me in silence.

As we walk on, stepping over fallen logs, bending to pass beneath low-hanging branches, we keep looking back over our shoulder. Is someone following us? She turns, her hands on her hips, her eyes narrowing. A bird flies up out of the bushes. We watch the light fall from the red spot on its wing as it moves along with us, tree by tree. Someone pulls playfully at my hair. "Mama?" I turn toward her, laughing, but her hands are deep in her pockets. And now, I, too, turn back, hesitating. We make our way slowly, down huge steps cut into the path with beams of wood. Whatever follows us seems to have gone on ahead.

A branch lifts up in the wind, we catch a glimpse of the lake. The path leads down and now as we round the curve, I see an old woman sitting on the wooden bench. I don't know her. She is wearing an old dark shawl, *valienki*. And yet, she looks familiar. Strange, I think, that someone else should be out this early in the morning. And then something like recognition rises up in me, howling.

My mother walks quietly next to me, holding my arm. She no longer turns back, she does not look ahead. She picks up a pine cone that is shaped like a rose; she is astonished by it, turns it over and over in her hand, marveling. And now, breaking the silence, she says, "In the shtetl we lived near the woods. I went walking there with my mother. I thought the flowers looked at me." She hands me the pine cone, reaches over to me, opens my hand and very gently places it on my palm. "My mother," she says, "loved to go out into the woods. There she would be happy. But walking in the woods I would not hold on to her hand. It would burn if you touched her. That is how big her happiness was."

When we reach the wooden bench it is empty. My mother and I sit down together, but after a moment she stands up, looking behind her. "Is someone here?" she says. She seems to be aware of something high up, far off. *"Unter dem kind's viegele,"* she hums, very softly. "What was that lullaby?" She tries again, *"rojinkes mit mandlen,"* shaking her head.

As we walk past the children's farm her mood changes. I feel her pulling away from me, closing herself off. A black goat comes up and pulls at my shoestring. A little girl with a whistle around her neck tears past us, raising dust. My mother notices none of this. She is frowning, the wrinkles settle back into her face and the lines return to their customary place between her eyes.

"Why did I leave the Soviet Union?" she asks, as if no time had passed since she fell silent late last night. "To that question you won't get an answer in three words. People ask me. But to you I want to be certain the answer I give is the right one. I have to go looking, after all this time . . ."

I look at my mother. A fine point of light opens into her eyes. And now she stares at me as if she could find the truth of her own life in my face.

"I remember, in 1934, the International Longshoremen's Union called for a general strike. This I read about when I was in Moscow. Right away I thought, Oh my God, we should go home. I wanted to get on a boat and go back to California. You see what I'm trying to tell you? The longshoremen were the most underpaid workers in the class."

Her voice is rising now. It is louder than the voice that has been in her mouth all morning. The soapbox voice, I used to call it. "For years," she says, "the longshoremen were never organized. They finished up a job and then maybe they would be without work for weeks. But now, these same men were able to get the support of the other unions. They could lead a successful strike."

Suddenly I feel an immense rush of love for her, this woman struggling so hard to remain more powerful than what she feels. But I am afraid to touch her. I think her hand will be burning, the way she said her mother's hand used to burn, as they walked in the woods. "Can you imagine what this meant?" she says. "I thought something we were waiting for, working for, dreaming for in America was going now to occur."

She stops walking. Her voice, even louder than before, comes in a rush. "As you know, we had a three-year contract with the Moscow subway. Your father was happy in Moscow. There he wanted to remain for the rest of his life." She looks around her, startled, uneasy, as if she might have betrayed herself, merely in being here. And now she begins walking, taking me by the arm, striding with all her formidable determination out of the woods.

The Sixth Story My Mother Tells
The Organizer (1934–1938)

When we came back to America in the summer of 1934 it was for a month's vacation. Our trip was paid for by the subway project. Naturally, we were expected to return to Moscow.

We went right away to Los Angeles. There both of our families were living at the time. We visited with everyone. Celia by then had already run off with Hank Doeff. She was living in South America. Gertrude was attending nursing school. Lillian was a teenage girl; she lived with my mother and father. She didn't talk much, but she liked your father. When he'd sit down and roll up the shirt sleeves, and tell about walking with Nina past the Kremlin, Lillian would put aside her book, come over without saying a word, and stand behind Paul, listening.

My father in those years was not so violent as before. But still you could see in that house, the quarreling, the shouting, my father's hand lifted against my mother. She would provoke him. She never got attention any other way. She teased him. He'd be sitting, reading his newspaper and he would threaten, "If you continue. I'll give it to you." Then he would hit her. She would run out into the street, shouting, "He hit me. He hit me." This is what I heard from my sister Lillian. She was sleeping in the same room with my mother, they shared the same bed. But, what could she do? Of course, if I would be there my father wouldn't act in this way.

I looked at all this. Do you blame me I didn't want to go back into it? I looked at them. Is it possible?, I thought. Here nothing has changed?

But America? In America everything was boiling. Any day we thought the whole system was going to topple. Here it was still the depths of the Depression. Fourteen million workers were out of jobs. Everywhere were the soup kitchens, the desperation. If you would walk down the streets of an American city you would see bread lines, apple stands, people picking garbage. The tenant strikes were still going on, the strikes against the prices of food. This was before the New Deal began to ease the terrible poverty of the workers. A steelworker then would earn maybe twenty-five cents an hour. They worked twelve, fourteen hours a day. It was impossible to see how capitalism could recover. We heard stories about fifteen people living in a three-room apartment, sleeping on chairs, sleeping on the floors. I had a friend who worked for the social services in New York. She was visiting in Los Angeles and she told me that people would call up the City begging for a box to use for sleeping. All over the country there were demonstrations by the unemployed. Their cry was "Work or wages, work or wages." Each day you'd hear about another rising, the most wretched among the working class becoming radical. This had not happened before. The Southern textile workers, who had been completely unorganized, suddenly went out on strike. In Aliquippa, in the great steel plant, the workers organized themselves into a powerful union without any help from the AF of L. And this was not just the Jewish trade unions, which already had been radical for a long time. This was the industrial worker, rising up against the conditions capitalism had produced.

In California, the farmworkers also were engaged in struggle. It, too, was very bitter. They were an exploited class of workers, without any form of organization. Every day people from Mexico poured into California looking for work. These were the *braceros,* men brought in illegally to work for starvation wages. They couldn't bring their families with them. They lived in shacks at the edge of the fields, six men to a shack, working from sunrise to sunset, six days a week. In the Imperial Valley the temperature could reach one hundred thirty degrees in the shade. They would work there for six months, maybe a year and then they'd be dumped back across the border. Alongside them worked the migrants, whole families doing stoop labor for ten cents an hour. They followed the harvest. Their children had no schooling, no medical attention. And they were starving.

At this time the American unions would not organize the agricultural workers. They were organized in the Confederation of Labor of Mexico. In order to talk with a labor-union organizer they would have to go across the border into Tijuana.

When I heard about this, what could I do? Sit enjoying my vacation? I went out into the fields. I wanted to see for myself. A year before we were traveling down the Volga River. And now who could believe here in America life for the workers could be so difficult? They were like serfs, close to starvation. Who can live with something like that? I heard that children were dying from malnutrition. Could I sleep at night?

During this time men and women organizers were going into the fields to help the migrant workers. Some of them were Communists, some were union members. Some were Wobblies, from the Industrial Workers of the World. The strikes began. California then was not California now. It was, let me tell you, one of the most reactionary states in the union. The farm owners formed themselves into vigilante bands. They hired any men they could get hold of. They attacked the workers and tried to break the strikes. The workers were beaten. This I saw with my own eyes, the men being dragged away, handcuffed, blood running down into their eyes. If they resisted they would be shot.

Fourteen men and women, union organizers, were arrested. They were tried under the Criminal Syndicalist Laws. The men were sent to San Quentin, the women to Tehachapi. What were the Criminal Syndicalist Laws? I'll tell you.

In 1905 the IWW had just begun to organize the workers. They wanted to form one large industrial union. They were very militant, very revolutionary, and they planned to call a general strike. They used to sing: "Tie 'em up! tie 'em up; that's the way to win. Don't notify the bosses till hostilities begin. Don't furnish chance for gunmen, scabs and all their like. What you need is One Big Union and the One Big Strike." The Wobblies wanted eventually to take over the government. And maybe they would have been successful. Who knows? They were growing into a powerful movement and then these Criminal Syndicalist Laws were passed. I was a girl in high school but we heard about these things.

You know the song about Joe Hill? "The copper bosses killed you Joe, they shot you Joe, says I. Takes more than guns to kill a man, says Joe, 'I didn't die.'" This song people were singing all over the United States. It tells a true story, and to this day every radical person knows it. But, who was this Joe Hill? A Wobbly organizer! A songwriter, and he led a strike against the Utah Construction Company in 1914. It was, believe me, very successful. So of course he made enemies. How else? He was framed on a false charge, accused of killing a grocer. And then this great man of the people was shot to death in the Utah Penitentiary by a firing squad.

Well, fourteen to fifteen states passed these Criminal Syndicalist Laws. They made it a crime to organize, they made it even a crime to advocate organization. And then with these laws they went after the IWW. With the indeterminate sentence they could throw an organizer into jail and leave him there from two to fourteen years. Naturally people were frightened. Thousands of members from the IWW were put in jail. Mobs attacked their meetings, the offices were broken into, and what do you expect? The movement was destroyed. This is our struggle. From it we have heroes, we have our own songs, we have stories, and of course we have this kind of telling, from mouth to ear, as my mother used to say.

But now you are wondering, what does all this have to do with my vacation in California? Well, here's the important thing. In 1934 believe it or not these laws were still on the book. And now they were used against our own organizers. Maybe to you the indeterminate sentence sounds like a good thing. Two to fourteen years you say? So, maybe they'll be out in two years? But we knew better. For every infraction of the prison rules time would be added. Very few people got out before the fourteen years were served.

So there I am, on my vacation from the Soviet Union. And here are the organizers, our own people. I knew some of them. They were Communists. I met them before we left for the Soviet Union. I started thinking, in jail for maybe fourteen years? You see what I'm driving at? It bothered me. It really bothered me. So, I decided to go over and talk to them. I went to Tehachapi, where the women were locked up. But of course I found them very disheartened. They had a high bail and no one could pay it. No campaign was being organized, there was no publicity for the case. They told these things to me and right away of course I'm thinking, No one to lead the campaign? Then, Caroline Decker, one of the women, says to me, "Rose," she says, "it's easy for you. You're living in a country where the struggle is completed. We're serving time and we'll rot here for fourteen years. What's being done on the outside to get us out?"

Caroline was the leader of the group. She was in there from a frame-up, a false charge. They said she signed names on a petition to support the farmworkers. Now I ask you, a woman like this? She was maybe twenty-two years old, tall and blond, a Communist organizer, and very beautiful. She of course was speaking in a voice I heard already from my own conscience. What could I say? For me it was indeed easy in the Soviet Union. There I had such a happiness as I before never knew in my life.

Finally I said, "Caroline, you know how it is. If it were up to me, would you be here tomorrow? But look what we're up against. How could I do anything about this situation?"

From my point of view the whole country was in a state of collapse. At a moment like that, the forces of repression grow even stronger. What could I do, one individual person, to get these prisoners released?

Caroline was meanwhile giving me a good long look. Then, I saw her smiling. "You can do it, Rose," she said. And her voice was calm. "You're an organizer."

I, of course, knew what I was. But it can happen someone tells you something and then you know it in a different way. This is what happened to me at that moment. I was, indeed, an organizer. From that point of view, what should I think now about my two years in the Soviet Union? It was a vacation. A time away from the normal time of my life. I felt ashamed that I wanted to stay there and enjoy the socialism someone else had already struggled for.

Caroline was watching me. "Rose," she said, "you know what it's like for an organizer to be in prison? For fourteen years, at a time like this?"

Tehachapi was then a new woman's prison. It was called an "institution" and it was supposed to be a liberal place. But, of course, there was the same awful food you'd find in any prison, the climate was dry and windy, it was the middle of the desert. Caroline was a married woman, with a son at home. So you will imagine, for a woman, for a mother, for a Party organizer, what those fourteen years would mean. I looked at her. We didn't say a word. But she knew, and I knew, the decision was already made. I remember. There was one moment I felt sorrow. Maybe, I thought, I never will see the Soviet Union again.

Of course your father was upset when I told him I was going to stay in America and organize a defense for the fourteen prisoners. We spoke about it. This talking went on for weeks. But you know how I am, I had an argument for every argument he raised up. I was very happy with your father. But I was thinking, the revolution will occur any day now. I was afraid I would miss it.

To you this is perhaps something to laugh at now. But America in those days you can't understand from your own experience of life. For us in those years it felt like the last days of the capitalist system. The way workers were treated in America made you feel they just couldn't go on without a revolution. Even to strike took an act of courage. The workers were beaten, dumped into a police wagon, they were shut up in a jail cell, they lost their jobs, they were fined. Even to join a union meant a worker would be spied on, blacklisted, discriminated against in hiring. How can I tell you what it was like to be alive in that time? All this that is so familiar to you — strikes, unions, organized labor, decent conditions on the job — was then still a very revolutionary thing. It was a change in the way the most oppressed people understood their place in the world. So I ask you, would someone who has worked for the revolution, who has lived for the revolution, and who sees now that it is coming, turn her back? How could that be? I felt ready to risk everything.

Finally your father said to me, "Rose. Don't you know I would miss you?"

"Paul," I said to him, "did you marry just a woman or did you marry also a Communist?"

Your father had a habit when he was thinking. He would pass his finger across his mustache. This he did. And then he said, "I'm not going to interfere with you. I understand your thinking. But . . . it will be hard for you."

Your father was getting paid in a special Soviet currency. Within the Soviet Union it would be valid but nobody could send it out of the country. Of course we had no money of our own. So the only way I could earn enough to support myself was to organize the campaign for the release of the prisoners. And get paid a few dollars as the organizer.

This was a big moment in my life. I knew the consequences. Maybe I would never see your father again. He loved the life in the Soviet Union. He had work there. Could I expect him to give this up for me? We parted for one year. Already I told you the way the women would go after him. Who knew what would happen afterwards? I thought about this, I was worrying but I said to myself, Rose, you are an organizer. Stay here and do your work. Your father returned alone to Moscow and my work in California began.

We formed two committees, one up north in San Francisco, the other in Los Angeles. I went over to Tehachapi to tell the people there we had a defense organization. "Rose," the women said to me, "we knew we could count on you." After that, I went every two weeks to Tehachapi and to San Quentin. I brought money we raised through our organizational work. I advised them to share it out among the other prisoners, to make good will. Each time the guards checked my identity papers, I had to sign the visitor's book, there was a body search. All the usual things. But then finally I came there so often they got used to me. "Rose," the guard would call out. "Still at it, Rose?" "Well," I'd shout back, "if you're tired of looking at me, just let them out of here and you won't have to see me again."

Right from the beginning our organization began to grow. The farmworkers would come into our office. We kept it open night and day. There was always someone to answer a telephone, or write out a leaflet. People came in from other organizations to offer support. That's how it was. In those days from every action we made the larger struggle.

You know that I had Nina with me at the time. Your father would have taken her back to the Soviet Union. But I wanted her to stay with me. Maybe this was not such a good decision. At first I didn't realize I would be doing so much traveling. In this type of an organization no one can ever limit the commitment. The organization grows, it makes demands. You discover more energy in yourself.

You become even more willing. This I have found out again and again in my life. But for a woman in this position it is very hard to care for a small child. You are always haunted by the idea she is suffering because of your involvement. You spend all the free hours with her, but the rest of the time she's with a babysitter. You tell to her exactly what you are doing. But always you are worried. Nina was an understanding girl. You, maybe, think I exaggerate when I am talking about Nina. Always, all your life you thought I loved her better than I loved you. From where do you get these ideas? I admit, she was an easier child. But better? Could I love anybody better than I love you?

Then she was seven years old. She used to talk to me as if she were grown up. When I would come home she would throw her arms around me. She would take my hand, we would go over to the couch. She always tried to assure me I should go on with my work. That's how she was. She would sit down next to me and say, "So, Mama, what have you been doing while you were away?"

Eventually I arranged for her to stay with some friends who had a small orange farm in Pacoima. I used to arrive in the evening three times a week. Whenever I could I spent the night there. On Sundays I would come early in the morning. She was happy, she ran about with the children, she ate oranges. When I left she would walk with me out to the road and hold my hand. But each time I went away from that child I could feel something tearing.

As an organizer one of my first tasks was to speak with the trade-union groups, to make them aware the Criminal Syndicalist Laws were a threat not just to the IWW or the Communist organizers, but to the whole of organized labor. I had to travel all the time. I went up and down the coast, addressing the labor councils, talking to all the other union bodies. In that time there were still two kinds of unions, the red unions and the conservative unions. The party was changing its policy to the Popular Front, but this move to unite the unions was only beginning. And I now had to speak with men who in no way were part of our struggle. But let me tell you, before we were done we broke through every trade union on the Coast. Believe me, every union. I was on the move constantly. I hardly slept. I talked myself hoarse, but was I tired? This is no exaggeration. A person who works for the people grows bigger than himself. If this is a miracle, there you have it, a Communist miracle.

On one occasion I went to Bakersfield where the Central Labor Council was meeting. It was the highest body within the union. So, in order to get there on time I had to fly. It was the first time I was ever up in a plane. It was a small plane and when we got up in the air, I thought, That's it, I'll never make it. This plane was shaking so much that soon the straps began to tear. To me it looked like everything in the plane would be coming apart. Then the plane began to dip. I thought, I had to become a Communist!

We traveled for two hours in that plane. When we came down I wanted to fall on the earth. I'm telling you, I wanted to kiss the ground. But this I couldn't do. We were already late for the union meeting.

I got a ride into Bakersfield, I arrived finally at the labor center. The sergeant-at-arms, who was sitting at the door, said to me, "You should know this, lady. Only the members of trade unions are permitted to address the labor council." He refused to let me in. Well, what can you do? A rule is a rule. But I had come a long way to speak. I didn't want to be sent back. "Listen," I said, "I'm the first person to respect a rule made by the union. But," I added, "I never yet heard about the rule that couldn't be broken." Meanwhile, someone went to get the chairman. He now comes out to speak with me. "Listen," I said to him. "I came a long way. Did I come for myself? Did I come for my family? I came because these laws affect the workers. It's you who could suffer from this thing."

Finally, I persuaded them to let me speak. You know how it happens? They adjourn the meeting early. They reconvene on a special order of business. To me, they gave five minutes. So, you don't make a revolution in five minutes, what could I lose? But I was worried about the time going by while I was talking. Suddenly, I looked at my watch. Six minutes had passed. I stopped abruptly. "These prisoners," I said, "were exercising their rights to strike and to organize. Brothers, in what way are they different from you? These laws are a threat to all of organized labor. Do you need me to tell you this?"

I was about to step down when someone called out, "Did you say your name was Rose Chernin?"

"Yes, Rose Chernin. That's right."

"Didn't you live in the Soviet Union?"

"I just returned. As a matter of fact, I ought to be there now. I remained to organize this campaign."

Another man spoke up: "Would you tell us about your experiences in the Soviet Union?"

"Brothers, I agreed to speak for five minutes. I've already gone beyond my time."

There was a cry from the audience. No one wanted me to go away. Well, I had a story to tell them. Why not? The chairman asked the men to vote. They decided to stay and listen to me talk. What a night it was. Suddenly I am a Marco Polo. They asked questions, I answered them, a discussion about socialism began. No one wanted to go away from there. Meanwhile, before my eyes, I could see the streets of Moscow. I could see even the frost in your father's mustache when we would be skating at the Park of Culture and Rest. I remembered the old man on the collective farm. "Did you know," I said to the union men, "socialist cows give more milk than any other cows?" And they just roared.

I went away from the meeting with the feeling that the labor movement and the Communist Party were drawing together. The men voted to support our campaign. A few months later, when we held our conference in Sacramento, every labor council from California was represented. That night I did not close my eyes. I lay there, in the small room at the back of a union man's house. And I thought, Yes, I was right to stay here. From this work, something very big is coming. In the morning up I got without two minutes sleep, and off I went organizing.

I met some wonderful people during our campaign. One man, a farmworker, became a friend of mine. I knew him from that time until he died a few years ago. This was no ordinary person. He came to California as a migrant worker, but he was born in New Mexico, to a family of miners. His father was a labor organizer. And he, too, of course as a boy went into the mines. These stories he used to tell me when we would be sitting in the office, working. He was lonely, he missed his family. He remembered the Friday afternoons when all the miners and their families would gather to eat, and to play music until the morning. It was called a *tardiada*. When he was a boy, not more than three years old, his mother dressed him up in a suit and he went out to dance all night. But now he couldn't go back to New Mexico. He had helped organize a strike in the mines. A deputy was shot. He and four other men were sent to prison, for life. But after five years he was released, on condition he would get out of New Mexico. His wife had left him while he was in prison. So now he came out West, to work in the fields. He was a man other men respected; he had a quiet voice, a certain kind of authority. He was a painter, a musician. He was living then at the edge of the fields with the other migrants. At night, he would go walking from shack to shack, talking to people about their conditions. After he came, the *braceros*, the migrant workers and their families, began to hold *tardiadas*, with music and dancing. He was always trying to get me to come, but I was too busy working. I used to joke with him. "Juan," I'd say, "in the first place I can't dance. And in the second place, my friend, who is to get the organizers out of prison while we're so busy dancing?"

I was earning then as organizer ten dollars a week. We had no independent source of funds for the campaign. We had to raise whatever we needed to keep the organization going. This situation brought me into contact with a wealthy woman. An heiress to the Crane Steel fortune. She was a liberal woman, she believed in the work our organization was doing. I made an appointment with her. She invited me to her house. So, why not? I'm always curious to learn something. When I arrived there I found a tremendous mansion. You had to announce yourself at the gate. The guard called into a telephone. Well, I thought to myself, I got past the union rules. Why not here, too? Kate Crane met me at the door. She introduced herself. She was a tall woman, very imposing. She was wearing her hair long, loose on her shoulders. And she was in a Grecian costume. *Bougemoi*, I thought to myself, so this is what an heiress is like.

We had lunch in a beautiful room that looked out to the swimming pool. There were Oriental rugs, antique furniture. A maid came in to serve us the meal. And there was a secretary who was sitting to the side, observing the scene.

I knew something about wealth, of course. I had heard about the czar. I knew something about the Russian aristocracy. But to sit there myself in that big room. Naturally, I was very impressed.

Kate Crane was aware of our activity in the organization. She told us she would like to pay the rent for our office. So of course I accepted. For us everything was very expensive. We were always counting the pennies. We never knew if we would have enough money to pay for the telephone, the paper we used, the trips to Tehachapi and San Quentin. But I went there to Kate Crane for something special. Now I had to talk about it. My voice came out different from what I expected.

"We want to hire buses to carry our delegates to a conference in Sacramento," I said. This part was easy. "But," I added, "we don't have the money for the deposit. Maybe when we get to Sacramento we'll be able to collect the money. Maybe we would be able to pay you back. But I couldn't guarantee it."

In my life I have found that always, if you are asking for money, there comes a silence. Very deep. This silence came now. And finally, a small voice went out from Kate Crane. "How much money do you need?" she asked.

That was in 1934. But I thought, Rose Chernin, you are a brave woman. And anyway, what's to lose? She's too polite to throw you out of here. So, I took a breath. I said to her, "We need five hundred dollars."

Kate Crane sat quietly. She had her hands in her lap. She was thinking, I could tell. Who knew what she was thinking? I looked around me. I wanted to see the door. But then she shook her head. "I'm very sorry, Rose. I would like to help you. But young Crane, my son, is traveling somewhere in Europe. Every time he writes he needs more money. What can I do? You can't strand your son."

I was thinking to myself: If only I had your problems. . . . But I said, "Mrs. Crane, I am so desperate I must say something which I think you would not like to hear."

"Please, Rose, say anything you like."

"I was admiring your paintings. Are they originals?"

She stood up very tall. She answered: "Originals? But of course they are originals."

"Well," I said. "Maybe you could take out a loan on them?"

Again came silence to the room. Where my breath went I don't know. I thought, I should be looking at this woman, straight into the face. But I knew I had gone too far. If I talked about our work I forgot to be intimidated. I forgot I was a poor woman, with no position, no title, no wealth. I saw only our necessity. All the work of the organization going to waste if we could not raise up the money for the buses. Finally, she said to me, "In the Crane family we never borrow money. Never."

The union had one rule, here was another. That's how it is in the world. I thanked her for lunch. I rose up to go. I was in a hurry. Now I had very little time to find money. When I was leaving I glanced once more at the paintings. Well, they were still beautiful, I had to admit. Maybe if they were my paintings I also would not want to take out a loan on them? But when I reached the door, Kate Crane called out, "Just one minute." She turned around to her secretary. She said to her, "Would you please look up my checking account? Tell me if we have five hundred dollars for this young lady."

The secretary, very dutiful, went out into another room. I watched this. I felt nothing. When she came back she said, "We have enough money."

"Make out a check for five hundred dollars."

Now I felt something. I grasped her hand. I was elated. She said to me, "I know how difficult this work is for you . . ."

"Oh no," I cried, "it isn't difficult. Now that we know the buses are going to Sacramento, nothing is difficult for us anymore."

I don't remember leaving the house. Maybe I floated out of there. The next thing I knew I was coming into our office. I was walking in there and I had in my pocket the five hundred dollars. I, Rose Chernin, from Waterbury.

~ ~

At that time my mother was living in City Terrace. I would stay with her whenever I came into Los Angeles. One day I heard her talking to her boarder. He said, "Wasn't this Rose Chernin who just walked in?"

"Yes, Rose Chernin."

"Rose Chernin the Communist?"

"Rose Chernin, my daughter."

Well, I thought to myself, this is going to be interesting. So far as

I knew my mother had no idea what a Communist is. But I listened and this is what I heard: "Mrs. Chernin, do you know that your daughter is a Communist?"

"Of course I know."

"And you? Are you a Communist?"

"I?" she says. "A Communist?" There was such a note in her voice. "How could I be a Communist?"

I was standing behind the door. Listening, the way I used to listen as a child. But when I heard this my heart grieved, it grieved for her. How she knew what I was, how she knew what a Communist was, I'll never know. I never talked to her about my activity. When I stayed with her I would say, "Mama, I'm going out now."

"Where are you going?"

"I'm going to make a speech at the plaza."

"Is it near City Hall?"

"Yes, near City Hall."

"Don't you go there."

She was always afraid if I went close by City Hall I'd be arrested. That was always her question. "Rochele, is it near City Hall?"

I would look at this woman and think about my own life. Hers was so small. And mine? Who could describe it? The revolution was coming, I would play a part. But I could never forget my mother's words. "I? A Communist? I am an ignorant woman."

For that whole year I worked night and day. We organized conferences in all the cities in California. But our biggest conference was in Sacramento. We expected six hundred delegates; we were sending them across the state in caravans of buses covered with banners and slogans. But when we came to Sacramento on a Sunday morning we had to get another hall to take care of the overflow. One thousand people came! From Los Angeles alone we carried ten thousand signatures on a petition. Members of the trade unions spoke, supporting the farmworkers. To the governor we sent a delegation with petitions demanding the release of the fourteen organizers from jail.

A few months later I was standing outside the woman's prison. It was still dark, the street was empty. It was almost dawn and I was excited. Here was the victory we had been struggling for. I closed my eyes. A year before we thought these women would be in prison for fourteen years. And now? For a minute suddenly I realized how tired I was. But then I opened my eyes. I heard sounds inside the building. My breath came faster and then the door opened. I saw the women walk out, in twos and threes. There was Caroline Decker, hurrying across the street to me. Another woman came toward me, also a prisoner. She was carrying a birdcage in her hand. Now, the sun was coming up. She put the cage down on the car and took my hand. We were all looking at the bird. Then, we looked at each other. I'll never forget it. She went over to the cage, opened the door, and we watched the bird fly off into the morning.

~ ~

During that year your father and I wrote to each other several times a week. We discussed the issue whether I would return to the Soviet Union. He was still very happy with life in Moscow. Maybe, I thought, he would decide to remain there. I could not imagine living with another man. But I knew also I would not give up my work. I knew this. To Paul I wrote we were building the revolution. He should come back, he should join us. It was his country too, I said. Who needed another Communist in the Soviet Union?

Finally Paul wrote to say he was coming back. He did not want to live even in the Soviet Union without me. I stood there with the letter. I held it up in front of my eyes. Not one word about the revolution. Paul Kusnitz was coming back to America for me. That much he loved me? And I thought to myself, Rose Chernin, is it possible?

When I told my mother Paul Kusnitz was coming back she took me into the cellar. She showed me the jars of jam. But still, no matter how much she had there it couldn't be enough. This was her love going into the jam. She went down to the grocery. She says to the man there, "Did you hear? My son-in-law is coming back from Russia. So today don't go talking too much. I'm going home, I should make him a bit of jam." Well, the grocer knows her by this time. He gives her a huge sack of plums. "Never mind," he says, "you'll pay me later. What if he would come and there would be no jam?"

"No jam?" she says to me and opens up the door to the cellar. "He thinks there would be no jam?"

Then she began to bake and to cook so that you thought she was expecting the royal family of the czar. *Hamentaschen* was your father's favorite cake. So now she made a whole drawer with *hamentaschen.* She would put in a napkin, fill up the drawer to the top, again carefully cover with a napkin, and close down the drawer. She'd say, "He's coming soon? Better he should come before the termites get them." She washed everything in the house. I could not convince her I was going back to New York to meet Paul. "Mama," I'd say, "he isn't coming to California."

"Nu," she'd answer. "You're here. So how are you going to meet him in New York?"

During that whole year she was worried about Paul. Each time I saw her she would take my hand. She asked me about him. She couldn't understand I had decided to stay with Nina in America because of my activity. She thought Paul had left me, the way Papa used to leave her. I would show her his letters, she would say, "So when is he going to send for you?"

~ ~

When your father came off the boat he was wearing a thick Russian coat. Nina took one look at him. All year she didn't speak a word of Russian. Now she ran over there. *"Tatushka,"* she yelled to him in Russian. "Did you learn how to talk yet, *Tatushka?"* He knelt down next to her on the ground. I remembered something. If he would try not to cry his nose would turn red. He picked her up, he whirled her in the air. I meanwhile was standing and looking. Was he always so handsome? I had forgotten the twinkle in his eye. And suddenly I was thinking, What if he stayed in the Soviet Union?

Then, he puts Nina on the ground. He knew me. He knew I didn't like scenes in public. He put out his hand to me. I took it. He was wearing fur gloves.

From the moment he came off the boat nobody could stop talking. Nobody could listen to anyone else. Nina wanted to ride on your father's shoulders. She, who was ordinarily such a good girl, insisted he carry her everywhere. Meanwhile, he and I would talk. I told him about Kate Crane. He talked to me about the subway. We walked all over New York together. After Moscow it looked so dirty. Paper all over the street, clothes hanging from the windows. The people coming by with weary expressions on their face. Everything we saw looked to us tired, old, worn out. I remember one little girl in a green sweater. She was carrying a big basket. Your father said something to her, maybe to help with the laundry. She gave him such a look I have never forgotten. Sharp, suspicious, tired was this look. I saw in it all the injustice of the capitalist system.

Later, when we were sitting down your father said to me, "Well," he said, "I didn't yet miss the revolution, anyway."

In New York my life as an organizer now went on. Nothing changed. I never grew tired. I became a full-time functionary for the Communist Party. I spoke all over New York, to women's groups, to worker's organizations, to tenant groups, to cultural clubs. But after all this speaking you think I learned not to be afraid? Don't you believe it. For me, it was always the same. But somehow I'd come to an end. And I'd hear the clapping. I knew then it was okay. I had not made a disgrace of myself. People told me I was a good speaker. Who knows?

Your father got a job as an engineer, he was active in the union, he taught classes in Marxism. We found an apartment in the Bronx, next to the park, on the fifth floor. We had a small elevator in the building. But the Third Avenue El ran right past our window. We learned to fill the glasses only halfway up. Every time we would sit down at the table the train would go by and everything would begin shaking.

Our whole life now was the struggle for socialism. In the evenings your father and your sister and I would go out walking. On the bench would be Sam, a union organizer. Walking along the path, Hannah, a student from your father's class. Farther on, behind a carriage, a woman who came out with me for the rent strikes. Across the hall from us lived the Stroms. Very active in our movement. Downstairs, my friend Sonia, a strong member of the ILGWU. At night, if I had no meeting, your father would read aloud to me from *What Is to Be Done?*. We would talk and argue until early in the morning. The Stroms would come over. "What's for tonight?" they would say. "What's the great debate going on here tonight?"

Nina of course was a part of all this. We had no reason to hide from our children what we were doing. Who wouldn't be proud of this work? We wanted to make a decent life for the workingman, a decent life for the workingwoman, for their children and for their children's children. Nina understood this. Naturally, she forgot Russian. But how could she forget her life in the Soviet Union? Her friends were all from our movement. They would meet together, they would go on outings: the museums, the theater. Always, you could hear them arguing. These were boisterous kids, with loud voices. You could sit at the table in the kitchen and you would hear this fresh voice going along the park, shouting, "Don't you tell me. I know what Marx said. I know what Lenin said, too. And you, what do you know?"

In the summer they went to Wo-Chi-Ca, a camp organized by the Party and a whole coalition of radical organizations. You know what Wo-Chi-Ca means? It stands for WOrkers' CHildren's CAmp. There they had all the activities you would find in any children's camp in the summer. But in addition, they learned all the revolutionary songs, all the people's songs, all the union songs. There you would see together Negro children and white children. Children from every color. At Wo-Chi-Ca there was a lake. With their blue skirts and pants, in their white shirts and the red Pioneer scarf, they would get together around this lake at night. The children made boats from bark. They would put candles in the boats and then push them out into the lake. When Mother Bloor would come to the camp the children would follow her about. Who was Mother Bloor? A great revolutionary. She lived to be a very old woman, and always, in our movement, she was revered. She was a labor agitator, a socialist, a supporter of Sacco and Vanzetti, she fought for women's rights. Later, she became a Communist, and she went to visit the Soviet Union. In the camp she told stories to the children. Stories about Walt Whitman, stories about miners' children in America, stories about children in the Soviet Union. The revolution, she told them, would be sure to come. In their own lifetime it would come. When Nina came home she could talk about nothing except Mother Bloor. "Mama," she'd say, in her grave little voice, whenever she saw me looking tired. "Don't you worry, Mama. The revolution is coming. Mother Bloor said so."

A few years later they had a celebration at this camp. It was called Old Timers' Day. We have an article about it from the *Daily Worker*. I remember it by heart. It says: "On Sunday, August seventeenth, Kenneth Spencer, distinguished Negro baritone, will be present at an Old Timers' Day at the camp. Memorials will be dedicated there to Wo-Chi-Cans who feel that people might live in freedom — a library room to honor Feifer, a music room to honor Gerald 'Whitey' Melzer and a vacation fund for needy youngsters to honor Meyer Finkelstein. These three staff members were victims to the fight against Hitlerism. An infirmary, honoring Nina Kusnitz, a young Wo-Chi-Ca camper, who died because of ill health, will also be dedicated."

That's what it said. An infirmary, to honor your sister, after she died. . . .

~ ~

This was our life. We were a powerful movement. The future was our future; we were making it ourselves. These young people most of all believed this. Your sister believed it. Her education, her social activity, her whole life was in the movement. At school she wore her Young Pioneer's scarf, a young Communist she called herself, very proudly. She was the future we were building, in her we saw the outcome of our work. You understand? She had a gentle nature, very thoughtful and our people loved her. You would look at her and you would think, Here is what a girl will be like under socialism.

Of course, we did not know she would die so young. Who could have known it?

~ ~

We were going forward. Every leaflet, every telephone call, every strike was to make this future come along a little bit faster. That is why you could not grow tired. You came home from a meeting. Maybe, it was late. Maybe you have been out speaking. The phone rings. Somebody didn't write a leaflet, and so they are asking, could you come down there, could you do this thing? Naturally, you are falling off your feet — but you think, maybe, from this, it will come . . . the revolution, a little bit faster. With this thought, where is the tiredness? You get on your hat, you put on the coat, you go out into the street. That was our dream. Our wonderful dream. Even today, who has lost it? This dream, I tell you, I believe in still.

The Rose Garden

The dream does not leave her face as we get out of the car and walk down toward the Rose Garden. I catch traces of it clinging to her eyes, the corner of her mouth, smoothing the faint traces of bitterness or grief which have left their characteristic mark, here and there, in the expressive tracery of her face. I am completely under her spell. The dream enters me, too. I feel what others must feel when she speaks in public. What I as a child felt, receiving from her this heritage. "In your own lifetime it will come," she used to say to me in moments of closeness. "Can you imagine? You will live to see the revolution even if I do not."

The day is warm. Arm in arm, we stand looking down over the rose garden at the bay. Below us, where the houses begin again, smoke rises in an unseasonal spiral and drifts in long, indolent wisps over the slate rooftops. It is early; few cars pass behind us on the street. The morning light is laid out everywhere like a sacrament.

She clasps my hand beneath both of her own, patting mine with a gentle rhythm as we walk down the steep, sloping concrete path between the first rows of bushes. But now at the edge of the garden she stops walking. "This, is the hardest work I've ever done. It might be easier to build the new society than to do every day this talking we are doing."

"To say nothing of the fact that we stayed up so late."

"What's that got to do with anything? This tiredness comes from remembering. All these years, some things I put away from me. Now in our talking they are coming back."

"Nina, you mean?"

"Nina, my mother, the dream we had. Everything." She repeats the names of the flowers from the small signs beneath the bushes. MARMALADE. GREEN SLIPPERS. And now she stops with pleasure. "Rose of Freedom," she reads, pointing to a dark, tense flower that has not yet opened. A trickle of water runs between the bushes; she bends down, wets her fingers, and sprinkles a handful of drops over the flowers.

Now, very carefully, she opens her purse, peers inside, rummages about until she finds a carefully folded handkerchief with a thin strand of pink and green embroidery at the edges. She pats her fingers dry and hands the handkerchief to me. "There," she says, "you can see the work my mother would do. If she would write me a letter always something would be folded inside. This one came maybe for your sister. Now I give it to you."

She is gazing at the flowers, her lips moving, repeating the names of the roses perhaps or finding the lullaby that has been haunting her all morning. And then: "Rose," she says, as if with this single word she brought them into being. "For this flower I am not certain we had a Yiddish name. But I, in my life, always thought the rose is for the nobility. Something to grow in their gardens. Not in ours."

"Oh, is that so," I say taking her by the elbow. "Well, my revolutionary, I've got something to show you. Are you ready for a surprise?"

She looks up at me with her eyes narrowed, trying to figure me out. Maybe they also did not have a word for joking in the shtetl? Or perhaps it is she who never learned it? I in any case have learned to wait patiently for her. And now, after a moment, she smiles. "You have a surprise? Show me."

We walk down the steps, past the tiers of rose bushes, thinking the same thoughts, feeling the same sensations, giddy from our closeness, playful and tender as we have never been before. When we reach the tier below the drinking fountain she is looking out toward the bay, rocking herself slightly, her arm around my waist. "Close your eyes," I say. I turn her gently by the shoulders so that she is looking uphill, away from the water. "Now look." And she clutches my hand.

She peers forward at the little plaque which dedicates the garden. She reads the inscription aloud and looks over at me, eyebrows raised. And then she repeats the words, declaiming now in her public voice. CONSTRUCTED BY THE WORKS PROGRESS ADMINISTRATION, 1937.

Joyfully, she claps her hands together. "Is this true?" she asks.

"Do you think I put the plaque here myself to fool you?"

"Well," she says. "Well, what do you know. This certainly makes me happy. This garden, put here for the people. This I approve of. This now I can enjoy."

As we walk on, her pace lightens. She walks with a lilting step, like someone who is learning to be a child again. "Ach, the people," she says. For a moment her hand touches her breast and then her arm sweeps out majestically in front of her. "What greatness," she cries out, "what love of beauty is in the people."

The sun keeps watch on us as we enter more deeply into the garden. "Here I am," she says, "seventy-eight years old. Maybe in my life I should have done more of this? But if I would go into a garden, right away I would think about all the suffering there was still in the world."

Our shadows spring out from the tips of our feet, casting onto the flagstone before us a shadow mother and daughter. All over the garden there is stillness, like breathing. And suddenly, in the same instant, we look up.

"Who's here?" she says, clutching at my hand. "Is somebody waiting for us?"

It is not her own voice coming now through her lips. Breathless, tender, deeply awed, it is a whisper of recognition.

A black man in a green uniform, a white golfers' cap, and dark boots walks slowly along a lower tier watering the bushes. Without even a smile on her face she calls out to him. "You like this work?" "Sure, lady," he answers, not knowing what to make of her. "Good," she says. "Good you should like the work you're doing." Maybe he laughs as he turns away, bending over to free the hose from a rock. But if so, he soon thinks better of it, carefully snips off a pink rose and brings it over to her. "For me?" she says, and then immediately hands the rose to me.

Suddenly, she stands up. She says nothing to me, but moves very quickly in the direction of the fountain. It looks to me as if she is hurrying to reach someone who is walking away. Soon I see her come out below the wooden trellis. She shades her eyes and looks out over the bay. Even from here I can feel the intense concentration in her face. And now I go to meet her. Very, very gently I take her arm.

"I thought, Mama . . ." she says but doesn't complete her thought. "Did you see?" she asks and breaks off in midsentence. A bird flies up, wings out over the garden, low, urgent. My mother looks up, cranes her neck, turns to watch this flight until the dark spot, higher and higher, where the bird was, vanishes before our eyes. "Ach," she says, shuddering deeply. "I want to tell you about my mother."

But then she says nothing. We walk on past the flowers. Finally she says to me, "A mother and a daughter. So much in this. How can I tell to you all I see?" She stops walking. She looks down at the earth, nudging a small black stone with her foot. "We are," she says, "four generations with the name Chernin. I never took your father's name. As Chernin I joined the Party. As Chernin I became known through my work. But maybe there was more to it than this? When you were getting divorced you wanted to change your name. Not back to Kusnitz, after your father, but to Chernin, after me. At first, I was opposed to this. Why should she suffer, I thought, with this name? For what does she need the name of a well-known Communist? But after, when you became Kim Chernin, I felt proud. Good, I thought, three generations of women all carrying the name Chernin. Then, when Larissa went into junior high school, she wanted to carry the same name as her mother. At first, I was opposed to this. Why, I asked myself, should she, an innocent child, suffer with this name? But after, when she became Larissa Chernin, I felt proud. Four generations of women. All carrying the name of Chernin . . ."

She breaks off, unsatisfied with what she has managed to express. I see this clearly in the way she reaches out for me. She takes me by the shoulders and indeed, her hands burn. Once, twice, she sighs deeply. And now, she tips up my chin, holding me in a grip so tight I am reminded of the power in this old woman who comes to the understanding of herself through me.

"You see? You see? It begins with my mother. With her, all this begins. From the shtetl, it begins. You see? And now Larissa, with her blond hair, still carrying the name Chernin . . ."

She is not accustomed to this type of thought. Ordinarily, it displeases her, is something at best to tolerate in a daughter who may one day put aside her metaphysical leanings and go back to her original, revolutionary understanding of the world. But she cannot thrust her thought aside.

"It's true," she says, "when I lived in New York, what was happening in my mother's life didn't mean so much to me. She lived in the past. For her there was still the shtetl, the czar was still alive. There was no future, not even, for her, a present."

She stoops down, gathering. They are large yellow petals, their tips curling where the rim of pink bleeds over in vermilion streaks. "From the same stalk," she says, "a bud, a flower, and these . . . what do you call them? Yellow leaves?"

"Petals," I say, sitting down next to her.

"From the same stalk . . . the generations," she murmurs, crushing the petals together in her hand.

The Seventh Story My Mother Tells

Letters (1938–1940)

While I was in New York my mother kept me informed about what was happening in the family. This is what I want to tell you about. With the years her letters grew more beautiful. Her English never progressed beyond a rudimentary stage, she wrote always in Yiddish. There was in her writing something to make you weep. I began to think, If this woman had been given the chance to develop, who knows what could have come of her? Your sister Nina loved Grandma's letters and she made me aware of this. She saved them all. If her friends would come over, Nina would read to them from the letters. My mother's view of the world was very limited. But she had that certain flavor in what she wrote down, suddenly you could see it before your eyes. And always it was between laughter and tears. When Nina began to write novels at the age of ten I thought, here is again the gift that was in my mother. You see? I am today twelve, fifteen years older than my mother when she died. I am older than ever my mother was. Now I find myself thinking about her. Now maybe I understand.

She was miscast in life. She hated housework, she hated the routine cooking. She wanted only to make delicacies, to bake, to make jam, to embroider, to write letters. When she was doing these things she would be peaceful. You could see she was contented with life. But of course she looked around, she compared herself to those women who were outstanding homemakers. This ability was always very highly prized among the immigrant women of her background. Compared to these other women, who hung out their clothes on Monday and ironed them on Tuesday, she seemed to herself an inferior human being. She hated the things she thought she should be able to do. And who valued the things she loved? We never gave her any encouragement. Who cared then if a mother would write a beautiful letter? We let her knit, we let her embroider for us. We read her letters, we smiled to ourselves. But did we ever really appreciate the things she made?

Her letters were all she managed to find for herself. Whenever she could take time, always you would see her, sitting at the table, writing. That is how you should think of your grandmother. This is how I want to give her for you to remember.

But there is something else. We are talking about the character of a person. So here's a mystery. My mother, I told you, was a broken woman. Broken by my father, broken by life. When I was living in New York, making speeches, fighting for the revolution, she was how old? Fifty-four years old maybe. Well, one day I received a letter from her, very enthusiastic. She told me a wonderful thing happened. Here, more or less, is the kind of letter she would write:

"My daughter Rochele, I am going to tell you how I went to become a citizen. Already I told you how I went to class, at night with other people and they also wanted to become a citizen. We studied civics. Then, I went to talk with the judge. He says: Mrs. Chernin. How long have you been in the United States? So I told him. I have been here, says my son, twenty-six years. But if you would ask me I would tell you, to me it seems maybe two years went by. He says, twenty-six years? How is it Mrs. Chernin you don't know English? And why don't you know your civics? These are the questions he asked. But who could answer such questions in English? So to myself I think. He is a judge. What I speak he will understand. And so, in Yiddish, I say to him, your honor, the judge, I will tell you how it is. I have five children. We are very poor. My children are brilliant. I have a son. He is a professor. I had to see to it all the children went to school. How else? I had to see to it they learned English. After all, they had to live in this world. As for me, what does it matter?

I am tired at night. You should blame me? In my civics class I fell asleep."

I ask you, is it to laugh or to cry? For this woman to go to school at night! Something in her would not be content, the same thing driving the rèst of us. She was diabetic, she was confused, she did not know English. But what happened? After she talked to the judge in Yiddish, a language he didn't understand, he gave her the citizenship papers.

Not all of my mother's abilities went into her letters. The stories she would tell you, if you went into the kitchen when she was baking, these nobody could write down. They have to be told by a mouth that is talking, a hand covered up with flour.

According to my mother, our grandfather was married first to a sterile woman. Now in Jewish law if a woman is barren for seven years the man has a right to remarry. So our grandfather got divorced, he married the sister of this woman. She bore him three children. And one of these children was of course my mother. But the first wife would come to visit. She would look at the children and she would cry. And so, for my mother, there were always two mothers. One of them weeping because these children were born from her sister. The other, a mother who had usurped her sister's place. Now what can we say about this story? To me it sounds like something right out of Sholom Aleichem. Maybe this was something my mother didn't talk about until she was an old woman, or maybe it was just a story she made up.

To every daughter my mother gave something from herself. Gertrude knew all her recipes, to Celia she gave the knowledge how to make a good story. Lillian, with her emotional nature, could break your heart. Just like my mother. I of course never thought I became a brave woman because of my mother. I judged her by the wrong standards. But, who knows? If you think about my mother as she was in those years, maybe you could say she was indeed brave.

Even then, in 1938, the women of her culture would stay shut up in their homes. But my mother didn't like this. In Los Angeles, she'd get dressed up. As Gertrude would say, she'd look like she came out of a flour bin. She'd pack dusting powder all over her face. Lillian of course would shout at her, "Mama, wipe off the powder." And she'd say: *"Es vert ainemen."* ("It will be absorbed.") She would take my father's sister Gita with her. Gita was a timid woman. "We don't speak English," she would say. "How will we get there?" And my mother would answer. "Ach, Gita, in America, everyone speaks Yiddish."

Sometime during those years Gertrude got polio. This, too, we heard about from my mother's letters. At that time, no one was allowed into the wards. But one morning my mother got up and she got dressed in her usual way, with the powder all over her face. Lillian asked her, "Ma, where are you going?" Pa was sitting at his place at the table. My mother said, "I'm going to see Gerty." Lillian said, "You can't go. Nobody is allowed in." But my father added, in his usual way, "Let her go. She's crazy anyway." Well, my mother answers, "Let me go. I'll try. It isn't possible a mother can't see a child." All this, remember, was in Yiddish. "I'll take some soup," she says. "I'll take the bread. I'm going."

So, what happened? A few hours later, she comes back into the house. She's triumphant. Lillian runs up to her, because she can see my mother is coming in there without the bundles. So, it turns out, my mother went into the ward, everybody ate the soup, and everybody ate the bread. She sat down next to Gerty, and there she stayed a long as she wanted. Now to my sister she says, "You see? If a child is sick who will keep out the mother?"

If I had kept my mother's letters I would have a chronicle, the story from the life of an immigrant woman. My father could never make peace with her, even when she grew old. My mother moved again and again when she lived in Los Angeles. We'd get a letter, with the familiar handwriting, the postmark from Los Angeles, but the address changed. So, what is it now, we'd think to ourselves? On one occasion my father gave her a bit of money and sent her away to live with a family near the beach. Then, later, he sent for her to live with him again. All this she would write to us, very knowing, with no pity for herself. "Papa sent for me to come to him," she'd say. "He must have wanted back the money to invest in the business."

It was through my mother's letters I kept in touch with my brothers and sisters. She wrote that Gertrude married a doctor. She said, "We don't like him. Papa says, only in America could a man like this become a doctor. In Russia, such a man wouldn't take care of horses." Another time she wrote that Milton came to visit her from Berkeley and brought his young wife with him. "A Jewish woman," my mother said, "with blue eyes." Later, my brother became a professor at the university and then, even a dean. For her, Milton was everything, the most important thing in her life. Compared to this son, what could a daughter matter? Every time Milton came in from Berkeley she would tell us about it. Later, when he was a top administrator in the state government, he would bring to her house all the people who were working with him in the state building. This was his way to give her, in her old age, a little pride.

During those years Lillian grew up. She became a member of the Young Communists League. She married an electrician, also a member of the YCL. They got themselves a little apartment in Boyle Heights. This was a wonderful Jewish neighborhood on the east side of Los Angeles. It had working people, it had trade unionists, cultural groups, a synagogue, kosher stores, a place where you could buy a Yiddish newspaper and books. One day my mother wrote and told us that she and my father together went to live with Lillian in Boyle Heights. When I read this I thought to myself, Hoie, they're right, life is stranger even than a story. And so it was. In Boyle Heights my mother suddenly became very outgoing, very social. She made friends all over the neighborhood, she knew everybody, all the merchants. You understand? In Boyle Heights my mother found the past again. Here, toward the end of her life, was again the shtetl.

And so now her letters had a new quality. They became portraits of life in a little Jewish neighborhood during the 1930s. "Rochele, my daughter," she would write, "Pesach, my dear son-in-law, and to you, Ninochka beloved, heartfelt greetings from California. This morning, early, I went for a walk. Uphill I went, past Sadie Feinstein's, with the red steps. There, from the open window, I heard chopping. Nu, I says to myself, what else? Gefilte fish. Then, on I walked past Fanya Bernstein's. There too, chopping. So, I think, again to myself, chopped liver. At Ethel Milchner's *knadlach,* at Gita Chernin's *tsimmis,* everywhere chopping. And now soon, here too, if you would walk by outside, also chopping. How else could it be? Today is Friday."

My mother wrote to us about my father. For him of course it was not a pleasure to go back into a shtetl. From this he had been running all his life. To the end of his days he remained a bitter individual. He felt sorry for himself. He, an intellectual person, saddled with a family, with a crazy wife. But she didn't listen to him anymore. With the powder all over her face, she put on a hat with flowers and out she went, all over the neighborhood.

But now there was something different from the shtetl. Here, in America, my mother could join the synagogue. My father was an atheist. An areligious man. He never wanted her to go running off to the shul. And in the shtetl of course where would have been a place for such a thing? Where we came from the women stood in a gallery, looking down. But now the old ladies from the neighborhood would follow her to the synagogue. In Boyle Heights you could see a whole procession of old ladies going down the street, with their hats and their sweaters and their heavy coats. My mother, with her big shape, walking in front of them, carrying the books. In the shul she would read to them. She was the literate one. She would tell them what was in the Bible. They would listen to her. They would repeat what she said. In this way she became very well known in the neighborhood. If these people would be alive today, you would hear them talking about her. Perle Chernin, a *chochma*, they would say, a wise woman.

In Boyle Heights my mother wrote letters for women in the neighborhood who couldn't write in Yiddish. Lillian remembers this. Again you could see her at the table, the way we as children saw her in the shtetl, the glasses at the end of her nose, tears pouring down her cheeks. Again she became the neighborhood scribe. Only now the letters, telling her little tales that never exactly happened, went the opposite way over the ocean.

Ach, I'm telling you, it's exactly like a story.

Then one day came a letter from California. It was not written by my mother. It was from Gertrude, telling me that Papa had died, asking us to send money for the funeral. We sent the money. But this was only for my mother. For my father I felt no regret.

My father left me bitterness from his life. It was all that survived him. Even today I feel hatred for him. When I received Gertrude's letter I thought, Good riddance. Should I deny it? If I could have written on his grave stone, this is what I would have said.

But now comes the sad part. Six months after my father died my mother had a heart attack. She was fifty-seven years old. All her life she could not live without my father. She followed him to America from the shtetl. She followed him to California. Now she was taken to Cedars of Lebanon. Gertrude and Lillian went in to visit her. She was recovering, sitting up in bed, in a bed jacket, a pink ribbon in the hair. As soon as they arrived she says to them, "Pack up. I want to go home." "Ma," they said, "they want you to stay a few more days." "I feel fine," she says. "I have a lot to do. Look at the life out there. I'll go home." So Gerty said, "Do they take good care of you?" "Yes," she says, "very good. These are angels here, not nurses." "So Mama, it's late. Maybe you'll stay overnight." "Gerty," she says, "it's enough already. Two days here. I'm such a young woman I can afford to give them more from my life?"

Finally she agreed to stay. They spent the visiting hour with her. Gerty lived then two blocks from the hospital. Five minutes after they got home, they were sitting there drinking coffee, the telephone rings. The doctor says, "Your mother passed away."

That was it. Your father and I were in New York. On that day we had gone out to celebrate our wedding anniversary. We went to the theater. When we got back, the babysitter told us there was a telegram. Right away I knew. Your father opened it. We learned my mother was dead. Later, we turned on the radio. We heard Hitler invaded the Soviet Union.

My brother, Milton, says it isn't so. It was my father, he says, who died in June 1941. Maybe he's right. He's the professor. But this is what I remember.

I felt sorrow for my mother. She never had a chance at life. But now we have to remember what she did against all the odds. The way her life ended. The stories people told about her. I remember my mother, the *zudhartkes* she took hot out of the oven, the way she put down an apple on the table when I was studying. In my mother's house, poor as she was, nobody went hungry. The pleasure it gave her to serve somebody a glass of tea. The sense of humor, the gentleness, the sweater she would knit for every occasion. How she would make from riding in a bus a little story.

When she was alive I didn't show my understanding. Now I remember. And most of all I remember the letters. About my mother's life my biggest regret is we never kept those letters. After your sister died they got lost. You, a writer, never read them. I look at you. I think about my mother. I think, perhaps in you her great spirit has another chance at life.

The Almond Giver

I wake from a deep sleep, fully clothed. My legs are stretched out in front of me, my neck is stiff. My head has been resting awkwardly on the side of my chair. My mother, too, has fallen asleep in the middle of our talking.

It is well past midnight. I listen to the slight whimper in my mother's breath, startled, embarrassed to be awake like this, lucid and attentive, while she is sleeping. Then, a vein of ice seems to pass beneath my skin and I notice, on the coffee table in front of me, a ceramic dish. It is shaped like a turtle and I look at it for a moment before I realize that it is exactly like the dish that stood on the table in our living room, broken by me one day in a fit of rage at my mother, lifted and smashed against the mantel of the fireplace, too shattered for even my father's painstaking repairs. I look up. My mother is sleeping with one arm folded beneath her head, her legs are tucked back, her right hand rests between her knees. When I was a child this dish was always filled with chocolate drops, raisins, and broken pieces of almond. Now, I reach out to lift the back from the turtle, wondering where my mother has found this replica of the shattered dish. But my hand, touching the glaze, suddenly burns, as if I had reached into fire. And then, as I raise my head, I see her standing there, leaning down from behind the couch. She is covering my mother in an embroidered quilt. My grandmother . . .

She turns her head slightly to the side, without lifting it. Our eyes meet as she touches a yellowing strand of hair at my mother's temple. As she gazes at me, I find myself recalling Yiddish words, and then the line of a Yiddish poem I learned to recite when I was eleven years old, and then the smell of almonds baking. I want to say something to her, but my eyes are drawn back to the ceramic turtle and when I look at it now the back has been lifted off. I see, shimmering in the same soft glow that fills the room, a gift from my grandmother, and I reach out, almonds, to put one in my mouth, and my mother wakes up.

She wakes, throws the blanket from her, looks around her, startled by the fact that we had both fallen asleep. *"Ikh hob gehat a kholem,"* she says, looking at me gravely, *"ober, Ikh gedenkt nit vos di kholem iz geven."*

"Mama, why are you speaking to me in Yiddish?"

She frowns; she seems to think I am mocking her and she says, sternly in Russian, "I was dreaming."

Now she is awake. I don't dare to tell her that Grandmother was here. "I dreamed, *weh's mir*," she says, "of Mama." Her eyes fall upon the dish of almonds, and she covers her face in her hands.

Now, for the first time in my life I take my mother in my arms to comfort her. I kneel down on the floor in front of the couch where she is sitting. I throw my arms around her and take her head against my breast. She is not crying, but I feel crying in her, a deep shudder. It rises across the entire length of her body and enters me. Now, I am weeping the tears she refuses. We are rocking together, and I realize in the rush of terror I feel that this is the closeness I have longed for all my life, the silent falling of barriers. Her head rests heavily against my breast. I feel the weight of it, as if an impossible burden had been given to me, and yet there is joy in this feeling. I have no wish to move.

And now I am remembering. But it is more than memory, it is emotion recollected in all the urgency of its origins. I live again a child and I grow younger, holding my mother in my arms. It is light, a beautiful radiance. I lie in my crib. Distinct forms begin to appear. There is my mother's face, surrounded by light. My mother and sister are bathing me. I am laughing and laughing as my sister's hand and the warm water awaken me to the world.

Am I dreaming? I see Grandmother leaning toward us. Her hair is white, very neatly combed back into a thin braid that sways slightly as she bends toward us and touches me with a cold, dry hand on the lips. My mouth fills with a peculiar sweetness, the almond disintegrates and all the restless hungers that have lived between my teeth are stilled.

My grandmother walks quietly around the room, putting things in order. She carries a large knit bag. Into it she places the ceramic turtle, emptying the almonds into her pocket, looking at me for a moment to see what I am making of all this. She has the most peculiar look in her eyes. For a moment I cannot name it. And then the word *roguish* comes to me. She is laughing at something, making fun of us perhaps, for all the tragedy we have woven around her life. She takes up the embroidered blanket, folding it carefully, fitting it into the bag. She is humming beneath her breath, a few words become audible and again fade away. *"Unter dem kind's viegele . . ."* she sings. I recognize, with a start, the words my mother was trying to recall, in the woods, this morning. I strain to hear them, but they hold themselves aloof, just at the edge of audibility. *"Dos tzigele iz geforren handlen."* And I feel that there is in these words something I am supposed to remember.

I watch my grandmother as she goes about her work, wishing my mother could see her like this, serenely humming to herself. She makes a gesture with her hands, as if she were calling small animals to come to her. *"Shtet a klor-veis tzigele,"* she sings and the glow departs from the room. And now the scent of almond grows fainter, the throbbing settles, the chill comes back into the room, and over my shoulder day returns.

I resist the desire to look over at the mountains. I do not want her to go, I do not want to open my arms from embracing my mother. But I feel powerless to resist, my head is drawn against my will, compelled to turn and look toward the window: a part of me is being torn away, I am severed from myself, divided. *Mayn kind vet zayn gezunt und frish.* For an instant the words walk through the air, a song, but no singer. And then my eyes open. A blinding silver sheen is laid upon the water. My mother is waking from my arms.

"Ach," she says. "I want to tell you what I never told you before." But then she sighs and says nothing. Our shoulders seem to share some common boundary. I look down at my hands, I move them, establishing the fact that they are mine, autonomous. But higher up, where my breasts are, I seem to grow out of my mother. I feel a tightness, an oppression in my breathing, as if her sigh were trying to pass through me.

"Why I never talked about it before . . . it's not that you didn't know these things. But to tell them, again, that is reliving."

Again silence. Something is happening between us that makes possible these silences we have avoided all our lives, which might have healed us. And suddenly I understand. This precisely is what we feared — this knowledge of loving, the depth of this love, our love so terrifying for us both. The last time, in childhood, we loved like this we both lost so bitterly. Finally now I understand my mother, this woman who was once a child. Now I hear this history of separations in her life, the loss of her first home, the shtetl, grandfather. The loss of her mother, who could not be a mother to her in America. And I think how very courageous we are to take upon ourselves this unmerciful greatness of loving.

"This part of my life," she says, "I never wanted to talk about. I didn't want to remember. The whole thing I wanted to cut away from me and be done with it. But the past holds on. We've gone this far, we have to go further. I'm ready . . ."

She says this without looking at me, but I know she is making good the promise we have both felt from the moment she arrived. Her fingers trace a line of blue thread in the arm of the couch and I watch her features set and grow firm.

"This," she says, "is the story in which you are born. You begin to grow up, you take your place in the family. After this story, you must start talking. What happens in my life after this, who I am, what sort of person I am in the world, we must hear later from you."

She clasps her hands in her lap and sits very still, her shoulders hunched. She has the look of a small girl, listening. And now when her words come it is clear to both of us they have been there, beneath everything else she has ever said, waiting for this moment.

The Eighth Story My Mother Tells
A Birth and a Death (1940–1946)

*T*he world in which you were born was not the same world your sister grew up in. During your childhood something happened in the world. And this, if you want to know, must have affected you. Right away, when you were a small girl, I knew there was something about you. You had a certain look in the eyes. I can't describe it. Nobody could keep a secret from you. You talked too early. A person could hear in your mouth such words, even a grownup would be happy to know. And wild? Never in all my life did I see a girl as wild as you were.

You were born in May of 1940. The early years of your life were filled with the war. Every evening, each morning, we were glued to the radio. Always, we were talking about the fate of the European Jews. Nina was terribly upset by what was happening in Europe. How else could it be? She was eleven years old when you were born.

I had serious doubts about bringing another human being into the world. I want you to know this. With the loss of the war in Spain, the success of Hitler, the formation of the fascist parties in Europe, everything we lived for disappeared. Instead of the revolution there came fascism to the world. We knew our struggle as Communists was going to be more difficult. We knew, as Jews, we faced a terrible catastrophe. The fear of pogrom was something we lived through already as children.

Many times, even today, I ask myself why in a time like this I gave birth to another child. I had doubts about myself as a mother. I wasn't sure I was capable of raising another child and still going on with my organizing. I talked to your sister about these things. Maybe this seems strange to you. But to this girl you could talk as if she were a grownup.

Now that I was pregnant I said to her, "You know, Nina, I'm an active woman. We have to make a decision whether I should have this baby. I'm almost forty years old, there's a war in Europe, we're not well off, and I don't know how well I can manage."

I'll never forget her answer: "Mama, if you have the baby I'll take care of it. You can keep on working, you can do everything you want. I'll help you, I'll do everything for you."

I can't describe the way she looked when she said this. She didn't plead, she didn't insist, but there was in her eyes something so deep it was hard to look into them. Of course, we didn't know then she would die so young. Did she have a premonition? I don't believe in such things. But still, you have to wonder. Looking back, sometimes I've felt she must have known she would never live long enough to have a child. When you were born that girl was like a mother to you. She was, in some ways, even more a mother to you than I was.

I was very busy during the pregnancy, active in the Party, making speeches, picketing, distributing material. I thought I was prepared for giving birth. I was a mother already, I was a strong woman. But I felt apprehensive. In my generation we always heard stories that glorified childbirth by describing how horrendous it was. I remember visiting my mother when I was pregnant for the first time with Nina. I said to her, "Ma, what does it mean when people say it's so terribly painful to give birth and that you go to death's door. Is it true what they say?"

"No," she said, "it's not. Here I am, your mother, I gave birth to you. And I gave birth to many beside you. You are going to give birth. And your daughters will give birth too. It isn't true that you go to death's door. It is painful, all of life is painful. And when your child is born you will know that this one thing at least was worth the pain."

But now, in my pregnancy with you, my mother was far away, in Los Angeles. She lived one year after your birth. You never met her.

By the time you took your first step my mother was not living anymore in the world.

The day you were born it was hot. Before Paul left for work in the morning I told him I would be giving birth. Nina went off to school. Don't be so certain, Rose, I said to myself. You can't know everything. But still, somehow I knew. I packed up a few things in a bag. I canceled my meetings. It was about three o'clock when I arrived at the hospital. They placed me in the labor room. I had a book with me, by Clara Zipkin, *On the Woman Question.* I was reading between the pains. The hours start to pass and I'm lying there. I heard the women screaming all around me. I thought to myself, I won't scream. I'll never scream like that. I went on reading and finally the pains began to subside.

I called the doctor. He said, "I could send you home, Rose. But since you paid for the day you might as well stay here. I'll be back later."

Now, the pains began again, but worse than before. The doctor came in just before dinner and examined me. He said, "The baby's too big. You won't deliver normally. I'll go home and have dinner, I'll come back later and give you a sleeping pill. Tomorrow morning we'll do a cesarean."

A few minutes later some orderlies came to take me to the x-ray room. When they were lifting me onto the table I said, "You'd better take me out of here because I'm getting terrific pains and I think I might be giving birth."

"Lady," they said, "are you the doctor?"

But the pains kept getting worse. I thought about the women screaming and I wanted to scream. Then they put me on the table and I still controlled myself. I said, "Well, you better hurry up because *something* is happening."

"Listen here, lady," he says, "your doctor told you the operation will be tomorrow morning." They continue with their work. They took the x rays and then put me back on the cart. My whole body was jumping. And the attendant says, "Stop squirming or you're going to fall off."

Then he wheels me downstairs and dumps me into the labor room. It seems to me that this baby is being born. I ring for the nurse and she doesn't come. I keep my thumb on the bell and keep ringing and finally she walks in. She was a middle-aged woman, very nice looking in her white uniform.

"Well, nurse," I said to her, "I don't want to disturb you. You're a hard-working woman and I know that. But I have terrific pain and it seems to me that I'm giving birth."

"Rose," she says (and I'll never forget it), "Rose, you know what the doctor said. He'll be back, he'll give you a sleeping pill, you'll go to sleep, and tomorrow your baby will be born."

Meanwhile, I hear all around me, in all the other labor rooms, this screaming. And I say to the nurse, "Do one thing before you go. Just look and see what's happening, because if I'm not giving birth it must be my insides coming out. Just have a look. That's all."

Finally, she picks up the sheet and says, "Rose, stop pushing. Doctor! Doctor! She's delivering."

One of the doctors rushed in and you were delivered in the next minute. I don't know if you were too big for me. But one thing I can tell you. As my mother said, that, at least, was worth the pain.

The doctor says (I still remember it), "You have a beautiful baby, Miss Chernin. We'll tell you in a minute how much she weighs."

"She?" I said. "I thought I was having a boy."

You were a beautiful baby. You had blond hair, like white silk. Your whole face was ringed with curls.

I stayed home with you for the first year and a half after you were born. It couldn't be otherwise. We didn't have the money to bring somebody in the house. There was a nursery for the people who lived in the cooperative, but otherwise there was none available in New York. And now I'm going to tell you something a mother can't usually say. It wasn't so easy for me after your birth. Should I lie about it? I loved you, of course, it's not a question of loving. But it was hard for me. I felt maybe I gave in to Nina, maybe I did what your father wanted me to do. He, as you know, always loved children. He loved especially girls. Most of the time, when you would wake up crying during the night, your father was right there to pick you up. How many men behaved like that in 1940? But now it was I who had to sit home all day with a new baby. Of course, I wanted to be a mother who likes to stay home with her children. You think anybody wants to feel like an unnatural person? But if you can't make a meaningful life from diapers and nursing, what's to be done? I ask you, what is to be done?

Nina, of course, could not do enough for you. For her, it was the happiest time of her life. As soon as school was over she'd run home to you. To her, this was no ordinary baby. You were more than her sister. She didn't want to leave you even to go play. She fussed over you all the time. She made up songs for you. When you were two or three years old she used to sit next to your playpen writing down stories you told to her. You had a story about Pedro the donkey. You gave him every sort of adventure. In one story Pedro went to help the miners in a strike. Another time he was part of a demonstration in a textile plant. Before you were three years old Nina had told you practically the whole labor history of the thirties. And then we'd see you, a little girl in the playpen, a very serious expression on your face, telling in a solemn voice how Pedro the donkey brought milk for the miners' children when they were starving.

Later, when Nina was older, already in high school, she would come home with her boyfriend and insist upon taking you with her to the park. I would say to her, "Nina, go alone. Maybe he doesn't want a baby with him."

"Well, he can go home then," she would say.

When you were a child we who were in the Party used to participate in activities with our children. It was still a common thing to see our baby carriages rolling down the street, filled with leaflets, the children helping to pass them out. One of my friends made you a pink bonnet and in the winter months I rolled you along and you would fold the leaflets while we were going. You were a plump little girl, always eating. To this day I can see you, with your pink cheeks, chewing on a Fig Newton. You made friends with the grocer, the butcher, with the cook in every restaurant on 204th Street. I'd wheel you in to distribute the leaflet and before we were back in the street there you were, with a big red apple, a piece of rye bread, some cheese in your fist. But of course you can't drag a little girl all over New York for the whole day. At home, I'd sit there while you were taking a nap, I'd get depressed. I had the feeling my life was over, I had accomplished everything I would ever accomplish. There was nothing more to look forward to, only the washing and the shopping and the cleaning and the cooking.

One day a leading woman in the Party came over to me and said, "Rose, we've been watching your work and we'd like you to return to full-time organizing."

"Sure," I said, "a full-time organizer with a full-time child in the house."

"Rose," she said, putting a hand on my shoulder. "We realize you have a baby. But we have an important job for you and we need you right away."

Nina walked in. She immediately sat down next to me. She listened for a minute and then she said, "Mama, go back to work. I'll help you."

I looked at them. This was my daughter, we understood each other. And this was a Party leader, who knew what the conditions of women were like. But still, how could I tell them what I was feeling? When you have a young child in the house you're convinced that she can't survive without the mother there. If you go outside, even for two minutes, you feel such an anxiety. You rush back in, you go into the child's room. You can hardly catch your breath, so nervous you feel merely because you took your attention away for a minute. So, how was I going to go out to a full-time job?

Meanwhile, this woman is trying to convince me. "Listen, Rose," she says. "We know that Paul will support you. Nina has just offered to help. You'll get a neighbor to come in, we'll find a babysitter. We want you to be the organizational secretary of the Bronx."

Well, when I heard that I gave her a good look and I started laughing. It was just like the time in the Soviet Union, when I was offered the job in the publishing house. How could I believe what I was hearing? We had five thousand members in the Bronx. I would be responsible for the entire Party membership and of course as the organizational secretary I would sit on the board. This position, let me tell you, was not often given to a woman.

But now I found myself on my feet. This time I knew it was a serious offer. And I saw that if I accepted I would have to get some kind of child care for you. I put on my coat. I saw exactly what I had to do. I was an organizer. So why hadn't it occurred to me before?

"Rose," says this woman, "where are you going? We need an answer from you right away."

I knew by then I could not blame my life on circumstance. I knew it was essential to fight for what you wanted from life. If you have doubt and conflict you have to master them.

"Sadie," I said, "you ask where I'm going. I'll tell you. My daughter needs a nursery. I'm going out to make one."

Naturally, there were other mothers to help me with this. It was a need we all felt, and now we acted. We rented the building, we paid for the teachers. A month later we had a nursery. That's how it was, that's how I became the organizational secretary for the Communist Party in the Bronx.

Soon I had the feeling my life was rolling along on exactly the right track. I was very active, very happy, the years began to pass very fast. Too fast, as I now realize. We began to see we would win the war. The world situation seemed to improve. The Soviet Union and the United States were allies and I hoped that America was becoming more tolerant of socialist ideas. We believed that in America we would be able to accomplish the transformation toward socialism. As you know, things didn't turn out that way. The time was coming when I myself would sit in jail, here in America, for being a Communist. And there was something else, too.

When Nina was a senior in high school she received a prize, on May first, for being the healthiest girl in her class. She had never missed a day of school because of illness. But shortly after this she began to complain of an itching on her legs. She began to lose weight and she had many sleepless nights. She would wake me and I would sit with her. You and she shared a room; we would cover the light with a blanket and whisper together in the dark. At first I thought she might have been worried about something; she was an adolescent and that can be a difficult time. But when she continued to complain about the itching on her legs I took her to our doctor. He assured me that it was an ordinary skin rash and gave her medication. But the rash did not disappear. It became worse and worse. Then we took her to a specialist. It was wartime and the doctors were all mobilized for the war. It was very difficult to get someone to see her but we managed it through Party channels. He examined her but could not find the cause of the rash. They took some tests and shortly afterwards I came into the office to get the results. The doctor was white as a sheet.

"But what are you suspecting, Doctor? Is it tuberculosis?" That was the worst thing I could think of.

"I wish it were, Rose. I wish it were."

He told me that she had cancer, Hodgkin's disease, that it was incurable, and that she was in a terminal stage. I thought, He has given me my death sentence. I sat there and felt that I was dying. Then I realized it was even worse than that. I was going to lose Nina and survive!

I stopped all my political work to stay home with her. The disease advanced very rapidly. We had no time to get used to the idea she was dying. I have not got used to it yet. Thirty years have passed and the idea still haunts me. I thought I had known what difficulty was but I had no idea. Nothing in my experience had prepared me. I thought I was a strong woman but I didn't think I could survive. We went from doctor to doctor, from hospital to hospital, looking for a cure which did not exist. We even contacted people in the Soviet Union. Maybe, I thought, they had a cure. But of course there was nothing, even in the socialist countries, nothing. Who's rational at a time like this? I tried everything. Special diets for her, vitamins, even healers with the laying on of hands.

She was suffering the torments of hell. A mother who sees a child suffer like this, a mother who sits there helpless, unable to relieve the suffering, can never forgive herself. In two months' time she couldn't eat and she couldn't sleep. She was on constant medication but it didn't help against the pain. Finally, the Party found a doctor who was a specialist in Hodgkin's disease. He was in the army but he came to see her. He was one of our people and to him we looked for what no one at that time could do. He told us straight out that it was hopeless, hopeless. There was no cure for it, she was going to die.

When she was in the hospital she wanted to come home. We would take her home but then she had to go back again. She didn't eat at the hospital and when she was home I would sit with her by the hour, trying to get her to take a little soup. I felt that I had to do something. It is your own child, she looks at you so reproachfully, as if you ought to be able to help. You feel that there must be something, there must be. But you can't find it. You sit there, you keep trying but you can't find the thing to do.

There is nothing worse than this. Nothing. I am not able to describe the continuous torture to her. That is what haunted me most of all. It drove me wild. I am a person who must act. But for this thing there was no solution. Nothing could be done. Do you know what this means? Until that time the concept had never existed for me.

We tried to keep all this from you. We never spoke of it. Nina never spoke of it. All your life you shared a room with her. Now, when you were asleep she would lie there and cover her mouth with her hand so that she wouldn't cry out and disturb you.

Every day it was worse. It became so bad that I began to wish that she could die and be free of the misery. If only I could have taken it all on myself. In all my life I have never seen anything worse than that. The seven months passed and she was dead.

Then I felt that I had no strength left to live. I used to sit every day and look down on the path she took to high school. I watched the children walking along and it became an obsession with me. I couldn't shake myself out of it. I would reason with myself. I tried to remind myself about all the people that had been killed during the war. Think, Rose, I said, about all the children that have suffered. But it was no good. The shadow that fell on the world at the end of the thirties dropped down on my life too, and I could not shake it off.

That was the time I became like my mother. I knew I could sink further and further. Something was lying in wait. I never admitted it before, but I knew it had always been there. Your father was quiet in his grief, he grew thin and he kept trying to comfort me. But I would stand there, looking down at the path, watching the children walk to school along the same road Nina used to take.

From the time she fell ill until she died I never cried for what was happening. Even after, to this day, I never let myself weep.

~ ~

At last, finally, I decided we should move to California to get away from the place where she died. We didn't know if it would be a visit or a permanent settlement there. We weren't sure Dad could find a job. We arrived in February. The weather was very mild, it was warm and beautiful. It seemed to me that we had left New York far behind and that here I could begin to involve myself in the world again.

But grief comes with you. If I forgot for a minute, I felt something running to catch up with me, I could not escape. I gave myself tasks, I forced myself to do them, the grief accompanied me.

The war was over and there was a terrible housing shortage. Soldiers were returning, people were coming out to California, looking for jobs. We stayed with your father's brother and sent you to boarding school. We slept in the living room in a tiny apartment and every day I went looking for a place to live. But nobody would rent apartments to a family with a child.

Finally, one night, when I was walking back after a day's searching, I saw a sign advertising a house for sale. I rushed home and said to your father that we had to buy the house. I didn't even bother to look at it. I knew that it was the solution for us.

We bought the house, we furnished it, we had you at home again. Now, I thought, now life will begin again. But nothing happened: the terrible pain had gone, but everything had become mechanical. Dad found a job, you went to school, and I had to face myself. Each morning when I awoke I had the same thought, even before my eyes were opened. I lay there and I said to myself, Rose, she's dead.

The people in the Party were pulling me back into activity. They were afraid that I would go down into a constant depression. But I had no heart left for struggling. If I couldn't save my daughter what was I capable of?

That was the time I began to understand my mother's life. I, too, wanted to kill myself, I wanted to drink ink. I thought such things, I couldn't stand them. Did this tragedy occur because I was an unnatural mother? At night, after your father was asleep, I walked about in the house. Sometimes I couldn't distinguish one thing from another. The war in Europe, the destruction of the Jews, even the fact the revolution didn't take place, Nina's death . . . this all seemed one occurrence. We kept nothing of Nina's. Her writing, the novels she wrote, the poems and notebooks we put away in a locked drawer. We bought everything new. Nothing to remind us came from New York. But still, everything I looked at reminded me of Nina.

I didn't think I could ever begin again.

But then, you know how it is, the months passed and I began to notice things. I saw that something was happening in our community. When we moved in there were many Jews in the neighborhood. Your father's family lived all around us. But now, very slowly,

Negroes were beginning to move into the community and the white people began to move out. Soon, only Barney and Sara were left, your father's oldest brother and his wife. And they were Communists. You would walk in the neighborhood and see all these nice little houses with a sign. It seemed to happen overnight. First there would be one house for sale, three days later six houses, after a week there were a dozen.

Every time a Negro family moved into our community there was a struggle in the neighborhood. One day a cross was burned on the lawn in front of a house several blocks from where we lived. When I heard about it I became enraged. I rushed out of the house, I took you with me. I ran down the block. You remember, when my mother moved to Canonsville, the neighbors burned a cross because she was a Jew? And now, in my own neighborhood, in 1946, the same thing was happening all over again against blacks.

That night and for many nights following we threw up a marching line around the house to protect the occupants. I organized for this. Many neighbors joined us and a community organization came into existence. When I came home the next morning, very tired, my hands sore from carrying the sign, I knew my life had returned to the struggle.

Without realizing it, I had been drawn back. I would go out to meet a family moving into the neighborhood and make them feel welcome. We began to organize the community to protect the Negro people who were moving in. And then we moved out into other communities, protesting the restrictive covenants, agreements drawn up among neighbors and realtors that no houses would be sold to minority people.

I took you on picket lines with me. I began to attend meetings at night. People stopped by the house, we made plans, the coffee pot was always brewing, we drew up leaflets, we called press conferences, and very slowly life began again.

Nina's death could not be altered. But there was still so much in the world that needed changing. I was an organizer. Nina was dead. But the world continued and I had to go on with it.

This is what I have to say. I could have died then, I could have killed myself, but I didn't. I went back into the struggle. I went back into life. . . .

PART THREE

The Survivor

414 East 204th Street

March 1980

"Nina is dead." I say these words I have avoided for a lifetime, and which were never spoken to me when I was a child. I repeat them, beneath my breath, then louder. I am walking by myself in the Bronx. If anyone looks at me I pretend that I am humming to myself, or singing. "Nina is dead," forcing the words against my own numbness. It is a cold day, people are walking fast, tucking their necks down into their collars. I wrap a scarf around my face. The wind is so strong I find it difficult to move forward. I hear the sound of the subway roaring past, shaking the ground all around me. I feel this same upheaval inside myself. I remember my mother's face, when she had lived through Nina's death again with me. It looked small and pinched; her eyes were timid. Then, she was weeping. A few tears at first, then more and more of them. But her face never changed. It didn't crumple, or wrinkle, she didn't sob or close her eyes. Her shoulders shook and I put my arms around her. It was the first time she wept because of Nina. The first time in thirty-five years. It was the beginning of mourning in our family because of Nina's death. And for me it was the beginning of memory.

I am standing here alone, on the corner of the street where I was born. "Four-one-four East Two-hundred-and-fourth Street," I say to myself, pronouncing each word very carefully, the way Nina taught me the first time I went to nursery school. She buttoned up my jacket, tucked in the scarf, and repeated the address for me. Then, she taught me a song to help me. *"Remember your name and address, and telephone number too, and if some day you lose your way, you'll know just what to do. Walk up to the first policeman, the very first one you meet, and simply say, I've lost my way and cannot find my street."*

I look at the three brick buildings across the way. I remember, in the one next to the park, on the fifth floor, Nina and I shared a bedroom. I stare at the house, wondering if it has the power to make me feel grief. Instead, I feel the most terrible aversion, a terror of it and then a fury. I hate that house, I hate it. I want to throw myself against it and smash it to the ground.

I walk past. I cannot bring myself to go inside. I go over to the steps at the end of the street and look down into the park. The old swings and the sandbox I remember are gone. There is a new playground here, and it is empty.

A few months ago, when I finished writing my mother's story of Nina's death, I sat in front of the typewriter and felt very tired. I kept hearing my grandmother's voice. *Unter dem kind's viegele, shtet a klorveis tzigele.* I didn't want to listen but the voice kept on and on. Finally, I realized it wanted me to remember. I went to bed and the voice came with me. *Mayn kind vet zayn gezunt und frish.* After a few hours I knew what the words meant. *My child will be healthy and well.* It was then I decided to come back to New York.

I sit here, looking down at the park. My hands are cold; it is hard to make them grip the pen. Across the street two birds are perched on the telephone wire. They bob there in the wind, but they are not singing. Very slowly, I remember. In the late afternoons Nina and I used to come here. She sat on the bench and I played in the sand. She wrote in her notebook. But when I called to her she came over and pushed me on the swing. "Hold on tight," she'd say. "Don't be scared. Hold on, you won't fall." She used to sing to me. She knew songs in Russian and Yiddish. "That's it," she'd say, "repeat after me," and then she'd grab me, flying up in her arms. One day I found a penny in the sand. I was very excited, I ran very fast across the gravel. I fell before I reached her. And she was there, crouching right down on the gravel next to me, even before I could cry out.

When we walked home, up the steps from the park, the light was long and our shadows went on ahead of us.

Nina and I used to come to this park every day when the weather was good. We had a favorite game. We called it grandmother. We pretended. There, on one of the benches, where the old women used to sit, feeding the birds, we would find our grandmother. She had come to take us back to the shtetl, we said. But it was only a game. We knew Grandmother was already dead.

There was a forest then in the Bronx park. When I was five years old I decided that Grandmother lived on the other side. All we had to do, I said, was cross through the forest and we would come to the shtetl.

But all of us had been told. We must not enter the woods. The biggest boys went in there, sometimes. The girls, never.

And then one day we sat on the ground, at the edge of the woods, playing with knives. I, a small girl, hanging around with older children. They used to throw the knives between their fingers, snatching them back, tossing them down again.

I wasn't supposed to play there, I shouldn't play with knives. But my turn was coming, I was scared, I was excited, suddenly someone called, the knives were snatched up, the group scattered, and everyone ran.

I walked into the woods. I held my breath, listening for footsteps. Grandmother, maybe, coming to meet me from the other side of the woods. I closed my eyes, walking along there. Dark faces, shaggy beards, fur hats, sheepskin jackets, black coats, stooped shoulders, spectacles. Snow fell, the little boy my uncle came from the bathhouse, Grandmother sat at the wooden table, writing letters, weeping.

I sang to myself. *Tsar Nikolai sidit na stoyle.* I went farther, I saw a bird. I sat on a tree with big roots.

Then, something happened. I never told anyone this story before. It was the most terrible thing that happened to me before Nina died. He stepped out from behind a tree. He was not wearing anything. I could see . . . his big thing. It was all pink and it was swollen. It pointed straight at me. He wanted me to touch it. "Come here," he kept saying. "It's fun, isn't it? Why don't you touch it? I'll give you a dime." I kept thinking, Just don't let him know you're scared.

Then, I was walking away. I kept telling myself, Don't run, don't run. I was walking slowly, I didn't cry. But my hands were sticky. I threw away the dime.

I close my notebook and turn back toward the street. The light is falling in long, silent slabs. Nothing moves; and soon, as I watch, the very idea of movement seems impossible. I face the building where Nina died. I take a step toward it and all at once I remember what it was like to come home to that house every day after nursery school. To walk toward it, knowing that inside Nina was dying. I would drag my feet, it seemed to me that I could not make them move forward, and yet somehow they went toward the house. It was the same when I walked down the hall. And when I came to our door, trying not to breathe, trying not to smell anything, I did not want to lift up my hand to knock at the door.

I cross the street and make myself walk up to the house where Nina died. I stand here shivering, spelling out the names on the bell plate. I am looking for our name, and it is not there. The door opens, someone comes out. A wild hope tears loose inside me. Thirty-five years after she died! I go inside, into the elevator, I am very small. In this elevator I am not more than three feet tall. I get off at the fifth floor and I walk to the door of 5E. I stand here, wanting to run away. The paint is dingy, there is no air to breathe.

Then I remember. A helplessness and a fury. A terror that cannot be spoken. Silence. No one spoke of the thing that was happening here. I stand here and I am a child. I feel responsible. I wring my hands.

Mama never told me Nina was dying. My mother, such a powerful woman. How could she let her die? I tried to save her. I stayed awake at night. I held my breath. I turned toward the door. I tried not to breathe. I turned back to the window, keeping watch.

At night, the door to our bedroom was closed. It was summer. It was stifling hot. There was a smell. And I lay there, in that room, across from her. I knew. I knew she was dying. What was happening to her could be happening to me. I wanted to break things and run out of there. I did not want to disturb anyone. I did not want anyone to know.

I woke up at night. I saw them sitting beside her; a scarf was covering the light. *Rojinkes mit mandlen*. My mother sang to her.

Unter dem kind's viegele shtet a klor-veis tzigele. Dos tzigele iz geforren handlen. Rojinkes mit mandlen. Rojinkes mit mandlen is zeyer zis. Mayn kind vet zayn gezunt und frish. My child will be healthy and well. Now I remember.

I woke up. Nina was scratching herself. The sound of the scratching, and the sound of the singing, woke me. I saw her lying there, in the morning, when I got up for school. And she was so thin. Her eyes were so big.

She would not look at me. She did not answer when I spoke to her. She never hugged me anymore. I did not want her to hug me. Who was this stranger? Her bones showing; her stomach, swelling up under the bed covers, blue shadows around her eyes? Her hands, on top of the blanket, turned blue. Her ears grew larger. They grew and grew. Her hair was wet and plastered against her head. I knew, Mama. I knew. There was on that side of the room a smell. It reminded me of the cellar. I walked wide when I went past her bed to get out the door, on tiptoe and not taking a breath, not to wake her, she might reach out to me, with her wet hand.

This was this sister I loved. This was Nina, turning blue. I knew. She lay there and sometimes you almost could not hear the sound of her breathing. Then, I would sit bolt up in my bed, I was trying to catch the sound of her breathing . . .

I knew.

And if I wished for Nina to die. If I longed for this dying to be over. If I wanted to leap out of my bed, to run across the room, to smash, to bite at my sister . . .

Forgive me.

~ ~

It is over, I've gone back outside. I have escaped, and this, walking down the steps into the Bronx park, this makes me want to weep. Everything I look at, the bare trees, the mud underfoot, the underbrush withering away, seems extremely desolate, desolate to ugliness, unbearable to look at really, as if it were dying (and no one would speak of it) or were already dead.

I go over toward the bare trees which were a forest. I can see past them, to the other side of the park, where the shtetl used to be. And I start walking. But suddenly there is a man, a very tall man; he looks down at me and he has just stepped out from behind a tree. I stop, frozen, I can scarcely breathe. And this time I cry, I shout out in terror, I run away. But when I stop at the park steps, and turn back looking, the shadow still seems a man's shape, standing there among the trees.

And now, if I am not yet free of this, if there comes with me still the sense of things dying, I think the symmetry is piecing itself together. I am leaving our street. I turn back and I see there are two street signs. DEAD END STREET. And the other, just at the edge of the steps leading down to the park, says (simply): END.

The wind has died down. I cross Hosier Boulevard. Here, the Bronx no longer looks like a ghost town. People are going in and out of the stores. There is an entire row of brick buildings that have been restored. There are green shutters on the windows, a freshly painted iron railing in front of each house. There is a newsboy standing on the corner, singing out the evening paper. A mother goes by holding her child's hand.

I am passing a bar. The door opens, there is a warm smell, faintly bitter. I hesitate, but then I walk inside and stand just in front of the door. The bar is filled with men. Here, in public, with all these men looking at me, I cannot bring myself back out of childhood. I am caught again.

And now, one of them, who is huge, the bartender, looks over at me. He looks at me crying. He leans over the bar toward me. He asks me what I want. I point to the telephone. And then, he reaches into his pocket and hands me a dime.

I walk out along 204th Street. I clutch the dime, holding it tight inside my pocket. It is the same dime I threw away into the bushes thirty-five years ago. But something inside of me has opened. I pass the bakery where the fat woman pinched my cheeks and gave me onion rolls. On the corner, there was a Chinese restaurant, where I used to go from table to table asking people to give me the shrimp from their chow mein. Here is the place where Nina and I waited for the bus the time she took me to see Rumpelstiltskin. And here is the place Daddy used to wait with me for the school bus, early in the morning, stamping his feet in the snow.

Then, all at once, I remember my carriage. My mother, walking behind me, pushing. I am folding blue papers. "Hold tight," she says, "don't let them go." We come to a place. There are mothers pushing. Children, holding blue papers in their hands. "Look," my mother says, "there they are." And then all of us, the children and the mothers, walk around and around in a big circle. The mothers are singing and they are carrying signs.

The Crossroads

Seven o'clock. The bell rings. Larissa races for the door. I hear her slow down as she crosses the tile entryway. I can imagine her straightening her blouse, her hair. My mother and I glance at each other. It never seems possible that this elegant young woman, with all her social grace, is our next generation. That easy sense of style in the way she dresses and talks, the laughter in her gray eyes, these are the qualities of the one who belongs. But we were always the outsiders, proudly, vulnerably, looking in.

The door closes. Footsteps, crossing the tiles, veering off into the kitchen. "Come on, Mama," I tug at her arm, "people are coming. We can't leave Larissa by herself."

My mother is standing in front of the mirror in my downstairs bedroom, where guests stay. It's a large room, looking out on the garden. Rain is dripping from the upstairs deck onto the porch. She's frowning at herself, putting on her lipstick. "How do I look?" She checks the buttons on the front of her dark dress. She looks formal, the way she always used to look when she was preparing to make a speech.

"Let's see." I put my hands on her shoulders, turning her away from the mirror. "I love that dress."

"This dress? You know how old it is?" She glances back at the mirror. "Not bad for an old lady," she admits, patting her belly. "You know what I did this morning? Did I tell you? I walked up that big hill. What do you call it?"

"Marin?"

"Up Marin. Before breakfast, even."

Above us, the door opens and closes again. I try to draw her away, but she clutches my hand.

"Tonight," she says, suddenly serious, "is an important occasion."

I wait, but I feel my face becoming tender.

"Tonight, for the first time, you are the one who will tell about our family."

I nod, keeping my face grave.

"And tonight, for the first time," she continues, "you are introducing me to a group of your friends."

"That's not possible. It can't be the first time."

"Don't I know what I'm talking about? I always thought you were ashamed of me."

"Ashamed of you? Me, ashamed of you?"

"So, why not? You are a very intellectual person. An accomplished woman. And your friends are cut from the same cloth."

I stand there, staring down at her with astonishment. And then I feel that something is about to be said which has never before been spoken between us.

"Listen to me," I say, "and you'll hear the truth. If I never introduced you to my friends it's because I thought you wouldn't like them. I thought they wouldn't be political enough for you. I thought you'd disapprove of us."

She raises her eyebrows and straightens her shoulders. Her head tips back. I can see she is about to disagree violently with me. But then she says, "Who knows? Maybe," and her voice is quiet, matter-of-fact. "Maybe that's what I used to be like."

We enter the room together. My mother walks ahead, very composed. Everyone falls silent, turning toward her expectantly.

I'm chattering. I hear everything at once. The piano, bright laughter, Larissa talking about college, the doorbell, someone arriving late, rushing down to apologize.

And then, for an instant, all of us are silent, my closest friends gathered here, with my mother and me. We are sitting together on the small sofa in front of the window, the manuscript lying quietly on our knees.

"My mother and I want to speak to you tonight about a book we've been working on together for the last six years."

My voice is surprisingly calm, but my lips are dry and my heart is pounding so hard I can scarcely hear my words.

"Tonight my mother will introduce the story I'm going to tell about our experience during the McCarthy years."

My mother leans forward. She holds up the manuscript and waves it in the air several times. "Ladies," she says, "tonight is an occasion. For the first time I am invited to a gathering of my daughter's friends. For the first time my daughter will tell about our life."

Her effect upon this gathering of women is unmistakable. There is a taut silence, a concentration. In her we see a possibility, a desirable way of aging. She is very wise, I think, suddenly astonished that this woman is my mother.

And she says, "Tonight my daughter is going to tell you a story. But, as my mother used to say, for every story there is another story, which stands before it. What is this earlier story I have to tell?" She hesitates, but only for a moment. "I had another daughter, Kim's sister, you know, who died."

Again, very briefly, a hesitation. "Kim," she says, "was a little girl at that time. She also remembers. In our life something ended with the death of Nina. That is what we came to understand."

Someone in this room is crying. But I am afraid to move or turn or look to see who.

"So, after this, if we were able to start over again, if we could find the way to make a new beginning, maybe there is some lesson for other people in what we found.

"My daughter Nina died in 1945. She was sixteen years old. By then, the war was over. But we, in America, did not come out of the war and move in the way some of us hoped. We, the Communists, thought maybe with the victory over fascism, the United States and all the Western countries will move toward socialism. That's how it is, you make mistakes.

"And I, who had seen with my own eyes life for the worker under socialism, should I blame myself that I began to hope?

"What am I trying to tell you? Am I saying this hope for humanity brought me finally out of my own grief? Maybe.

"Am I trying to tell you my life as a Communist, a fighter for justice, saved me? Perhaps.

"Grief is a very selfish thing, very private. For me, the despair I felt was something to drive me away from people.

"So it was. For four years, after we moved away from New York, my life was recovering. I worked, I organized in the community, I involved myself with people, but in those years, to tell you the truth, I was not completely alive.

"Then came October 1950 . . ."

I watch my friends as my mother talks. She, too, is looking at them, weighing her words. And now: "Forgive me," she says, in her most charming voice, "but I can't go a word further if I don't tell you a little history. Of course, you are women with a political consciousness, that we take for granted. But this history I'm going to tell you not so many people know about, even the educated ones. It's the story of the deportation attempts during the McCarthy period, and it is in this area of work I finally got involved. Because of course, if the government was going to try to take away citizenship from radicals, or to take residence permits from foreign-born people, and deport them to any country willing to receive them, someone had to protect these people. Don't you agree?"

We nod eagerly, leaning towards her. But I cannot hold my attention steady. Tonight, I am stepping across a line I always felt it was forbidden to cross. It was my mother who foresaw, and planned, this moment when the voice in these family chronicles would pass over to me. But first she has a story to tell, and it is the political background to my childhood.

"In 1950," she says, "the government passed the Internal Security Act. Would you believe it? They make a law stating that the Communist Party advocated the violent overthrow of the government, and never mind whether they have to prove it. So here suddenly we have a piece of legislation that allows for the deportation of any foreign-born person who has been a member of a so-called subversive organization. The act was passed in October and in that same month we had already four people arrested for deportation in Los Angeles."

My mother's voice breaks off as we go right on listening. But I know why she hesitates; soon she will catch herself up, she will continue, overcoming her resistance.

"I don't like people to think I'm boasting," she says. "But if I tell people about the McCarthy period, and I don't tell them what I've done, they begin to look at me. So, why not? After all, only two kinds of people have these facts sitting in the pocket. You know what I mean? Radicals and stool pigeons. So, I figure I'd better tell you which I am."

Now, she glances over at me and winks. Storytelling makes her playful, the way she never is at any other time.

"In 1950," she repeats, and I can hear how many times she's used that date before, "I founded an organization to protect the people arrested for deportation. It was called the Los Angeles Committee for the Protection of the Foreign-Born. At that time, we already had a national organization, active since 1941. But now I established a committee to handle the cases of people arrested on the West Coast. And believe me, we had our hands full. In 1952 the McCarran-Walter Act was passed to aid the government in its deportation effort. And then, before the McCarthy period was over, we had almost two hundred denaturalization and deportation cases. But I am proud to tell you, most of these we fought right up to the Supreme Court. We stopped the deportations. So I ask you, who had time for personal troubles?"

My mother is no longer talking. Slowly she moves her gaze around the room, a conductor in that moment of acute suspense before the baton is lifted. And now when she knows that we are all perfectly attentive, she turns toward me, a deliberate gesture. She intends to remind me, my turn is coming soon, the story has led back out of history into our own personal lives.

And then she says, "There's another date I'll always remember. July 26, 1951," with that cadence of the storyteller who has come upon a tale that has long since proved to be everyone's favorite. "July 26, 1951, is an important date in my life."

But now, at the second repetition of this date something happens to me. Recalling it later, it seems to me that the room disappeared for a moment. And then I see the door to the house in which we lived when I was a girl. I see the red steps leading up to it. A child in braids runs up the steps, shouting something. The door swings open and the image fades.

My mother's hand rises to her earlobe, toying with an earring. Her eyes are cast toward the ceiling. "I got up early," she says, "Paul and I had breakfast together, he prepared his lunch and I read the newspaper aloud to him. Who could have expected it? He left for work, I began to straighten up around the house. I prepared something for dinner and then . . . I heard a knock at the door.

"I opened the door. I saw two men standing there. They were dressed very conservatively. They asked me if I was Rose Chernin.

" 'Yes,' I said, 'I am Rose Chernin. But who, gentlemen, are you?'

"The men showed me a warrant. I looked it over, I was satisfied. FBI. I was arrested. And for what? For forming a conspiracy, they said, and advocating the overthrow of the government. By force and violence, no less. That was the Smith Act. But of course I knew at once it was all because of my work with the Foreign-Born Committee.

"Well, I said to them, 'Gentlemen I am going into the house to change my clothes and to say good-bye to my daughter.'

"They agreed, they began to follow me into the house. But I said to them, 'Gentlemen, stay right where you are. Into this house you are not taking one single step.'

" 'Oh no? Then you're not going in either.'

"They arrested me.

"I looked behind me. I saw the gate to our back yard was open. Three men were standing there, with rifles. I walked out onto the porch. Our entire block closed off. It was early in the morning. But most of the neighbors were on their porches, watching. There were some men, they were walking up and down the block. These, I thought, are FBI agents. A car was parked across the street. From that car emerged a nurse in a white uniform and two men. They were coming toward us. We met in the middle of the street. They got into another car with us and then we were driving away.

"Kim was asleep when they came to arrest me. Everything happened so quickly. I couldn't say good-bye. I hoped our neighbors would see what was happening, they would go and tell her. But the faces didn't look familiar. I thought, they are all strangers.

"That was July 26, 1951. That summer my daughter became eleven years old."

I am aware of a desire not to cry. I am in the grip of something. It is old, it is powerful, it makes me want to turn away and to go toward it. It is fearful, I lost it long ago, and I desire it.

"What was it like for her? How did she first learn I was arrested? Had she expected this thing? That is what she will tell us now."

It's called memory, the child rushing up the steps, the door swinging open. But to me it seems an immense, inarticulate rush of feeling. At first I am afraid it will eat up my words. Then, I open my lips and it makes language:

The First Story I Tell

Hard Times (1947–1952)

I heard them talking. I heard them, even before my mother was arrested.

Frank, the lawyer, came to our house. "Sit down, Frank," my father said. "Have some coffee."

My mother was on the telephone.

Frank sat at the table. He put his elbows on the table and leaned against his hand.

Frank said, "They call, they keep coming. Our own people. Terrified."

My father listened, he shook his head. I heard him jingling the coins in his pocket. I sat next to my father at the table. I pretended I wasn't listening. I looked at the comics page in the newspaper.

Frank was talking. "What do you make of it, Paul? Why would this bastard come to tell me if he wants to croak to the committee?"

My father considered. "He thought you might tell him it's all right to save his wife like this. He wanted approval."

"From me? Approval? I could wring his neck."

There were other words. People used them and their voices had an edge. The Attorney General's List. The Blacklist. McCarthy. Red-baiting. Witch Hunts. The Loyalty Oath, they said. These were words they didn't want children to hear.

I heard them talking. My father had a friend who used to stop in after dinner. When he came I brought my schoolwork out of the bedroom, I lay down next to the heater on the living-room floor. He was a screenwriter, he told stories. Actors who came drunk onto the set in the morning. People who went swimming at night in their clothes. An actress who was found naked in a place you'd never expect to see anyone naked.

One night he told another story. From this story I got the impression the committee had called someone, who was an actor, and he had trouble because he smiled. I was seven years old. And that was in 1947.

When John left I took a good look at my father. He was putting his chess set back in the drawer. I decided to risk a question. "Daddy, why couldn't Robert Taylor smile?"

My father looked surprised. "You know what the committee is?" he said. With my mother I would never confess ignorance. She thought I should know everything even before I was told. But my father liked to explain. "By 'the committee' we mean the House Un-American Activities Committee. HUAC, we call it for short. The committee is trying to intimidate Communists and other radical people. It calls people up, it asks questions."

"And then?"

"Sometimes they lose their jobs."

"What's wrong with Communists?"

"Well, from our point of view, of course, what could be wrong? I'm a Communist, Mama's a Communist, Aunt Lillian and Uncle Norman are Communists, Frank and Gene are Communists. But the committee is out to expose people, to get Communists out of responsible positions."

My father waited for me to think things over. He liked children. He rolled down his sleeves and fastened the buttons on his shirt. I thought about what he said. I considered it for a long time and he wasn't in a hurry. Finally, I had a question. "Why couldn't Robert Taylor smile?"

My father sat down at the dining-room table. "Ach," he sighed. "Robert Taylor was playing in a film about Russia. The committee didn't want people to think Russians smiled." Then, he added, "About socialism."

"You were born in Russia. You smile."

"These are hard times. Things just don't make sense until you give them a political explanation."

I thought I could understand the explanation.

"Sometimes, people turn against their best interest. They don't develop the right consciousness of their political situation."

"Will they turn on *you?* Will they turn on *Mama?* Will they turn on Frank and Gene and Aunt Lillian and Uncle Norman? Will you lose *your* job?"

"Let's hope it doesn't come to that." He got up, put the queen back into the chess box, and closed the drawer.

~ ~

I divided my life. On the surface there was a little girl. I made a mess in my room and straightened it up when my mother yelled at me. I taught my dog Lucky to play dead. In the mornings my mother braided my hair.

But inside I had already grown old. There, I figured out my sister was never coming back. The dying, that no one had talked about, had gone so far it couldn't turn around anymore.

I figured things out. I figured out there was some new danger in the world. The fascists had gone. The concentration camps were gone. The Jews had gone to Israel. Now it was the turn of the Communists. We were Communists, it was our turn.

Alger Hiss was attacked by the committee. He was a good man, I found out, but I kept forgetting. His name made me distrust him. Hiss. I thought he was probably a snake, a stool pigeon. I was eight years old then. That was 1948.

"That snake-in-the-grass," my mother said one night at dinner. "Would you believe it? Sam Kichle. The membership director of the entire Los Angeles County. A stool pigeon. He had the name of everyone who joined. Their Party name and their real name. Very convenient. He turned over a carbon copy of every membership list to the FBI."

Adele came over for dinner. She always brought a little bag with cottage cheese and fruit. On her way in, she'd pick a fresh sprig of mint from our garden.

One night she arrived and she was pale. She was a Negro woman, but she had light skin, and this time her skin was even lighter than my father's. She said, "We know where they came from. They went through everything. Smashing, breaking." My father looked grave. "Paul," she said, "Paul. A children's bookstore."

~ ~

I didn't sleep very well at night. Sometimes, my mother would get up and sit next to me. She'd sing: *"Ticha smotret mesyats yasni."* For my sister, she used to sing in Yiddish. For me, in Russian.

One night I began to pray. I knew my parents did not approve of praying. I hid my folded hands under the covers. "God, keep my mother and father safe."

I had learned to pray in the boarding school where they sent me, after Nina died, when we first moved to California. "Jesus loves me, this I know, for the Bible tells me so." I hated that school. My mother hated religious songs. One Sunday, when they came for a visit, I sang to her. The next week they brought me home.

Then I was a Communist and at that time you could tell it to other people. It was something, my mother told me, to be proud of. We had a fur pillowcase with a hammer and a sickle. We had a picture of Nina as a little girl, wearing her red Komsomol scarf.

Now it changed. It was 1950. I was ten years old. I wasn't supposed to open the door to strangers. I had to ask first, making sure, before I opened the door. I wasn't supposed to tell the kids at school. I shouldn't repeat anything I heard my parents say at home. The kids said they were Democrats, they were Republicans. I said nothing.

The second time the committee came to town my prayers grew longer. "God, keep Aunt Lillian, Uncle Norman, Aunt Sara Barney's safe. God, keep Lucky safe. God protect the other Lillian, and Dorothy, Sam and Eva, Helen and Ben."

I was horrified about my prayers. Did they work? Did they help? I began to repeat them, beneath my breath, even at the dinner table. I took huge portions of potatoes. "Eat the string beans," my mother insisted, leaning over to take some potato off my plate. Without warning, suddenly, I picked up a glass and threw it against the wall.

After dinner, when I was helping my father with the dishes, I broke a plate. "Look at her," my mother insisted, "she's doing it on purpose."

A cup knocked against a dish in the drainer. The handle broke.

My mother's nerves were bad during that time. My nerves were bad, too. "I can't stand it, Paul," my mother yelled, "I'm telling you, I just can't take any more." I ran out of the room, I slammed the door. "Hush, Rose, she's only a child." Later, my father came into my room. "Try," he said to me. "She's nervous. These are hard times."

The hard times we were living in made everyone nervous. Lillian and my mother had fights on the phone. Lillian and Gertrude and my mother stayed up till all hours talking. My father got up, he went to the living-room door. "Please," he said in a soft voice, "please. I've got to go to work in the morning." For a moment the voices got softer, then they came up loud again.

I stopped sleeping. I lay awake and kept watch on things. I kept watch on the shadows that filled up my closet. I kept watch to make certain someone had left the light on in the hall. I listened to my mother and father whispering in their bedroom.

One of my mother's comrades came over to visit. They were talking in raised voices in the living room. I opened my bedroom door, I crept down the hall.

"It's a question of conscience, Rose. I'm leaving the Party. I can't and I won't accept that from the leadership."

"Three years ago you could accept it? Something's happened to your conscience all of a sudden since the committee came to town?"

"Rose. You know better than that."

"Do I? Do I?" There was a silence. Then, my mother said: "So where will you go? Let me tell you. For us, there's a concentration camp standing ready."

I crept back down the hall, I closed the door to my room. Inside, it was dark. I opened the curtain next to my bed. The light came in from Crenshaw Boulevard. Very quietly I started packing. I put an old pair of jeans, a sweater with a hole in the sleeve, and a heavy flannel shirt into the gym bag I made at school. I added a book by Laura Ingalls Wilder. The next day I added a chocolate bar.

Every night, before I said my prayers, I checked to make sure everything was okay in that bag. I never ate the chocolate bar.

My prayers grew longer. Sometimes I would fall asleep in the middle of my list but I woke up a few hours later, in the dark. I was covered in sweat. I started reciting. "Dear God, keep Sonia and Peter and Freddie safe."

My father came into my room. He walked on tiptoe. "Are you awake? I heard you talking."

"I wasn't talking. I was asleep."

He sat down at the edge of the bed. "Don't worry too much," he said to me. "Maybe we exaggerate. Who knows? Maybe it will still blow over."

My father had a big garden in back of our house. He grew corn and radishes, cucumbers and schav. He also had flowers, roses and camelias and a large cactus, he said, that bloomed only at night.

"I want to show you something." He brought me my bathrobe and my knit slippers. We went out into the dark. The grass was wet. The moon was shining. We went over to the cactus. There was a big white flower. I looked at my father, I took hold of his hand. Before that I never believed the cactus bloomed at night.

~~

Aunt Lillian was called before the committee. My mother put down the telephone. "Paul," she shouted, "Lillian. My sister Lillian."

We were proud of Lillian. She gave no names. "Risked everything," my mother said. "Stood fast."

We baked a turkey, we chopped liver. Lillian and Norman, Terry and Paulie came over to the house. Terry started running around the room, he was wild, he liked to climb on the furniture. Paulie watched him with a secret smile. Norman took Terry outside into the garden. "Rose," Lillian was saying, "the world is not all bad, I tell you."

Lillian was working at that time in Orange County. Her supervisor read her name in the paper after she went to the committee. Her supervisor stood up for her. She said, "Lillian's my best nurse. She always does the best job. She cares for people. Communist or no Communist, I'm not putting Lillian out of her job."

Lillian said, "You see, Rose? That's a brave woman. You know what she said to me, Rose? She said, 'Lillian, the only thing I regret is, you didn't tell me you are a Communist.'

" 'I should tell you?' " Lillian's eyebrows flew up. She looked just like my mother. " 'How could I know how you'd respond?' "

My mother said, "Did you notice? The committee always arrives in the winter. They come from where? From Washington, of course. And in Washington it's not exactly summer in the winter.''

Some men were following my mother. She and the other Rose, a lawyer, were driving to a meeting one night. My mother turned this way, she turned that way, the car still followed her.

"Paul," she said. "I'm not exaggerating. Paul, I'm telling you."

I heard them talking.

"Who knows where it will stop?"

I heard them talking.

"Who knows what it's headed for?"

"You remember the Palmer raids? So, what's new about this? We'll come through this. Everything will be normal again."

"That's what the Jews in Germany thought."

~ ~

One night the telephone kept ringing. It was dark in the house, someone forgot to leave the light on in the hall. My whole room was dark. I heard them getting up, their bedroom door banged open. The light came on in the hall. I heard my mother's voice.

"Who? Don't tell me! Who? Where? Who else?"

I sat straight up in my bed. She put down the telephone. "Five people," she said to my father. He was tying the belt around his bathrobe. "David Hyun. Frank Carlson. Harry Carlyle . . . without bail, on Terminal Island."

I went into the closet and got my hands on the gym bag. I slipped on my jeans and my Eisenhower jacket. I came back to watch them from my door. My father took my mother's hand. "What next?" he said.

"Deportations, Paul. Now already, it's deportations."

I went over to my closet. It was the only hiding place I could think of. I climbed up on the shelf, but I had to be quiet. The closet had a small inside window. It opened into another shelf, in my parent's closet, in the room next to mine. On my shelf there were extra blankets, for the winter. I tried hiding myself under them, piling them up on top of me.

My parents came back into their room. "The Party wants me to organize a defense. They want me to start an organization," my mother was saying. "I'm going to call a press conference in the morning."

My father sighed. "First they deport the foreign-born. And then?"

My mother's voice snapped, it was a whip. "Paul," she said, and she could have been talking through a microphone. "These people will not be deported. I'm telling you. We're going to fight."

The next day I was late for school. For weeks now I had been coming late so that I could miss Current Events. Usually, if I came too early I raised my hand and went out to the bathroom.

In Current Events they said there were prison camps in Russia.

In Current Events they said the reds were a menace. They said Communism was spreading out all over the world.

That day, in Current Events, they said that five Commies had been arrested. The teacher said it was a good thing. Now, she said, they could be deported.

One of those Commies she named was my friend. He was a Korean architect, he used to come over once a week in the late afternoon to give me art lessons. Sometimes, we went to his house for dinner. They served us spicy food in little bowls and David Hyun taught me how to eat with chopsticks. My mother had told me that if David and his wife were sent back to South Korea they would both be killed. I thought maybe I should raise my hand and say that to the class. But I looked around at them, these kids I'd gone to school with since the first grade. What difference would it make to them that David Hyun taught me to draw?

Tonio was another of my mother's comrades. He drove the Good Humor Truck. At home, we used to laugh with Tonio, at dinner. "The Communist Ice Cream Man," we called him. "Don't you give out propaganda with the ice cream, Tonio," my father would joke.

Tonio used to pick me up after school. I had a warm jacket and a thick scarf. Even on a cold day I could sit up front with Tonio, ringing the bell of the ice-cream truck. The kids came running after us, all over the neighborhood.

One night after dinner we saw Tonio coming up to the back door. He was wearing a police uniform. My mother wouldn't let me go out there. She wouldn't let me talk to Tonio. She wouldn't let me go anywhere near him.

"But why did he come here? Why did he come?" I yelled and

yelled. I pounded on my bedroom door. I was furious at her because Tonio had betrayed her.

"He wanted me to give names," she said.

~ ~

One day when I woke up in the morning a neighbor was standing next to my bed. I reached up to hug her. My mind raced. Our neighbor began to speak. I knew, even before she said a word to me. They had taken my mother. I was eleven years old.

It was summer, I put on my shorts. I got my bike and rode over to my friend's house. Her parents were Communists, we went to day camp together.

"Jessie, they arrested my mother. She didn't even get to say good-bye. No, I'm not kidding, are you kidding?"

Sara Kahen came out of the kitchen. "What are you whispering about?"

"They arrested my mother. This morning. I was asleep."

She got on the phone. "Sam? Rose was arrested. This morning. No, she's fine, she's not even crying."

Jessie and I got on our bicycles. Sara Kahen made us a big lunch. She chucked me under the chin. "What's the matter? You don't miss your mother?"

"I never cry."

In the afternoon the newspapers had the headline. Jessie and I saw it when we were riding home from camp. FIFTEEN COMMIE LEADERS ARRESTED IN CALIFORNIA. There were names, pictures. I saw my mother, wearing my flannel shirt.

"Jesus, Jessie, look at that. They didn't even let her change her clothes."

Jessie Kahen used to call herself my cousin. We had known each other since grammar school, we were best friends. But the day after my mother was arrested, Jessie Kahen told all the kids at camp we weren't really cousins.

"The hell with her," I said to myself three times. Then, I rode home from camp alone, without crying.

That night Aunt Lillian came over to the house. She talked for a long time with my father.

"Paul," she kept saying, "listen to this, Paul. They need someone to take over the work at the Foreign-Born Committee. I told them, how could I take Rose's place? But someone's got to do it. They won't stop arresting the foreign-born just because Rose Chernin is in jail."

My father put coffee and cookies on the table. "Sit down, that's better, take off your shoes." He poured a cup of coffee for her. "To begin with, why shouldn't you take her place? You're a brave woman. That we know. I advise you, take over as director of the Defense Committee."

Aunt Lillian had brought dinner for me and my father. She was gathering up clothes for my mother, in jail. "What do you think?" she said, holding up a polka-dot dress. "Does she like this one?"

My father warmed up the dinner. "Lillian," he said, "you'll understand, I'm not very hungry."

I was very hungry. I ate more than they ever saw me eat before. I ate my dinner, and my father's dinner and Aunt Lillian's dinner.

"Look at her," Lillian said. "She'll eat for all of us."

The telephone kept ringing.

"Eight o'clock this morning," I said. "Sure, I was at home."

People kept coming to the house. Aunt Sara came, with a dish of stuffed cabbage.

My father gave her a hug. "Thank you, Sara," he said, "but you'll understand. Tonight I'm not very hungry."

Sara was plump. She carried a red purse. When she came in the door you could go over and take a look into the purse. There was always something, a cookie wrapped in a napkin, some chocolate, a little game.

I loved Sara. She never forgot. "So come," she said, when she saw me looking. "You're too old all of a sudden to give a look in the purse?"

In Sara's arms, for the first time, I cried. With my father, alone, I wouldn't cry. "Tell me," he'd say. "Talk to me. Why should you have all this alone? Tell me, what are you feeling?"

"I'm all right," I'd say in a furious voice. He had let me down when my sister died. "Just leave me alone," I'd say, "I'm okay." Now he couldn't even keep my mother safe. Why should I talk to him?

One night he told me that bail for my mother and the other

defendants was one hundred thousand dollars. He told me that meant they couldn't get out of jail. They had to stay there until the bail was reduced. He said, "How could we raise one hundred thousand dollars?"

"Well," I said, figuring quickly. "We'd have to divide it by fifteen, right? That means, for each one, less than seven thousand dollars." I went right on thinking. It didn't seem so bad. There was Uncle Max and Aunt Anne. They were wealthy. There was cousin Sol, who had bought the shopping center. There was Dorothy in New York, who had loaned us the money to buy our house. I became excited. I couldn't figure out why he looked so grim. "Come on, Dad. You're making a big deal. You could get on the phone, start calling, you'll have the money like that." I snapped my fingers. I began to prance around.

"Listen, listen," he said, trying to grab me. "You don't understand."

"What? What?" I was scared now.

"One hundred thousand dollars each."

"Come on." I couldn't believe it. "Just come on. They couldn't do that. It's not fair."

"Ach, fair." He sat down at the table and looked tired. "A fair world we haven't yet been able to make."

I shook him by the shoulder. I didn't want to see him like that. It was the same when Nina was dying. I began to shout.

"Goddamn it," I yelled and my voice thundered. "We won't let them get away with that." I was eleven years old, I knew something about the law. "It's unconstitutional," I screamed. "And we're going to fight it."

We fought. The hearings lasted six months. The lawyers also thought it was not constitutional. My father said, "In these times, who's going to protect the Constitution?"

"Daddy," I shouted at him. "We're going to protect it."

We were standing in the garage, stacking up newspapers for the school paper drive. "Daddy," I yelled, and I just kept on yelling. "We won't let them get away with that shit." He looked up startled. Then he smiled. That night, he talked to his brother Max on the telephone. "A fiery one," he said, and he had the same smile on his face. "Just like her mother."

I didn't tell him I hated going to school. I didn't tell him how one day, when I walked up to the school, I saw my friends gathered together, standing in a little group, whispering. When I came up there was a funny movement. Something that had been there disappeared. And now nobody had anything to say.

Then someone was talking. "Hey," he said to me, casuallike. "What's your mother's maiden name?"

My mother's maiden name?

The kids were all smiling. Then someone was holding the newspaper clipping in his hand. Oh yeah, of course, it had to happen. ROSE CHERNIN, COMMIE LEADER, ARRESTED IN LOS ANGELES. Sooner or later someone had to figure it out.

Who cares? I walked away, shrugging my shoulders. Then it came to me: now things were different. If I denied who we were, that was betrayal. It was not keeping her safe. I turned back. "Rose Chernin," I said. My voice was loud. "My mother's maiden name is Rose Chernin."

I never told anybody how much I hated going to school. Every day I passed through the front gate and my eyes itched. My mother said I was a fighter. I made a fist. The other kids, their gossip, that passed over. But my biggest fear was, I knew things I shouldn't know and I was afraid I might tell.

I knew the name of a man who had been deported. I knew he had come back secretly and was living in Los Angeles again. I heard them talking. He was underground, they said. If anyone found out, my mother said, he'd be sent back to South Korea. They kill Communists there.

There was a girl named Zoya Kozmodemyanskaya. I had a book about her. Adele gave it to me one night when she dropped by with her bag of cottage cheese and fruit. Zoya was a partisan fighter in the Soviet Union during the war. The Germans caught her, they pulled out her nails, they put matches against her, and they hanged her. She was only thirteen years old. Later, her brother came with a tank battalion and found pictures of Zoya. Hanging. But she never told them, she never gave them a single name.

Would they torture my mother in jail? Would they torture me? Would I tell the names I knew? Would they put needles under my nails? Would they hold a burning match under my chin?

I knew the name of everybody who came to our house. I knew if you started talking you'd tell everything. "He sang his heart out," my mother had said one night at dinner before she was arrested. "Once he started, he never stopped. He gave even his wife's name. The name of his sister."

The fascists put children in gas ovens. They put children in cattle cars, separate from their mothers.

Once a week I wrote her a letter. "Dear Mama," I said. "Everything's just great here."

I didn't want my father to find out and tell her. I didn't want her to worry about me.

At school my old friends drifted away. If they saw me coming down the hall they turned and fiddled with a locker. They went into a bathroom, they walked into one of the empty rooms. I looked back after I passed, I saw them come out again, whispering.

Then, for a while, I didn't have any friends at school. I didn't try to catch up with the other kids in the morning. At lunchtime, I sneaked out of the playground, so I wouldn't have to sit by myself eating my lunch. Tonio no longer picked me up in the afternoon. I hung around in the halls, or I sat by myself on the back staircase. That way no one would see me walking home alone. At home, in the afternoon, I clipped articles about my mother out of the newspaper and pasted them into my scrapbook. My dog Lucky and I went out for a walk in the Baldwin Hills.

But then one day everything changed. One day in class there was an incident. A boy hadn't done his homework. The teacher was exasperated. She turned away from the blackboard and she said: "Keep on like this and you'll end up collecting garbage." Before she could turn back to the board a book was flying across the room. There was a silence and then she went over and took the boy, James Grove, by the shoulder. She pulled his sweater and dragged him over to the door.

"Take your hands off him." I was on my feet, shouting. My voice cut the other voices in the room. "I threw that book."

"Sit down," she yelled back. "Don't even try. I saw him."

"I threw that book. If someone's going to the principal, it better be me."

That boy had a strange look on his face. He had light skin and gray eyes and we thought he was real cute. "Hey, hey," I saw him saying with his lips, under his breath.

It was a restless class, people whispered and wrote notes and made cootie catchers. If someone happened to know the lesson, when they stood up to read everyone else started talking. But now it was awfully quiet in the class. Everyone was looking at me and the teacher.

"Prove it," I said. "Prove he threw the book and I didn't."

"All right," she said. "If you're so eager to go to the principal, you come, too."

We sat outside in the hall, waiting for the principal. We sat in her office, waiting for her to get off the phone.

"Who threw the book?" the principal said.

"I did," said James Grove and I.

"You both threw the same book! Okay, you're both suspended. Tell your mothers to come to school."

"Hey," I was going to say to her. "Hey, my mother can't come to school. She's in jail."

But something happened to the principal's face. Before I could say a word a look crossed over it. James Grove saw it and I saw him see it.

She knew already that my mother was in jail.

She fiddled about with the charts. She looked inside and read over our records. "Well," she said, "you have good grades. Both of you. Take this as a warning."

James Grove put his arm around me when we walked back to class. James Grove opened the door for me when we came to the room. The teacher was at the blackboard and some of the Negro kids got to their feet. They stood there, girls and boys I hardly knew, cheering as we walked into the room.

In our school the white kids all left by the front gate. The Negro kids and the Mexican kids and the tougher Oriental kids went out through the back gate. James Grove was a Negro kid. And now I went out through the back gate with him. There, behind the school, were older boys from the neighboring high school. Policemen often came cruising by in patrol cars. Fights broke out. There were knives, gangs, secret clubs, violence. Once, after school, at the back gate, someone took a basketball and threw it into the gym teacher's window.

My new friends never asked me about my mother. They never whispered about me. I went to parties and the boys lined up to dance with me.

At school, the white kids stopped whispering. They just looked at me when I went down the hall, walking with my new friends. In class, I sat with the Negro kids, and the few Mexican kids and the Oriental kids.

Then, one day, the teacher called on a white boy for Current Events. James Grove stood up by his desk. "Ah shit, teacher," he said. "Ain't nothin' new 'bout this ol' world."

The next day she called on someone again. James Grove was on his feet. "Didn't I tell you, teacher?" A white girl was standing up, her newspaper clipping pasted on a piece of yellow paper. She looked at James Grove. "You hear?" he said. And she sat down again.

It was late by the time we got home from school. We stood around at the corner, shifting our books and kicking pebbles. The boys smoked, passing the cigarette behind their backs. The girls wore two pair of socks, one color turned down over the other. The boys had their shirts open to the waist. We didn't talk much, we were cool. But when I went off to go home alone, a girl said: "Don't worry honey. You got friends."

The next day and the day after and then every day for a week, the teacher called for Current Events. But each day one of my friends stood up. "Teacher, don't you know by now? Ain't nothin' new in this ol' world."

~ ~

One day a boy kissed me. He put his arm around me at the back gate, we walked all the way home from school. His name was Roni Takata, he was a beautiful boy. He had black curls, he had dark eyes, his lips smiled even when Roni Takata wasn't smiling. At home, in the living room, we sat down on the gray couch with the long shag. Roni Takata put his hands inside my pants. A feeling came and I hid my face in his chest, embarrassed.

When I went to the bathroom I saw blood. I didn't want to tell my father. I waited for him to come home. There was more blood, I rolled up toilet paper and held it tight with my legs.

"Daddy," I said, when he came in the door. "I have to tell you something."

"So, tell."

"I'll write it on a piece of paper."

He read the paper. "You're a woman," he said. "Don't worry."

"Dear Mama," I wrote, "I got my period. Dear Mama, here everything's just great."

But my father said, something was building. At night, the covers were never tight enough. At night, I recited my mother's name two hundred times in my prayer.

He said it to Aunt Sara on the telephone. "Something's building in that girl," he said.

He was right, something was building. It couldn't be fought down anymore. Once, I almost started crying. My father and I were doing the dishes. "You worried about Mama?" "I'm not worried. I know she's okay." "Tell me," he said, drying his hands on the apron. "Why should you have all this alone?" "It's nothing, I mean it. Just some dumb boy at school, you hear?"

Sometimes I had to call out for my father at night. He came and sat next to me on the bed. He didn't know any Russian lullabies. "What's wrong with you?" I yelled. "Is something wrong with you? Didn't you have a Mama? Couldn't she sing?"

At my uncle's house, where my father and I went for dinner on Sunday nights, I yelled at my father. "You old goat," I shouted, for no reason at all.

I ran out of the room, no one came after me. I ran into the bathroom and locked the door. "You old goat," I screamed again. But that time I was crying. I sat right down in a heap on the tile floor, my shoulders started shaking. "It's not fair," yelled a hoarse voice. "It's not fair," it shouted in a terrified whisper. "It's not fair, it's not fair, it's not fair, it's not fair . . ."

I stayed in that bathroom for a long time. After a while, I heard them talking. "How can you blame the child?" my father said. "Six years ago she lost her sister. Now, her mother's in jail. Did you ever think," he said to his brother, "how the world must look in the eyes of this child?"

One day he came home early from work. He parked his car in front of the house and he came up the driveway practically running.

"She's coming home," he said. "She's coming home."
"Hey, what happened? She escape from jail?"
"The bail's reduced. She's coming home."
My father had bought me a new dress, organdy.
"Come on, Daddy, I'll wear jeans."
He bought me a pair of patent-leather shoes.
"You kidding, Daddy? I'm twelve years old."
"You're happy?" he said and he touched my hair.
"Sure I'm happy, what d'ya think?"

Take a Giant Step

"Who would have thought it? I ask you, who could imagine?" My mother looks at the women in the room. But she doesn't see them. "Always," she says, her voice breaking, "always we thought we could protect our children from knowing. Now we find out it was the children protecting us."

~ ~

Then we are alone in the kitchen, preparing a light supper. The last guest left over an hour ago. Larissa has gone out to a late movie with a friend. We heat up a pot of cabbage soup, slice a loaf of barley bread, toss a fresh salad, and put out baked apples with yogurt.

"You want butter?" she asks, setting the dish down on the table. But her voice has a flat, leaden quality. She is upset because of my story.

"Sure." I am trying to keep my voice cheerful, but I am fooling no one. "How about you?"

"No. No butter."

I look at her as I eat. She is stirring her spoon around in the bowl but she is not eating.

"You need salt?" I want to express my concern, my anguish at the thought that I have hurt her. But she is remote, inaccessible. The mood she has no doubt been trying to fight off since I first began to read tonight has now apparently taken over.

"No salt," she says, "it's fine." It has happened before; her wonderful bravery, thrusting her past her own limits while people are present. But suddenly, when we are alone together, the past claims her.

I listen to the kettle heating on the stove. The motor in the refrigerator turns itself on and fills our silence. Any moment, I know, I am going to start chattering, on and on, about nothing at all.

"It's Larissa's favorite bread," I venture, trying too hard, unable to stop myself. "And the soup? You remember? The same one Aunt Gertrude used to make."

She takes up a spoonful of soup and blows against it very carefully. But then she puts the spoon back down into her bowl. It is a very familiar gesture, and it affects me deeply. Suddenly, I am a little girl again. My sister is dying. My father sits at the table trying hard to pretend that everything is all right. Very slowly, with an immense effort, he eats the food my mother has put before him. But she sits silently, with this same stony silence, her face grim, her features drawn, all the light in her killed off. Every now and again he reaches out and pushes her plate very gently toward her. She does not look up at him, but her hand springs up from her lap and pushes the plate back.

I would come running into a room, looking for my mother. Even at the time I could feel the incredible force by which she tried to drag herself back into the world and pay attention to me. But the memory of this, more painful even than the memory of my sister's death, has remained even more carefully hidden. And now, as it returns, I realize how often, in our life together, I found her, in an unexpected moment, brooding so desperately. It was, I knew, a secret she kept. Even from my father. It was, I felt, a side of her I alone knew, our special bond. It was different, deeper, more tremendous in its suggestion of an unhealing wound, than her behavior at the table. It was dark and awesome, very disturbing and strangely beautiful to me, because it kept her at home with me. Yet I feared it. I thought she was going to die of her despair.

And I realize that all my life I have been afraid to jostle her down into this tremendous sorrow.

"You want salad?" she asks, pushing the bowl toward me. "You're not eating."

"I'm trying. It's you who haven't touched a bite."

She seems surprised at this and glowers down at her bowl. "A good soup," she says, taking a mouthful. "It was Mama's favorite. Also for a rainy day."

I can tell, from her voice, that she is trying to reach over to me again. She holds out her plate as I offer her the salad. And now, before I can set the bowl down, she reaches out and pats my hand.

"Mama," I say, and I try to forgive myself the eagerness in my voice. "Talk to me."

"Talk to you." She repeats the words with her flat, despairing tone, and I see in this one moment everything that has gone wrong between us, repeating itself, again.

The kettle begins to whistle. She gets up to turn it off and stands next to the stove watching the steam. She is trying to straighten her shoulders, but the effort it takes makes her look crushed and broken. This powerful woman, so completely helpless. And still so sternly, so militantly refusing to share her mood.

I go over to her. Years ago, maybe even a year or two ago, I would have been walking from the room and slamming the door in rage. I have never been able to forgive her for this insistence upon bravery. Now, I put my arms around her. She stiffens, drawing away, but I hold on to her.

"Talk to me."

She touches my hand; her fingers are very cold.

"If I hurt you I want you to tell me." My voice is scarcely more than a whisper.

But now I can feel her, gathering herself, focusing. I can feel that my struggle has reached her. She, too, wants us to change. Her whole body becomes taut and finally she says, "I didn't want to make life hard for you."

So that's it? That's why she withdrew? I should have known it. She has carried this guilt, as a mother, even before I was born. This awful sense that she has hurt her children by being a Communist. But I had wanted to give her this story of our life as a gift; as a reparation even for Nina's death. And now it turns out that what I have just read to her she sees as her public condemnation.

We are both sinking; it is a perceptible sensation; we are falling back into that silence which used to be so terrible between us.

"Listen," I say, "it can't end here." My voice cracks, breaking through its hostility. "I'm thirty-nine years old. And I don't blame you for being a Communist. I never did. No one has an easy adolescence. I, at least, had a mother I could be proud of."

She turns around and looks at me, straightening her shoulders, as if she were making a speech. "I closed you out. From the time Nina died. I know, you don't have to tell. How could I tell to a five-year-old child about such grief?"

But her voice is not the voice of an orator. It is simple and naked. It speaks what we have both been waiting a lifetime to hear.

And now I hear in my voice the same simplicity, a truth, spoken with feeling. "I couldn't forgive you for letting Nina die. I hated you for falling apart. I hated you because you loved her better. I thought I killed her."

"You?" she says. And then she repeats the word in a tone of stunned and urgent disbelief. "You?" We do not look at each other, but we both hear, in this single word, the echo of all the lonely guilt and horror that always, until now, divided us. She, too, blamed herself for Nina's death.

I would like to put my arm around her and look out into the night.

"We're not done yet," she says. "There's more coming. I know it."

I glance at the clock. It is still early, not yet nine thirty. Only an hour has passed since Larissa shut the door behind her, calling out, "Don't stay up talking all night this time."

"I gave you the impression I wasn't a strong woman?" she asks. "You want me to read?"

"Read, tell, what does it matter?"

I smile, almost convinced. There is so much I still want to tell her. But I don't go down into the living room for the manuscript. She watches me, that stern, self-mastering look in her eyes. And then she says, very seriously, "I want you to do something for me first."

"Anything. Just ask."

I stand there, my whole being reaching out to her with eager hands. I would fly up the chimney if she wished for it.

"So, sit," she says. And then she's on her feet, moving over to the stove. "You'll eat a bite first. What will it hurt you?"

The Second Story I Tell

A Communist Childhood (1952–1957)

*T*he day my mother got out of jail I wore the organdy dress and patent-leather shoes my father bought for me.

I smiled and I kept on smiling, letting my father hold my hand as the elevator door opened and a group of men and women came down from the Federal Building, and one of them was my mother.

She was different than I remembered. She was not taller or shorter, or plumper or thinner. Her face was, I suppose, the same. But something inside me, bravely smiling, was saying: Who is she? What does she want of me?

This woman, with gray hair, wearing a neat dress with a belt, walking with a good, firm, dignified stride into my father's arms; taking my hand to draw me along beside them; this woman, who spoke my name twice and pulled me against her, was an acceptable person to be proud of (and I was). But the woman who had gone away to jail six months before had taken my feelings along with her. And now, having by this time forgotten how to feel, I had lost my mother.

We could hold hands, we could walk cheerfully down the street, waving good-bye to the others. We could get into the car the way we'd always done, my mother in the front, I kicking my heels in the back. But it was only pretending. This woman, coming home with us, was not my mother.

~ ~

During the six months my mother was in jail my father and I had roast beef every night for dinner, except for the nights we had dinner out. We had roast beef warm, roast beef warmed over, roast beef in cold pink slices, roast beef cut into small pieces and stirred in the pan with onion. For six months we had roast beef. And that night, in celebration of my mother's homecoming, we had roast beef.

I set the table, putting out rye bread and butter, the tomato juice in little glasses. My mother went in to change her clothes and when she came back into the kitchen I could tell from one look at her face that she wasn't happy to be at home with us.

"Good to be home?" my father said, taking her hand.

My mother stiffened. "Of course, Paul, what do you think?"

I watched her. I kept my eyes on her all through dinner. She liked it better in jail, I thought to myself, she can't fool me.

There was, without doubt, a strain in our little family gathering. The conversation just couldn't get going. My father talked to her about the prospects for the trial.

"They'll have paid witnesses, what else?" my mother said.

We heard the sound of knives and plates. My dog came over to beg at the table. I threw him a piece of roast beef.

"You feed the dog now at the table?"

My father put out his hand to touch my mother on the arm.

"All right, Paul," she said, impatiently.

I saw what I shouldn't see. That was the problem. Before, when she was in jail, I knew what I shouldn't know and I felt what I shouldn't be feeling. But now, I just could not stop my eyes from seeing. They saw the way my father jingled the coins in his pocket all the time. They saw he was afraid to lose his job. He smiled too much and when he said something he put his hand to his mustache and stroked the hair back from his lips. He did that a lot; before he only used to do it when he was nervous.

My mother didn't like roast beef. I could tell. She was cutting irritably at the tough meat.

"It's great, Dad," I said, in a false voice. I always defended my father.

"Rose," he said, with his smile, "if you would count six months and then multiply by thirty, you would know, give or take a few days, how many times she ate roast beef while you were away."

My mother tapped her spoon against the coffee cup. "Years ago, I told you, Paul, shouldn't you learn how to cook?"

I heard myself shouting. "I love roast beef," I yelled, and these words were so loud you could feel them hit the wall and come back, vibrating. "I hate fish. I hate chicken. I like roast beef and potatoes and string beans and salad. And if you don't want to eat them, you can just go back to jail."

There was a silence after this outburst. My mother sat with the spoon in her hand. My father looked at his plate. And then I knew for sure she was not really my mother.

"All right," she said, "sit down." She spoke in a whisper. "I'm on edge," she said and my mother never would have admitted that. "You think it's been easy?"

~ ~

After dinner Aunt Lillian and Uncle Norman arrived at the same time as my father's brother Max. Gertrude came later, with her inevitable bag of delicatessen food. The phone kept ringing and our comrades started dropping in.

My mother sat in the living room, on the gray shag couch, her feet curled up beside her. We turned on the television to watch the news story about the release of the Smith Act Defendants from jail that morning. My mother and Dorothy Healey came out of the elevator. They were handsome and smiling. If you didn't know better you would think they were dignitaries returning from a European tour. I watched them and thought it was funny the way they were, and were not, the women I knew so well. Then, even before the news was over, my mother started telling stories. She had a cup of coffee in her hand and it just stayed there and got cold while she was talking.

My father and I sat across the room from her, watching. That was when she became my mother again.

"I used to think," she said, "about being arrested. These days, who doesn't? I used to ask myself: Will I be able to take it? Will I be able to overcome the fear of going to prison? Will I break down under the strain?"

My father held my hand. He had a certain look on his face when he looked at my mother. He loves her, I thought to myself, seeing things I would only understand fully years later. He would not have found it difficult to come home to us. For him, she was the great love of his life. His work, chess, his friendships, even his relationship with me or with the Party, would always come second. It was a fierce passion for such a gentle man.

Of course, she was spellbinding. No one could ever resist her. I fell in love with her all over again that night. But I went right on seeing.

She would always find it hard to step back into domestic life. We limited her, we tied her back down to the earth. She was made for larger confrontations, for crises and battles. And I, seeing this, knew I was exactly the same. Someday, when my time came, I would be just like her.

She said, "So we're driving away. I was nervous. Who knew what to expect from the FBI? And certainly, I was worried about my daughter. Well, I know myself. When I get nervous I talk. When I start talking, who knows what I will say? Sooner or later, I thought, they're going to question me. The only thing for me to do is to shut up my mouth now and not to open it again."

She clenches her fist. "I am a determined woman," she says, "as you know. I had made up my mind. I would answer no questions. So now the nurse says to me, 'Rose, would you like to borrow my lipstick?' Because you can believe me I looked a sight. I was wearing clothes my daughter had thrown away a year before. I didn't have a chance to comb my hair or put on make-up. These are the clothes you put on for cleaning up around the house in the morning. They are not, I assure you, the clothes you choose to be arrested in. Then the interrogation proceeds. 'Rose, would you like some coffee?' But I had decided to keep my mouth shut and that's exactly what I did. I was arrested at about ten minutes past eight and from that time until twelve o'clock, when they came for me, I didn't say a word. I don't remember any other time in my life when my mouth was closed for four hours."

During the laughter that follows my father goes out into the kitchen for another pot of coffee. Aunt Lillian goes along with him, taking his arm.

"So, Paul, how does it feel to have Rose home again?"

"Lillian, Lillian," he says, patting her hand. "Can I tell you?"

And meanwhile, my mother is talking. "As a woman, as a mother," she says, "you feel so much guilt because of your political involvement. You're torn apart. You're afraid, merely in being away from the child, that she is suffering."

The women shake their heads, sighing sympathetically. That was always the way with my mother, I think. She could say exactly what people wanted to hear. But, did she mean it? Did she really think about me one bit when she was driving away?

Shut up, I say to myself. What makes you so mean? Shut up those thoughts. You're angry and you're jealous. Now she's the center of attention. She comes home and now everyone pays attention to her.

For that whole evening I was as clear and transparent to myself as a crystal ball. I was only twelve years old, but for those few hours I had the introspective insight I would develop fully many years later. It frightened me, and it fascinated me. It reminded me of the machine at Sears, where you could gaze down at your feet and see the way your toes fit into your shoes.

My mother calls me. "So tell us," she says, "what was it like for you when I was in jail?"

The whole room swivels around to look at me.

"What was it like?" I repeat. Not for nothing am I her daughter. My arm moves exactly like hers. My hand sweeps out — that intimate, rhetorical gesture. "It wasn't so bad. The kids talk, they stop talking. I'm not exactly the type you make into a victim."

I think about the other kids who waited outside the Federal Building this morning. What are they saying tonight, in all their houses, all over the city? Richard Healey might tell the truth, but that was the trouble with him, I decided. He could still feel. No doubt he was even capable of crying.

"Come," says my mother and holds out her hand. I walk across the room, proudly; for the first time I am happy about the organdy dress and patent-leather shoes, the little-girl disguise my father has given me. I sit down on the floor at my mother's feet, next to the gray shag couch where Roni Takata discovered me a woman.

My mother puts her hand on my head. It rests gently, but I feel it as a tremendous weight, making its claim on me. For her, I am brave and loyal, beyond the reach of those fears and doubts that trouble me at night, in darkness, in silence. She wants a model child; a girl who can make a Communist proud. A child about whom it cannot be said that it was too great a strain being raised the daughter of a Communist mother. Never, never must she be allowed to suspect how difficult her choices have made life for her daughter. I reach up and cover her hand with my own. I'm taller than she is now, my hand is larger.

She pulls my head over toward her and I rest it against her shoulder. And she, nodding her head, continues to tell her story:

"Well, you might say, what is so terrible about being in jail? I'll tell you. In the first place, who knows what will happen to you when you go in there? You're a free person, you have your own dignity. But now they've taken away not only the freedom but the sense of your own decency. You want to know what I mean? There is of course the fingerprinting, the photographs, the body search. They make you take a shower and always someone is standing there to watch. Little by little, you see, they are stripping away. The tone of voice, the rough hands pushing, those cold eyes. These things work on you. Naturally you're frightened. Who knows what these people will want to do to you? After the shower, you come out and dry yourself on a rough piece of cloth. They give you a dress to put on. The prison garment. In another situation maybe it would be funny. And why? Because to me, a little person, they give a long dress, a huge, drab blue, cotton, shapeless sack that is just hanging off of me. But to Bernadette Doyle, a big woman, very tall, with a large shape, they give a garment that hardly reaches to the knees. But funny it's not. It's part of the work they do, to intimidate, to take you from yourself. They lead you into the cell. The door claps shut behind you and you think, That's it, it's all over, I'll be in here forever."

~ ~

That night I had no idea it would be I who one day would give to my mother's stories their final form. I knew only that she had begun to work on me with her old enchantment. She had been taken off to jail and had entered history. When the story of the McCarthy period would be told, someday, her life would be part of it. And that, I saw, forgiving her, was why she found it difficult to come home again, to the rye bread and tomato juice, the tough roast beef, the little girl in the organdy dress and the gentle man who jingled the coins in his pocket and worried about losing his job.

I forgave her. How else could it have been? She would live, for the next five years, before I graduated from high school and left home, uncertain whether she was going to prison. She would, during those years, be called up before the House Un-American Activities Committee. She would be the first person in America the government would try to denaturalize and deprive of citizenship. And I, although I suffered in my own smaller world of childhood, because of these things — I was fiercely proud of her.

To this day I can recite the knowledge of her work I acquired when I was twelve years old. The words came easily from my lips; when I spoke them I would look around at my audience. They were, for the most part, kids in the Labor Youth League, the radical organization I had helped organize. "Do you know what the McCarran Act is?" I would ask. "Do you know what an outrage such a law is in a democratic country?" I discovered that I, too, could hold an audience captive. I listened to the rise and fall of my voice, rounding itself out with rhetorical flourish.

"Just think," I once said to a group of students from the college division of the League. "My mother has led the perfect radical life. What does it matter if the revolution hasn't occurred yet? Look what she has done in the last few years." They looked at me, their smiles fading. I was a fiery kid, and I knew how to take myself seriously.

I was proud of my mother. "How many girls," I would say to myself, "have an example like this?" "How many Young Communists," I would say to my radical friends, "can look to their family and find a woman who was a Communist before they were?"

I was a master of rhetoric. And I used every ounce of my rhetorical skill to make up for the quarrels that were always breaking out between us. She arrived home in the late afternoons; she found a spot on the red carpet I had vacuumed for more than an hour, and right away she and I would start yelling.

"She's under such terrible pressure," my father would say. "Maybe you can think about it and you'll forgive her."

Suddenly all my sophistication dropped away. I stamped my foot. "Why does she have to pick on me?"

He wanted me to keep my voice low. "Shah," he'd whisper, "she'll hear you. Why do you want to upset her?"

"Nothing's good enough for her," I screamed. "She comes into the house and right away she finds a spot."

"She's nervous," he said. "Who wouldn't be?"

Those were nervous times. Every morning my mother drove off in her car, still forgetting to put a napkin in my lunch, but now she was going down to the Federal Building to sit in court, on trial for being a Communist.

The headlines said: TRIAL OF L.A. REDS. JURY CHOSEN TO TRY 15 COMMIE LEADERS. The trial began on February 1, 1952. Six months later they were found guilty. They were fined ten thousand dollars each, they were sentenced to five years in prison and the government put a lien on our house to guarantee it would get its money. My father said, "Now even the house is no longer secure."

I was in court the day the sentence was pronounced. I saw my mother and the others being taken away, the men handcuffed together. My mother turned and looked back at me and I didn't see her again for five weeks. I was scared then; the sleepless nights came again, and the newspaper headlines. I thought she would be away for six months, I was afraid maybe she would not be permitted to come home at all before she was sent to prison. Our local newspaper said: AREA RED ONE OF 14 SENTENCED. But five weeks later they were out on bail.

At dinner, that first night she was home, my mother stopped eating. She carefully placed the fork down next to her plate and she looked over at us, with our tense faces. Far back, behind that fierce sparkle in her eyes, there was something that ached and worried. "Don't fuss," she said when she saw me staring. "It's not over yet." I liked her fierceness; I felt, looking at her, that she was a woman who could not be broken. "The case will go to the court of appeals. And then, if necessary, we'll fight it right up to the Supreme Court. It'll take years," she said. "We're in no hurry to go to prison."

It took years. In 1953, they were found guilty again in the court of appeals. Her name, her photograph, the story of the trial, appeared again in the newspapers. The headlines said: RED DEFEND-ANTS SMILE AT U.S. WAY OF JUSTICE. And meanwhile, all over the country Communists were going to prison. Other people disappeared and went underground. People moved to Mexico and Europe. There were Hollywood writers living in France, writing film scripts under assumed names. The phone still rang with stories of jobs lost, people questioned, names given or withheld, new immigration trials, friends detained on Terminal Island and threatened with deportation.

I knew everything that went on. I eavesdropped on every conversation. Secretly I listened in on meetings and overheard telephone conversations. I no longer prayed.

Gradually, I discovered that the newspapers told stories our own people wanted to protect me from. For a while I kept clippings of every Communist arrested or jailed in the United States. But one night I destroyed most of them and kept only the articles about my mother's trial. I felt guilty knowing all these facts no one really wanted me to know. I burned the clippings and flushed the ashes down the toilet, but the knowledge remained.

I knew that Communists had been tried and sentenced to prison in Hawaii, in Oregon, in Utah, in New York, in Colorado, in Pennsylvania.

I knew that Robert Thompson, the Party leader from New York, was captured by the FBI after he'd gone underground. I found out that he was tied up to a tree and left for hours in the hot sun. Later, when he went to prison, a prisoner attacked him with an iron bar.

I heard of another Communist, Philip Frankfeld, who was beaten almost blind by his fellow prisoners.

There was a poll published in our newspaper. It showed that the majority of Americans were in favor of sending all Communists to prison.

By that time the Smith Act case of the New York leadership had been heard by the Supreme Court. I knew that the decision of the lower courts, finding them guilty, had been upheld.

My mother would go to prison. That seemed clear. And would she be beaten?

During those years, the Communist world, in which of course we had always lived, made itself even more visible. A clothing manufacturer my mother knew gave me an expensive suit for my junior-high-school graduation. My dentist stopped sending us bills, our doctors refused to charge us, and now at Christmastime a mysterious Santa Claus began leaving gifts in front of the door — extravagant presents, which it later turned out were left for the children of all the Smith Act victims. Then, we began to laugh and joke about the Communist Santa Claus. It was the first time I'd been permitted to celebrate Christmas.

~ ~

As children of the left we had always known we had a meaningful place in the Communist vision. We were the hope and the promise; it was we who carried the hope of the revolution they had expected in their youth. Later, when for some of us the vision collapsed, it left an emptiness that reached back into the earliest experience of childhood and shook the very fundaments of memory.

It would be hard to forget the Sunday afternoons, walking between my parents down Pico Boulevard, where there was a cinema that showed Soviet films. And yet, for many years after I gave up being a Marxist, I had to make myself forget the happiness I felt as we strolled along there, catching sight of one friend after another, waving, calling out greetings, gathering in little clusters of two and three to exchange comments about the world situation.

"So, Rose," people would say, hurrying to catch up with us, "what do you think about the situation in _____?" We would stop, my father would look thoughtful, my mother would make her pronouncement, and on we would go, drawing further with each step into that safe and familiar world of radical feeling and thought.

In those years my mother's committee began to hold their annual celebrations, the Festival of Nationalities. Hundreds, sometimes thousands of people came, even then when everyone knew how dangerous it was. All over the picnic grounds people walked about in their national costumes. There was folk dancing, decorated booths, display tables with folk art and exhibits. Even when I was a teenager, growing tougher and harder with every year, those great, ceremonial celebrations of radical solidarity would tear me open and make me a child again. I would catch sight of my mother, strolling along with the committee's defendants, people whose lives had in many cases been saved because of her work. I loved the way people looked at her, the way they reached out to touch me, Rose Chernin's daughter. Halfway across the picnic ground I could hear her voice reciting the list of cases the committee had won. She reached up and took the hand of a tall, dark-haired woman standing next to her. "And here we have Fanya," she exclaimed, "threatened with deportation to Czechoslovakia." Everyone looked serious. "But let me tell you," my mother boomed out, "we're going to keep her with us."

In that smaller world, I felt safe and secure. I was very popular, my mother was admired, and I would go home from a weekend or an event feeling very courageous and optimistic about the future. I took my radical commitment very seriously in those days, and planned to become a civil-rights lawyer. Of course, it didn't work out that way. But how could I foresee the terribly difficult times my mother and I would pass through as I tried to turn away from political life and become a poet? That was several years ahead of us. Now, during the McCarthy period, if we were ever tempted to draw too far apart, the political danger she faced always reunited us. We would be sitting at the table and every time there was a knock at the door we would fall silent and look at one another. By then my own feelings had begun to run ahead of events, and I could frequently sense trouble or danger before anyone had spoken about it. I remember one night when she came in late for dinner. My father and I were sitting at the table. I heard something in the sound of her footsteps and I was already on my feet when she walked through the door.

"Guess what, folks," she asked, in that deliberately casual way we'd all begun to talk whenever there was trouble. My father looked startled. I picked up her tone. "What now," I said, "are they planning to send you to a concentration camp?"

"Smart mouth," she answered, smiling grimly.

"So? What?" My father wasn't as good as we were at keeping his voice cool and steady.

"So, I've been subpoenaed. What could you expect?"

My mother's appearance before the House Un-American Activities Committee became a source of stories we would tell over and over again. Many years later, when she had almost finished with it,

I picked it up. It had become by then, during the resurgence of radical feeling in the 1960s, a story for a daughter to brag about. It was, of course, dramatic and fiery. And the first time she spoke about it, a few hours after it had taken place, there was a contagious excitement in her voice.

"Was I nervous?" she asked. "Who knows? I walked in there with my attorneys. John, of course, was still counseling me about strategy. For weeks, as you know, we'd been talking. But now, 'John,' I said finally, 'I won't give names. We both know that. I won't hand over membership lists. So, who needs strategy?' "

She stood there in the kitchen, her purse and jacket still in her arms, holding a stack of leaflets from her defense organization.

"So, I'm called up to the witness stand," she went on. "I'm sworn in, of course, the usual things. Then Congressman Doyle, the chairman of the committee, asks me to hand over the files from our membership. Naturally, I'm not exactly ready to hand over the files. I have a prepared statement and I begin to read it. 'Mr. Chairman,' I say, 'I will not give names to this committee.' But right away he interrupts me, to insist again I tell him names. Well, naturally, John Porter is on his feet to object. And now this Mr. Chairman turns to him and shouts, 'Comrade Porter, instruct your client to answer the questions.' So again, John objects, what else? A member of the legal profession to be called Comrade Porter? The chairman orders him out of the hearing room. The guards come forward, they stand next to him, and John is led out. Al Wiren from the ACLU gets to his feet. 'Mr. Chairman,' he says. And then he protests this treatment of John Porter. The chairman calls him Comrade Wiren. And him, too, he throws out of the room."

I laughed, of course, because I could see she wanted me to. But my father stroked his mustache, shaking his head and making a tch-tch sound that irritated her.

"I'm going to call the president of the Bar Association," she said and went off into the bedroom.

I looked at my father. "Well," he said, speaking showly, "she has to have an attorney for Monday's hearing. And these days that's not so easy. If John Porter has been thrown out, and Al Wiren has been thrown out, by Monday she has to find a new lawyer to defend her."

She came back into the kitchen. We looked up expectantly. "I'm telling you," she laughed, "he just couldn't believe it." She made her voice deeper. " 'Just a minute, Miss Chernin,' " she mimicked, " 'are you telling me that at a congressional hearing Mr. Porter, your attorney, was actually thrown out of the hearing?' "

"What now?" my father asked.

"So, he'll try to find me an attorney. But these days," she added, her eyes veiled, "we shouldn't expect too much."

I kept watching her face. Oddly enough, she didn't look worried. I looked at my father. Now he, too, was smiling. And then, her eyes triumphant, she said, "He told me, if he can't find someone over the weekend he'll come right into the court and represent me himself."

Monday night my father and I were home early. My mother drove up just when the potatoes finished cooking. She was talking as she came through the door.

"This you should have seen," she called out. "The minute we went in there, Mr. Gray insisted the chairman apologize to my two lawyers and reinstate them. But don't you ask me to describe this Mr. Chairman's face. You maybe would look like this if you swallowed an ashtray. But of course, what could he do, with the chairman of the Los Angeles Bar Association standing there? John Porter is reinstated. Al Wiren, reinstated. And then, what does Mr. Gray do? He walks up to the bench and he announces he's going to stay right there in the courtroom and observe the conduct of the hearing."

I could see the way she'd been that day, pulling herself up straight and powerful. Her voice boomed. "I will not give names to this committee. My board and I cannot see any connection between the ostensible purpose of this committee and its methods of intimidation and harassment. When there is a proper legislative committee, seeking to gain information for the purpose of passing laws, I shall be ready to testify before such a committee. But this present committee is perpetrating a witch hunt. Nothing else. It does not have the legitimate congressional authority to cite anyone for contempt."

"Whoopee," I shouted and danced around through the living room with my dog. "Watch the coffee table," she called after me. "Paul, stop her," she cried out, laughing, "a *meshugana* like this one, who needs?"

I grabbed her around the waist and danced with her. It was like moving a ton of bricks. "Come on, Mama, dance," I kept insisting.

She pushed me on the shoulder, took a few little steps, looked over, shaking her head at my father, and finally broke away and sat down on the couch.

"Would you believe it? I didn't surrender the records from our organization. I didn't give names. I didn't hand over our literature and pamphlets. I'm sitting here at home, and no citation for contempt. And that, if you ask me, is all because of Mr. Gray. How else will you explain it?"

I remember her face. She was fifty-three years old but at times like this she looked much younger. "So that's it, my friends," she said, and gestured for me to come take the pamphlets out of her hand. "Because they threw John Porter and Al Wiren out of the hearing room on Friday, I am a free woman today."

That is the way this story always ended. Whether she told it, or my father told it to his brothers, or I told it to my radical friends, it always rounded itself out in this victory for justice, triumphantly.

And then, for a while, while this story was being told, things settled down in our lives. I grew older. Breasts grew on my body. I entered high school and in my sophomore year I suddenly grew three inches.

It was, for a brief time, a fairly normal adolescent life; there were all the usual confrontations, about my messy room, my late hours, the dark circles beneath my eyes, and the heavy make-up I'd begun to wear. In the late afternoons, my friend Carole Drake and I used to do Afro-Cuban dancing.

Like most adolescents, I had begun to lead a divided life. At home I involved myself in politics, made my little speeches, and was active in the Labor Youth League. I still sold the *People's World* on Sunday afternoons with my father in the neighborhood, and on Sunday nights I prepared lectures on Marxism for my Marxist study club. But in my school life I was a wild kid, who stayed out too late and wandered about on the streets with other kids, cruising from party to party. Exuberantly, I became what I thought of as a typical teenager. And then, for a while, it was almost possible to forget these were the troubled times, the McCarthy years, and that my mother was in danger.

But one night, when I came home for dinner, I saw several cars pulled up in the driveway. It wasn't the usual night for our open house and it scared me. What now? I wondered as I ran up the steps. My dog came to the door, leaping and frisking. "What's happening?" I called out, pushing him aside. Everyone turned to look at me.

My mother held out her hand. Her face was bright and excited, her eyes hectic and flashing with that fervor I felt so often in myself. "I was driving to work," she was saying, tightening her lips emphatically, "a usual morning. I turn on the radio to get the news. And, what do you know? I hear the voice of the attorney general. He's holding a press conference. Suddenly, he says: 'One of the things we are prepared to do in order to rid the United States of subversives is to denaturalize ten thousand naturalized citizens and deport five thousand of them. And the first we are going to denaturalize is Rose Chernin.' Well, I say to myself: Rose, hallelujah. Of course, it made sense. This was my work, fighting deportation. So wouldn't you expect them to denaturalize me and try to deport me?"

I saw, of course, that once again a good story was in the making. Cups were poised in the air, breath was held, someone, reaching out to light a cigarette for Aunt Gertrude, left his hand suspended. In all the room, only my black dog jingled his license, scratching irreverently.

"Well, you know, my friends," she said, putting her arm around me and drawing me close, "no one's going to deport me. Against people with no citizenship papers they haven't been very successful, as you know. So now what? Do they think we'll let them attack the rights of naturalized citizens?"

The next morning the press showed up at my mother's office. "What are you going to do now that you'll be deported?" they asked her.

"Who says I'm going to be deported? Attorney General Brownell? And who is he? He didn't bring me to this country. I am a citizen of the United States. He is a very arrogant man to play around with citizenship like this. I shall continue the work I am involved in because we are organized to stop deportation and we intend to do it. And I say this to Attorney General Brownell himself. You go tell him. We will not permit him to denaturalize a single citizen! To do so, gentlemen, would be to threaten your citizenship as well."

We laughed about that one for several nights, and I saw the way, once again, these attacks against my mother were drawing us closer as a family. Now, for a while I came home in time for dinner and did my homework in the living room, where my father sat, with his shirt sleeves rolled up, reading.

My mother's denaturalization trial lasted for seven days. The government had to prove that in 1928, when she applied for citizenship, she was already intending to join the Communist Party. Therefore, they claimed, she had perjured herself when she swore on her citizenship application that she was not a member of a subversive organization.

It was, even for those years, an outrageous charge, and it required the government to prove, beyond reasonable doubt, that they knew her state of mind almost thirty years earlier. At any other period in American history a case like that could never come to court.

My mother and father discussed these things with me every night at dinner. And I myself was in court one day when the government witness, who claimed to have known my mother during the twenties, insisted that he could easily identify her even today. My mother frankly could not remember the man and we decided he was probably confusing her with some other organizer from the Bronx. Or maybe, my father suggested, he was paid to lie and it simply didn't matter whether he ever knew her at all. For my father, that was a severe degree of cynicism and he spoke it with the first edge of bitterness I'd ever heard in his voice.

Unfortunately, he wasn't with us that day in court when the witness stood up and went striding through the courtroom, to stand, his finger pointing, before a small, gray-haired woman. "This," he boomed out triumphantly, "is Rose Chernin."

"Will you stand please," the judge requested, nodding his head at the woman who had been identified.

She stood up, clearly struggling not to smile. "Are you Rose Chernin?" the judge asked.

"Lord no," she cried out, putting her hand to her cheeks, and all of us burst out laughing.

Because of course we had planned it that way. "That stool pigeon," my mother had said. "You think he would know me from Karl Liebknecht?" And her friend Frances Williams added, "Let's try him." And so another middle-aged woman, with gray hair, had been found to sit in my mother's place. And now the government witness carried himself back across the courtroom with a distinct air of deflation.

He made other efforts to incriminate my mother, but it was clear that he had never met her before and had been coached. When asked about the crucial year, 1928, he insisted that he'd gone regularly to meetings with her and that she had told him she was planning to join the Party as soon as she became a citizen.

I listened to his testimony with a feeling of outrage. I was fourteen years old, and it scared me. The government of the United States dared to come into a federal court and present this man, this paid, professional liar, as their witness against my mother?

John Porter, her attorney again for this trial, was cross-examining the man. He was asking whether he'd noticed anything different about my mother during 1928. But the witness shook his head and said there had been no significant change in her.

I could scarcely sit still while the cross-examination was proceeding. What changes had taken place in 1928, which the witness should have remembered if he'd known my mother? Baby books were brought into court; they were submitted as evidence and it was established beyond any doubt that in 1928 my mother had become pregnant with my sister Nina.

The trial was a mockery, and after seven days the judge refused to denaturalize her. The newspaper said: RED LEADER TO KEEP CITIZENSHIP. The judge told the government that it could not prove its case against her and had presented no evidence of guilt. Then he went further, and I cheered for him under my breath. He reprimanded the government and cautioned them to be more careful how they handled citizenship. It was, he said, a very sacred right.

I'd give a great deal to be able to describe my mother's face at that moment. Triumph? Vindication? Relief? No doubt all of that was apparent. But I saw something else, which affected me deeply. It was, I think, the rebirth of her optimism after a time of unacknowledged doubt. There was a clear, fierce light in her eyes. A return of belief in her own power to fight, to overcome, to beat back institutional injustice. She looked over at me, her eyebrows raised. I lifted my hands over my head. And silently, from opposite sides of the courtroom, we shared this feeling of victory.

But for us, in those years, such moments were rare. Usually, we passed each other, going and coming; I returning from a party, she on her way to a meeting or coming home late. Most of the time I felt for her that brooding resentment so typical of adolescent life, a sense of violent rebellion against any authority and all restriction. It was only in court that I could feel the strength of my devotion to her, my unshakable loyalty. There, I was always dressed in my best clothes, carefully and conservatively, unrecognizable as the kid who went to school wearing huge earrings and tight skirts which caused my mother grief.

I was always getting into trouble in school. I came late to classes; I made up excuses for cutting on Fridays, so that I could go watch the high school football game across town; I talked too much in class and rarely handed in my homework assignments. But somehow, I managed to get excellent grades and could not be expelled, no matter how often that was threatened.

I was a rebel, my gym teacher said. And in my own way I carried on a relentless fight against "the system."

In the afternoons, I used to walk out of school surrounded by a loud and rebellious group of boys and girls, mostly Negro. Outside the building we lit up our cigarettes and began our slow, hours-long ramble through the neighborhood streets, turning over garbage cans, stealing license plates from parked cars, and once or twice, on a quiet street, setting a palm tree on fire.

My constructive rebellion took the form of an outspoken protest against racism. At dances I would stand in the part of the gym where the Negro kids gathered. They were my oldest friends; we'd been together since grammar school. But it took courage to dance with them on the high-school campus. The other white kids looked on and whispered. Most of them came down to school from the Baldwin Hills. They were wealthy, they were bigots, they told stories about me and gossiped that I slept with Negro boys. Once, when I was dancing with James Grove, the algebra teacher clapped me on the shoulder and asked us to stop dancing. My mother called the school of course, to protest its racism. And I carried on my own warfare with the teacher after that.

He was an old man, who would otherwise have inspired my compassion. His hands shook when he stood at the blackboard. One day, when the class had gone completely out of control, Mr. Alimon came striding down the aisle, pointing his finger at me. He stopped in front of my desk. "You're the ringleader," he yelled, spittle gathering in the corner of his mouth. "Get out of my classroom. You're a disgrace to your race." I stood up, smiling. He was not a tall man, but he was at least a head taller than I was. I cocked my head to the side. "Mister," I said, and my voice was ominous. "I wouldn't spend three minutes in your class if it was the last place on this earth where I could get an education." I grabbed my purse and headed for the door. But in the last moment I stopped. He was still standing next to my seat, stunned and silent. "You're a vicious racist," I called out, my voice level and steady. "And you ought to be expelled from the school system."

I slammed the door shut behind me. "It's you who will be expelled, young lady," he yelled after me. And I realized, before I had gone ten steps, that he was probably right. I whirled around and came back into the classroom. I walked over to my seat and stood next to it. "Mr. Alimon," I shouted, "no one's going to expel me from school. I'm here to stay and just you try to budge me." I sat down in my seat, folded my arms, and stared up at him. The class was going wild. Cheering and hooting and shouting. Even the white kids, from the Baldwin Hills, were laughing. And then, finally, the bell rang for the end of period, and I strutted from the classroom, radiant with triumph.

That event changed the next years of my life. For a long time now my friend Carole Drake and I had been performing Afro-Cuban dances at school assemblies. I knew that the kids from the hills thought our performances were outrageous. But when we danced off, tossing our heads and leaping wildly, a thunderous applause from the "other side" of the auditorium would always call us back onto the stage. Now, however, my continual rebellion against authority gradually changed my status among those wealthy kids. When I received an invitation to a large party in the Baldwin Hills, I went without a moment's hesitation. A week later one of those boys invited me out on a movie date and finally I received a formal invitation from the most popular social club to attend its yearly dance.

That invitation flattered me. It stirred something in me I had never known existed before. I had to borrow a formal from a girl in the

Labor Youth League. I wasn't used to wearing heels. I had learned
to dance from Negro kids, who would not have been permitted to
enter the club in the valley I now walked into, holding my date by
the arm. I felt uneasy and I felt guilty. But as we stood at the door,
waiting to hand in our invitations, I had an overwhelming sense of
the ease and privilege of their lives. In their most casual act, there
was a quality of serene self-assertion. These were the desirable ones;
and I suddenly realized that I could pass for one of them. As we
walked into the ballroom I caught a glimpse of myself in the huge
mirrored wall. I saw a pretty girl who moved with a fiery grace, eyes
flashing and shining. No one, looking in at us, would ever imagine
what a different life story was hidden away behind her smile.

When I arrived back home at four o'clock in the morning, I knew
that I had crossed a barrier. I sat down on my bed and fell immediately into an ecstatic doze in my crumpled ball gown. But the next
morning I woke up feeling dreadful. That glorious night, with all its
clever conversation and laughter, was in reality a betrayal of my
oldest friends.

Their loyalty had been tested and proved over and over again
since those early days when my mother was first arrested. At each
new outbreak of publicity about her trials, when the gossip started
up again, and I became, among the white and wealthy kids in our
school, an object of comment, the Negro and Mexican kids I knew
rallied around me. They built a protective circle, within which I had
a relative degree of safety.

But now I turned my back on them. Little by little, knowing
perfectly well what I was doing, I began to shift away. I changed my
hairstyle, got rid of my large earrings and tight skirts. I began to eat
lunch in another part of the schoolyard. I rode home from school
with a pimply-faced boy driving a new sports car. And when these
new friends of mine told their racist jokes, I sniggered and laughed
along with all the others.

One day I found myself laughing at a dialect joke. And a week
later I was rolling my eyes and telling one. I remember the shame
and terror I felt. That night, I could not eat dinner.

By the time of my senior year, I was cutting my old friends when
they passed me in the hall. In class, I sat in the front of the room,
raising my hand like a good little girl to answer the teacher's ques-

tions. There were even rumors that I would be invited to join the Delphinians, the most popular social club in school. And then, a few months before graduation, one day when I walked onto the campus, I saw my own picture up on the bulletin board. I had been selected as the OUTSTANDING GIRL OF THE WEEK, a distinction settled once or twice a term on some proud young lady. We all knew it was really a question of having the right friends. And I, apparently, had acquired them. I knew everyone. And now my own face, with my stylish haircut, and my big phony smile, stared back at me from the central quadrangle of the high-school campus.

Then it happened again. My mother's name, her picture in the newspaper. The news that the Supreme Court had reversed the decision on her trial. She was free now, the government's case against her had not been proved, she would not go to prison.

It was June 1957. And the date would later become significant in the history of the McCarthy period. With this decision the Supreme Court reversed its earlier rulings on the Smith Act cases. Now, for Communists to be found guilty of advocacy, the government would have to show that they were advocating action rather than belief.

Formally, the case was known as *Yates* v. *The United States*, but the newspapers reported it in their own way: REDS BOASTFUL AS 14 WIN IN SUPREME COURT RULING.

In fact, the decision in my mother's case affected all the Communists who were on trial all over America. Within months the government dropped its cases against the Boston Seven, the Cleveland Six, the Pittsburgh Five, the Philadelphia Nine, the St. Louis Five, and the Puerto Rico Eleven.

It was the beginning of the great reversal that would, a few years later, make me a heroine among my college classmates because of my mother.

At home, we celebrated. People began to drop in. My father made vodka martinis, we put out plates of chopped liver and whole-wheat crackers, my mother sat on the gray shag couch, which had by that time witnessed some pretty torrid love scenes. She took off her shoes and tucked up her feet. I stood leaning in the doorway, watching her.

"Well," she said, clapping her hands, "I'm not sorry that I won't be going to prison." Lillian nudged me; she had come out of the kitchen, carrying a coffee pot. "But," said my mother, "I also want you to know that I was prepared. After all, I've been inside. I know what it's like behind bars. And let me tell you, if we have to, we'll survive even that again."

I stood there watching her. She was a distilled essence, a fiery elixir. The consistency, the dedication of her life was visible in her every line and gesture. And suddenly I felt heartsick, as I realized just how deeply my behavior during the last two years had betrayed her. I, who had always wanted to be loyal to her, and to the Party, had gone over to the enemy. I had made fun of everything I loved and cherished. I had pretended to believe the worst stories about the Soviet Union. I had nodded my head when someone said we could win the cold war. I seemed to have felt that if I lied enough, and made enough racist comments, people would forget that I was a Jew and my parents were Communists. And for a year or so it had actually worked. Everyone seemed to have forgotten, or not to care.

But I cared. I cared desperately. I could remember back so clearly to that other night, five years earlier, when she had come home from jail. How eagerly, how wildly I had thrown myself into being what she wanted me to be.

The next day at school, during the midmorning break, a girl from the Delphinians came up to me. She pulled a newspaper clipping out of her purse and held it up in front of me. "Is this your mother?" she asked. "It's her maiden name," I answered, remembering all this from six years before.

At lunchtime, I started to walk out into the section of the yard where my new friends ate their lunch. As I approached, I felt that terrible chill they know so well how to draw over themselves. I kept walking, and I walked so far that I found myself out of the schoolyard during lunchtime, a violation for which one could get expelled.

The following day it was better; a few of the boys talked to me and walked along with me between classes. At the football game on Friday, I seemed welcome enough among our crowd. And then I heard that invitations had been given out to the Delphinian dance. I had been expecting mine, and now I realized that it wasn't coming.

When I got home the phone rang. It was Carole Drake, calling to tell me she was happy to hear about my mother's victory. We had never spoken about the trial. I never knew for sure which of my old friends knew that my mother was a Communist. But now, during the next days and weeks, a few of them came forward, in the hall, or after school, to let me know they had heard and were glad. I felt I could have gone back to them, and been friends again. But I was too proud, and too ashamed, to accept their help once I had turned on them.

For a few weeks my days in high school became very similar to that time, years before, when my mother was first arrested. Again I walked home alone, choosing streets that I hoped would be empty. I lied to my parents about my Saturday nights. I went out by myself and drove around all over the city, pretending to them that I was going to a party.

One night when I came home after dinner there was a telephone message. My father had taken it down, writing everything very carefully. It was from Stanley Konig, telling me he couldn't make it to the prom. I called him, but he didn't elaborate. He couldn't make it, he repeated, and hung up.

I had other boyfriends; one of them was in the navy, he came into town for weekends. I called him, but he was unable to come to the phone. I tried again, several times, during the following days, but he was always unavailable. Then I called a few other boys I'd dated that year.

No one bothered making excuses; and of course no one ever told me the truth. Many years later I realized that someone had gone about urging the boys and girls from the social clubs to ostracize me. It was, I think, a girl named Marianne, who belonged to the Delphinians. But at the time I refused to believe it was my mother's political life that had deprived me of a date for the prom. I was desperate. I called another boy, but after the tenth call I finally gave up, feeling broken and shaken; an outcast.

Finally, there was a boy. He was rather short, he had a blond crew cut, he'd just come back from the marines, and he lived in the Baldwin Hills. I met him three days before the prom. I made up some story about my date being ill, I apologized for asking him so late, and we laughed about how lucky he was, coming back into town at just the right moment. His name was Mike. Somewhere, there must still be a picture of us, all dressed up in our formal clothes, Mike with his arm around my waist. The picture doesn't show his face when he found out who he had taken to the prom. And I, of course, did not see it at that moment either. After the prom, in fact, I never saw him again.

I had decided some months earlier to attend the Seventh World Youth Festival in Moscow. For weeks I had been counting the days until I could leave Los Angeles. Now there were five left. I got up early and went downtown with my mother. Years before, whenever I was off school, I used to meet her at her office and we'd go out for lunch. Then, I loved to go to Roy Rogers movies, and we would spend the afternoon together, eating popcorn and holding hands.

Now, a few days before I was leaving home, we decided to go into all the old places we'd gone to when I was a kid. We stopped at the juice bar, we went into Clifton's Cafeteria, where the water was still pouring into the fake stone fountains. When we had finished lunch I suggested to my mother that we stop in for a movie. We checked the papers, but Roy Rogers had long since gone out of style.

Instead, we went shopping. I needed clothes for my trip to Europe, and the two of us needed to spend time together before I left. She knew something was going on for me at school, but she had never asked me about it. I took her arm when we crossed the street. And suddenly she said, "So who ever told you it was easy to be the exception? At your age, especially? But a year from now you'll look back, you'll be with a whole new group at college, and all this will be something to smile at."

She was wrong; she, who never needed to be told, who could always figure it out, was wrong. I would never forgive myself for that one. The dread of it ran too deeply through the generations of our family, this repetition of the impulse to make a sacrifice of the mother.

We walked on; past the Mexican shoe store where my mother bought her shoes. We passed the newsman, one of our comrades, who slipped the paper under her arm, winking at her, as we went by. We rode up the hill in the funicular, completing the whole ritual I had loved so much when I was a child. And then, as we started to cross the street at the top of the hill, a woman walked up to my mother. She was a beautiful woman, with dark skin. The minute she caught sight of my mother she whirled around and opened her arms. "Auntie Rose," she cried out, "Auntie Rose." I saw some people

258 In My Mother's House

turn to look at us. They were talking together, laughing and holding each other by the hand. "I've got a regular job," the woman was saying; "I'm on my own feet again, Auntie. I'm not on the street anymore." My mother was squeezing her hand. "You call me," she was saying. "You know where I am." And then she gave me a good, long, hard look and said, "I just kept wondering. What kind of daughter would Rose Chernin have?" She reached out to shake my hand. "Your mother," she said, and her voice became severe, "she saved me."

We stood there watching her walk away. "Was she a prostitute?" I asked. My mother looked at me. "We were in jail together."

We walked on silently for a few steps. And suddenly I had the most tremendous longing to have my mother tell me a story. "Was she there the day you had your birthday?" I asked. My mother tipped back her head and gave me one of her deep looks. "Did I ever tell you that story?" she asked. And then we both roared with laughter.

"Ach," she sighed, "to think what we've been through." She had a way, even then, of telling the most familiar story as if it were the first time. "Those were hard women," she said. "Their lives were hard, they were bitter, very angry. Remember this and then listen to what I will tell."

But then her story took a new turn. She frowned and shook her head. "This woman you have just met? Did I save this woman? Of course not. She was a tough one. She sat all day playing cards. When the others would talk to us, she would look over, the eyes angry. Then, one day, she and I began talking. She could tell, right away, I had no sense of us and them. We were people together, prisoners. She saw in me, a possibility, no more, no less. I was something different, from another world. When she got out of jail I gave her the name of an attorney, I told her to look up someone to ask for a job. The rest, believe me, she did herself. From that day to this day I never saw her again."

I squeezed her hand; for the first time since she had been arrested I felt a tickling in my nose. And I realized it was the way you feel before you are going to cry.

"Well," she said, slipping her arm through mine, "that wasn't the story you asked for. But who can determine? You open your mouth, who knows what will come out of it?"

I saw her watching me from the corners of her eyes. I knew she was drawing me to her, easing the way between us. And then, sure of me, her voice moved out along its well-worn track.

"It was September fourteenth, seven o'clock in the evening. We were sitting in our cells, Dorothy Healey and I together. The lights were on, everyone was walking back and forth. We heard whispering, more commotion than usual, and, finally, someone called out, 'All right, we're going into the first cell (the cell of the trustee), let's go everyone.'

"I noticed there was a lot of activity in the tank. Our trustee was going in and out, the women were going over to the first cell and I figured, why not? I went out of my cell and right away they all surrounded me.

"Someone shouted, 'All right, let's do it.' And then from all parts of the tank, in loud voices: 'HAPPY BIRTHDAY, AUNTIE ROSE.'

"Everybody moved forward into the trustee's cell, dragging me along with them. There I saw a table set up in the center of the cell and on it was a birthday cake. But this scene you will only find in a county jail. The chair had become a table, the towel became a tablecloth, the birthday cake was made up of cookies, and the candles were from matches. They had nothing at all with which to make this celebration. But somehow they managed. They got some hot water for tea, they got permission for spoons, they collected all the chocolate bars they could put together, and it was a party.

"They were singing songs and they had presents to give. Now you must wonder what these women could possibly give to anyone, and I will tell you. They had nothing. Nothing. But they managed to get something together. One woman crocheted a tiny set of teacups and saucers. A work of art. The other women gave, for instance, a few hairpins, a scarf that one of them knitted. A hairnet, the few pennies one of them had. We had a party. We sang. But suddenly there was weeping. Everyone was weeping. Yes, believe me. Everyone."

We stop walking. For some reason, I was still trying not to cry. I felt the wetness on my cheeks and I wiped impatiently at my eyes. My mother grabbed my hands. "So weep already. Weep. You have to be harder even than they were?"

I stood there sobbing, laughing at her, trying to get my hands free. She held them in her eagle's grip. Her mouth tightened. She nodded her head.

"Never tear yourself from the people," she said. And her voice was not more than a whisper. "For us, our strength is with the people. This is our meaning. This is how we survive."

A Knock at the Door

*O*ccasionally, when the fog is heavy late at night, it is possible to hear sounds from a great distance. The cars on the boulevard near the bay seem to be passing along my own street. Voices, a loud knocking at an unknown door, a child waking in an invisible house, footsteps that seem to be walking up my own stairs, or the sound of a train from the old station that was torn down, more than twenty years ago. At times, I sit straight up in bed, ready to run or to defend myself. But usually I find myself strangely soothed by these disembodied noises that bring together what is past with all that should be inaudible.

Tonight I hear the bells on a church across town. It is very late and I have been sleeping fitfully. The heater comes on with a subdued roar. I am tired, I don't want to risk more. I have spent almost seven years on this work, in order to make her a gift. And now that we have accomplished so much, I find myself suddenly aware of a danger larger than any we have faced so far. There is a story I did not want ever to tell her. I found it so difficult to write down that once, a few weeks ago, I actually left my notebook in a gas station where I'd gone inside to make a telephone call. The owner came running after me as I was walking down the block, but I had already turned back, my shoulders aching with the awareness of what I had almost done. And then, a few days later, when my story about my trip to the Soviet Union was complete, I left the manuscript in a coffee shop. That day, I got all the way back to my car before I realized that I'd gathered up my empty notebooks but left the written pages behind.

Since then, I've taken the notebook with me when I move about from room to room. When I go out at night I wrap it in tin foil and put it in the freezer, in case a fire should break out in my house. I am terrified of my impulse to destroy this confession. It is the story of how I stopped being a Communist.

Why is it so hard for me to tell her the truth? Is it because, after a lifetime of faith, she needs to believe as she does about the Soviet Union? Because she was persecuted, jailed, and tried for her belief during the McCarthy period? Because this ideological apostasy of mine is a betrayal even worse than what I did to her in high school? Is it the dread, once again, of the family pattern? All my life I have admired her loyalty to the ideal, the dream vision of world peace and justice, decency and freedom. The trials and purges of the thirties, Hungary, the Khrushchev report, the work camps, the gulags. It took strength, I thought, the power of sustained belief, to remain loyal no matter how hard the jagged failures of reality pushed her. I always disliked the ones who fell away, the weak ones, as I saw it. How could I be one of them? From the days when I loved Zoya Kozmodemyanskaya, girl heroine, partisan fighter, defender of Moscow, I always planned to become a woman just like my mother. And now, what am I, awake at midnight with my guilt?

The manuscript, typed in its first draft, is on my desk. I pull the papers together and write down a title. I have been considering it for days, but have resisted it. Now, it makes clear that on my journey to the Soviet Union I saw everything she was unable to see twenty-five years earlier. I'm moving fast. When the time comes to risk, I don't know how to move with care. I lose all sense of delicacy and timing. There is, I know, much to criticize in this impulsiveness that insists on waking up an old woman who has had a long and difficult day. But I'm going to do it.

The door to the downstairs room is not locked. There is a crescent of light on the stairs, and I make my way easily. I walk softly, but I hope that my footsteps will wake her. Or maybe she's not yet asleep? I've known her to lie awake reading a newspaper or a book until the early hours of the morning.

Tonight she sleeps. The lamp is on next to her bed, the newspaper is open on the pillow beside her. She is propped up in bed, frowning, her glasses atilt at the end of her nose. She looks much older than I've ever seen her. I stare at the wrinkled skin on her breast, where the pink nightgown opens below her neck. Her hand is clenched tight, balling up the blanket.

I sit down in the wicker chair next to her bed. Carefully, I place the manuscript on the chair beside me. I cannot regain a sense of my own life. This room, where I once hammered up the oak walls, seems strange to me. Suddenly I remember a critic saying that no real woman would ever burn a manuscript, the way Hedda Gabler had done.

And then, she turns toward me. The newspaper crackles. I reach out and very gently remove her glasses. I put a lace cloth over the lamp but I do not turn it off. My tenderness has released me.

When I look back from the staircase I see this little composition I have arranged. The veiled light, the old woman asleep in the large bed near the window, the manuscript waiting on the wicker chair, her glasses resting beside it.

I can feel from my own love for her the certainty that nothing can destroy the bond between us. It is stronger than ideology, unshakable in its binding. It is not the birth bond which made us a mother and daughter; that we could have trampled down, in our impatience and confusion. This bond is a comradeship, won from the work we have done together. It comes so rarely to a mother and daughter, but once it is achieved it tangles itself in with all the nature and shared flesh. And then even they, if they wished, could no longer pull it down.

As I open the door she says something incomprehensible. I strain to make it out and I realize it is I who have never really forgiven her for remaining a Communist under circumstances that drove me away from the Party and destroyed my faith. But tonight, in a rush of urgent awareness, I understand that the value of her life's work did not depend upon the triumph of socialism anywhere in the world. When I am eighty years old, I shall be happy if I have managed to remain true to myself, against all the passionate contradiction that cries out in my nature. And suddenly, rushing back down the stairs to her room in an anguish of love, I feel like a small child again, brushed with my old longing to grow up someday to be just like her. But now, I stop at the foot of her bed and I do not wake her.

She will read my story in the morning.

The Third Story I Tell
Motherland Revisited (1957–1967)

*L*ong ago, long after the time I ceased to think of myself as a Marxist, for years past that time, the words *Soviet Union* brought tears to my eyes. But that had begun when I was a little girl and my mother would say to me, in that way she had; "So guess what? We have a surprise for you. Do you know what it is?"

"Something to eat?"

"Even better."

"To see?"

"Yes, to see."

"From the Soviet Union?"

"What else?"

Usually it was a film, sometimes a dancer or a musician. When the pianist Emil Gilels came to Los Angeles for the first time, she got me a box seat so that I could sit on the left side and watch his hands.

"Someday we're all going to the Soviet Union," she'd say, and I believed her. "Someday, we, too, will have a worker's revolution, just like the Soviet Union." That, too, I believed. "While we were living in the Soviet Union, during the thirties," she'd say and then I could go over and sit next to her on the gray couch and put my head in her lap.

Then, the day came. I graduated from high school and left for the Soviet Union. Falling asleep on the train that crossed through Poland

I heard her voice and it spoke clearly. It murmured again between dream and awakening, repeating its stories. I was going home.

It struck me suddenly when we changed trains near the Polish border. All at once I knew that I would cross the border and be at home. Everything looked familiar, the landscape drawing away into the distance, the trees around the station, the plump women dancing together, the steaming samovar: Russia near the Polish border, Vitebsk, Chasnik, my mother's home — wasn't it somewhere near?

I stood in the open space between the cars, holding myself in a precarious balance so that I could be away from the others, undisturbed in my contemplation of this extraordinary landscape, the likes of which I had never seen before and yet seemed always to have known: forests of white trees, stirring up in me a feeling so profound I suddenly did not know who I was; surely it could not be I who felt this way?

One of our interpreters came looking for me, to tell me that we had crossed the border and were now in the Soviet Union. But I had known it and had already begun to cry. The young man put his arms around me and I wept against his shoulder, trying to tell him something I could never possibly have expressed.

I was seventeen years old. It was 1957, the year after Khrushchev's report to the Twentieth Congress. Thousands and thousands of people were thronging into the Soviet Union from all over the world. The Russian people rushed out to greet us, the delegates to the Seventh World Youth Festival. All the way to Moscow, hundreds of people would arrive at every station our train passed through. Their ecstasy, that unrestrained outpouring of the heart, made me myself again. On the train I wandered from car to car, meeting people from the various delegations. It was exactly what my mother had promised. It was her own trip all over again. And I saw that she had been right. Here, something had happened to the world, people came together as sisters and brothers. We believed in the Russian Revolution, we believed in the revolution we would make in our own countries.

In Moscow the ecstasy continued. We had arrived several days before the official opening of the Youth Festival, and I used them to explore Moscow. Here, too, everything was just like my mother had told me. I saw the gleaming steel of the Mayakovski subway station, and I told everyone, very proudly, that my father had worked on its design. I walked in Red Square, I looked at the Kremlin. Here the May First Celebration had taken place. I stood in line to see Stalin and Lenin, lying in state, in the Mausoleum. The crowd of people moved steadily past the biers, but I stopped dead in my tracks and stood there, looking at the waxen face of Stalin, with his big mustache. Was it possible? He looked just like the pictures my mother had shown me when I was a child. And I remembered my sister had been invited into the Kremlin to meet this man.

There was a beautiful song people were singing all over Moscow that summer. You heard it everywhere, in the People's Park of Culture and Rest, in the Agriculture Exhibit, on the streets at night. It was called "Moscow Nights," it was a love song to Moscow, and I learned to sing it with a throbbing heart.

Day and night people thronged the boulevards in national costumes, with instruments, with flowers, with arms full of gifts. The Russians threw themselves into this festival as if every stranger were a kinsman, returning home. They flocked around our buses, they forced the buses to stop, they rushed to the windows, took our hands, pressed them and shouted out to us: MIR Y DRUGBA, "Peace and Friendship," that ritual call no one who attended that festival has ever been able to forget.

We lived, during those weeks, in a large hotel in the Agriculture Exhibit, a vast park with permanent exhibits from all the nationalities of the Soviet Union. It was warm during the days of August, we sat outdoors; large women with kerchiefs served us our food and each of them, taking me by the arm, fussing over me, became my mother.

There were, of course, organized activities at the festival: delegations meeting together, performances of national music and dance, tickets to concerts and the Bolshoi Theater, meetings with famous Russians, ideological discussions and debates. I attended many of these, but always in a state of extreme distraction and with a great restlessness. I wanted to rush back into the street; I loved the moment when, at the end of a formal meeting between delegations, presents were exchanged and people came together to shake hands and embrace one another.

One day several people from our delegation went to call on Madame Kozmodemyanskaya, the mother of Zoya, the partisan girl who had been tortured and killed by the Germans during the Second World War. I was beside myself when I heard that she was still alive. Zoya's mother? My heroine's mother, still living? We carried huge bouquets of flowers and stood in the street below her window, singing to her, while she leaned forward and looked down at us. In that moment, I felt that my whole life came together and made sense. My old childhood idealism came back to me and I felt that I, too, would be capable of the heroism and sacrifice Zoya had shown.

But then, one night, two days before the opening celebration of the festival, something happened. At the time, I did not consider it very important, and was completely unaware that it had any lasting significance. If it had taken a physical form I could now say that it shattered me. But it was instead an emotional blow and its effects went so deep I couldn't afford to know they had occurred.

On the surface, the event was slight — such events usually are. One of the girls in the English delegation had relatives in the Soviet Union. They were Jewish and one night after dinner we set out across Moscow to visit them. It took us time, of course, because people kept stopping us and inviting us to join them for drinks. But finally we were walking up the steps of a large apartment block. Several floors above us we heard a door open, and then the head of a girl about our age leaned over the railing and called down. Soon, the whole family was trooping down the stairs, their arms open. There was an initial confusion about which of us was the niece, but then no one seemed to mind very much or to pay much attention to the distinction. When we got in the door, the commotion grew even greater; everyone had to be hugged and kissed all over again, the table was covered with food, we were eating dark bread and cheese, drinking tea in glasses, the spoons were tinkling and we were shouting in Russian and Yiddish and English, everyone talking at the same time.

The mother of the family was handicapped, she had been injured on her job and after dinner she showed us the work she did at home, for full pay, sorting colored bits of industrial glass. Then letters were brought out; they were carefully stacked in wooden boxes, and they went back to the beginning of the century, when Hyla's family had gone to England. Each one was carefully dated in ink, on the envelope, and we could see how often the family had moved around from the repeated changes of address. But I could also see that the mood in the room was changing. Hyla's aunt was becoming more and more silent. Her two daughters were trying to keep up the conversation, but their English wasn't very good. Her son, a boy of seven or eight, translated for us, but it made him impatient, and he would suddenly turn and glare at his sisters for talking too fast. Then, in an uncomfortable silence, Hyla's aunt sighed. She said, "So, you're here. You've come. It's good." She leaned forward and took both of us by the hand. But then she said, "It's good you're here and it's good you'll be going away again."

We both looked at her with astonishment. What did she mean? I said, putting my hand to my heart, fervently, "I could stay here forever."

"You like Moscow?"

"I love it. It's my home. I've never been happier."

"You're a foreigner. Don't believe everything you see."

Hyla and I looked at each other. We were both part of the Young Communist movement. And now we were proudly wearing the festival pin on our collars next to a Soviet Young Communist badge. Hyla laughed. She patted her aunt on the hand. "Just like Mama," she said affectionately, "always looking on the dark side of things."

But it was clear to me that something serious had been said. The young boy was whispering with his sisters, translating our conversation. I looked over at the older girl, a beautiful woman with blond hair and blue eyes. It was hard to believe she was Jewish. She nodded her head vigorously at me while her brother was talking.

"What?" I said to her. "The Khrushchev report?"

I had read it, of course, several months earlier, and it had made me shake. But why now? Why should we be cautious now not to receive the wrong impression?

She looked right at me and spoke to me in Russian. And then her brother's shrill voice repeated everything. I'll never forget it, such a terrible meaning from a child's lips. "So you think now that we've had Khrushchev everything's changed? Don't you believe it. To be a Jew in the Soviet Union I wouldn't wish on my worst enemy. What's changed? So now they'll take Stalin out of the Mausoleum, maybe, and put him in the Kremlin walls. Who cares?"

Then, for a few minutes, there was a flurry of movement. The aunt must have seen something in my eyes I myself could not acknowledge. "Never mind. You're happy here. And you're right to be. Maybe, it's a new day beginning. Who can say?"

Fresh tea was poured, little candies in colored wrapping were passed out, and the conversation drifted back to family gossip. But the bitterness in the cousin's voice had chilled me. Because of it I now recalled the day I read the Khrushchev report a few months before, alone in my room. It was the first time in my life I did not turn to my mother for reassurance about the politics we shared. I had stayed there, frozen on my bed, watching the dust in a beam of sunlight. Could I believe that in the Soviet Union, in that world of justice and equality I had loved since childhood, millions of innocent people had been killed? By the Communist Party? By Stalin?

Once, when I was in the third grade, a teacher had insisted there were slave labor camps in the Soviet Union. I ran home from school that day very agitated, but my mother reassured me. It was Capitalist propaganda, she said, and of course I believed her. Never believe anything you read in the Hearst papers, she said. And I never did. But now, all at once, because of the look in a woman's eyes, I saw that the Khrushchev report had been true. I saw what the terror and horror of the Stalin time had really meant. And for this there was no more running home to Mama.

By the time Hyla and I left their house the last buses had stopped running. The subway was closed and we had to walk back to our hotel. A few people came down the street toward us, stumbling and holding themselves up against the buildings. *"Mir y drugba,"* they muttered, and the gay words seemed strangely tarnished. I had not taken my jacket with me, and now I was terribly cold. We sat down at a bus stop and put our arms around each other's shoulders. My teeth were chattering, and it seemed to me that we were very far from our hotel. I looked around at this city that had seemed to be welcoming me home and I felt that I had never in my life been so cold before. Hyla was wearing a scarf around her neck and we took turns holding it over our hands. "We should have left earlier," I said. "We certainly should have." There was an ominous sound in her voice. She, evidently, had taken my words differently than I'd intended. "I'm so tired," I said, clarifying, "I can hardly walk." "Yes," she murmured, after a moment. "We're both worn out." Again, her words seemed to imply something, but I couldn't bother to figure it out. We got up and started walking. The streets were deserted. In the dark, the tall buildings suddenly took on a grim, barren look. "It's an awful part of town," she said, suddenly angry. "Yeah," I agreed. "It doesn't even look like Moscow."

And that was it. We never repeated a word of what had been said to us. We didn't discuss it. In fact, after that night we drifted apart. The next time I saw her she was drunk and was walking with a boy in a small park. There were lights strung up in the trees and I had gone there to dance. We were sitting in a little pavilion when Hyla came by. I was trying to pour down a small glass of vodka with a raw egg yolk in the bottom, but I kept gagging. The boys were encouraging me, and we were all laughing. Then I looked up and saw Hyla waving. She looked terrible, her hair was wild, and she was laughing in a shrill, unconvincing way. "Americans no can drink good," the boy on my right said to me. "She's English," I answered. He shrugged, it was all the same to him. Then he picked up my glass, made a blurred ironic salute to the Youth Festival, and swallowed it down, raw egg and all.

Suddenly, I was very depressed. My companions were getting drunk. They were telling jokes to one another and laughing raucously. They kept pushing each other out of the way to sit next to me. "You like jazz?" one of them kept asking me. "Ella Fitzgerald? Louis Armstrong?" But his accent was so strong I couldn't make out at first what he was saying. Then, I realized, they were trying to tell me something. Jazz wasn't supposed to be played in the Soviet Union. It came through on Voice of America. And it was blocked out. But they evidently had some way of hearing it, they listened to Voice of America, they had learned English that way. I looked at them more closely. Who were they?

One of them was dressed in what looked like a very expensive suit. His father, someone said, was a leading member of the Communist Party. Earlier in the evening, when we were going up the elevator to his family's apartment, he had suddenly taken me by the shoulder and put his finger to my lips. Then he pointed up to the top of the elevator. I raised my eyebrows. What? He pointed to his ear. Then, he mouthed the word *microphone*.

The boy sitting next to me was wearing jeans. He seemed to be very proud of them, and kept tugging them smooth and carefully creasing the cuffs. He had bought them in the black market. Yes, he insisted, when I looked skeptical, you could get anything in the black market. Even money. He offered to get me a better exchange for my dollars but I gave him a look that shut him up for the rest of the night.

And now? One of the boys, whom I liked, asked me to dance. He was a tall, dark boy with beautiful eyes. He was quieter than the others, his name was Tolya, and he looked at me with a shy, adoring expression. We walked around the lake together, and I finally found the courage to ask him something. "Tolya," I said, "do you like living here? I mean, really?"

"In Moscow?"

"In the Soviet Union."

He looked over at me and raised his shoulders. He was studying to be an engineer; he reminded me of my father. He was a good dancer, and he didn't drink. But now he said, "For me, Soviet Union is good place. I have good education. I have one day good job. But for you," he shook his head, "don't stay here." I had already told him I wanted to stay on after the festival, learn Russian, and go to Moscow University. "Why not?" I asked, but I didn't really want to hear his answer. "Go home," he said, putting his arm around me. "I'll arrange, I'll to visit you. It's better."

The next day was the official opening of the festival. The members of delegations rode in open trucks, wearing national costumes. The streets were filled with people. There were times when the whole vast cavalcade came to a halt because the people that pressed around us formed so dense a mass it was impossible to continue.

The procession lasted most of the morning; it was a slow event with an accelerating momentum. But from the first moment I climbed up on the cab of the truck, I knew that there was nothing more to worry about. I lifted my arm, waving the American flag. I shouted out, *"Sovietzky, Amerikansky drugba* — American, Soviet friendship." People in the street answered with a great roar. This was socialism. This tearing down of the separations between people. What was there to fear or doubt?

A strange sort of ecstasy began to mount in me, something I had never felt before. Excitement at first, it became a wild exuberance.

But then it was a calm; I felt that I was weeping with joy, and a peculiar, aching sadness.

This ecstasy grew greater as we entered the stadium. There, delegation after delegation marched around the field, waving flags, spreading banners, wearing national costumes, playing instruments, dancing, beating drums, carrying paper dragons.

I looked up as each new delegation entered. I thought, Here I come. Here I come.

These thoughts kept darting into my head and each time I felt tears pouring down my face, although I had no idea why I should be crying. Something was happening in the crowd above us: I looked up and saw that people were still standing and waving but there was now a silence settling upon them. And in the vast arena too, where I was standing, although everyone was still dancing, here, too, a quiet was settling.

I saw that clusters of balloons were rising into the air, a huge flock of white doves was released, I watched them climb, they fluttered upward, over the stadium, over these people who had come from all over the world, and suddenly I understood: I, too, was mounting upward with the doves, I was lifted above the crowd, spread out over it, while at the same moment I stood among it and felt the most extraordinary sensation: one heart was beating within us. For an instant, quicker than thought, I imagined I had been swept up in the same enthusiasm that possessed my mother, almost thirty years before. But then, as my feet hit the ground, I suddenly saw that she was wrong. The revolution had not occurred.

A great change was coming, but it would take much longer than she imagined. It would not happen first out there, in the social world. It would happen slowly, to one human being after another. It would be subtle and overpowering and would take the form of a gradual change of heart.

I wrote enthusiastic letters to my parents and I told them the whole story of the festival. But that was the official version; what I left out was the real story, and it is difficult for me to write even today. For I was, in the next weeks, to learn even more about this country that had once inspired my greatest childhood passion.

Traveling in a bus with Tolya, one night I saw two women standing outside the subway station. He told me they were prostitutes and at first I wouldn't believe him. How could there be prostitution in a socialist country? I looked back, and what he said seemed true. They looked like prostitutes anywhere. For a minute I closed my eyes and put my hands over my face. "*Shtotakoy?* What is it, little friend?" he asked. "Something hurts you?" "Prostitutes," was all I could say, but there was a lot in my voice if he cared to hear it.

One other night he took me to a poetry reading and told me, on our way there, that it was dangerous for us to go. Did I want to change my mind and go back to the festival? "Dangerous?" I said, laughing at him. I was used to people exaggerating, especially at our age. And anyway, I liked the idea of danger.

It was held at Kostya's house, where things were safer, Tolya said, because his father was so high up in the Party. When we walked in, someone had just put on a Miles Davis album that would be played over and over again, religiously, through the night. There were paintings on the wall, but they would be taken down, Tolya told me, before the evening was over. The artists would lose their jobs, he said, if anyone knew they painted abstracts. I looked at them, without going too close. Personally, I preferred the Socialist Realism which was the accepted school of art. I shrugged, what did I know about painting?

Tolya was very excited; he said everything in a high voice and I saw that he and everyone else felt they were doing something very daring. A few girls came in and were introduced to me. I realized that as an American I was a guest of honor. And not because my parents were Communists. The boys wanted me to teach them to dance. They knew the waltz and the fox-trot, but they wanted to show them how to jitterbug. They caught on very quickly, and for a while I couldn't tell if I was in Moscow or back at home in Los Angeles. Then the record player was turned off. The man who was reading first went up to the table, tossed off a glass of champagne, and threw his head back to get his hair out of his eyes. The Russian boys wore their hair cut short at the sides, with a long sweep of hair on top, the way my father wore his. As soon as they got excited, the hair would fall forward into their eyes. They had a way of tossing it back which I found very attractive. Several of them were wearing jeans, one of them even had a flannel shirt. Naturally, I didn't think any of this was at all dangerous. Music and poetry, jazz and blue jeans. What could happen to people because of that?

One of the boys showed me a silver icon, a triptych with a hand-worked hinge. Everyone gathered around to look. It was very old, and the work on it was very fine; even I could tell. Tolya told me it had been stolen from a church, but I didn't really believe him. Then Kostya came over. "You like it?" he asked. He talked with an Oxford accent and his English was excellent. "I'll send you one," he promised. "But don't you ever tell anyone where it came from. Promise?" He made a gesture of cutting his throat. In fact, it arrived a year later in a plain brown package, without a note. It was a brass icon, and it looked very old to me. I hid it away in my drawer and never showed it to my mother. By then, I believed a whole lot of things I denied while I was in Moscow. And the icon seemed to make visible all that I never wanted my mother to know.

That night, when we were leaving Kostya's house, Tolya put his arm around me. He was a very polite boy and he never made advances. Probably, he could see that I was feeling disturbed. "You don't like jazz?" he said, evidently trying to figure out my ideological orientation. "My parents lived here in the thirties," I answered. "They loved it here." And what, after all, did I want him to understand? That I was disappointed because the Soviet Union was not perfect? Not the ideal world my mother had promised me? Was a world, instead, where people could lose their jobs because they listened to jazz, where women sold their bodies, where Jews were persecuted, where people were afraid to tell the truth to foreigners?

But what truth exactly? What truth?

"*Smotretye,* look darling," Tolya said. "Don't blame. You think people talk? Even to ourselves not."

Somehow, because he had to struggle so hard with English, I found myself trusting him. "But how could they live here and not know? How is it possible? My mother especially. She just takes one look at me when I walk in the house and she knows exactly what I'm feeling."

I was saying to him, a stranger, the thought I had kept from myself for many months now, since that awful day I read the Khrushchev report for the first time and my mother came into my room and found me so unhappy. And of course it was too much for him. He couldn't figure out why I was so disturbed, he didn't know what to say to me. And I think it was because of this that he acted in a way not at all typical of him.

We were close to my hotel by then and Tolya suddenly suggested we walk down to the parkland near the river. I nodded and followed after him, walking quickly. There were large trees there, with branches that came down almost to the ground. "Not talk anymore," he whispered, taking my hand and putting his finger to my lips. We passed a few other couples embracing, hidden under the trees. We went farther, both of us awkward, a new mood between us. And we were both eager for it.

Finally, there was a place for us, near the river. Tolya took off his jacket and put it on the ground. He sat down and offered me his hand. I was looking over his head into the trees. And then I was unbuttoning my blouse.

I heard him draw in his breath. His excitement from the poetry reading, his tenderness, his struggle to understand me, were all still apparent in his face. But there was something else as well, which made me feel very powerful. I had never gone all the way with a boy before and now I wanted to. He stood up, pulled me against him, and unfastened my bra. Then he drew back to look at me and I heard him gasp. I had never been with a boy who was less experienced than I was. It made me feel capable of anything. I wanted to take off my clothes and chase him through the trees. But he had knelt down in the wet grass. His hands were pressed against my back. He kissed my breasts as if he were worshiping me.

"Take me Tolya," I said, in a hoarse voice I had never heard before. The words embarrassed me, but they wanted to be spoken. "I want you," I whispered.

"Yes?" He hesitated. "Yes?" And then, without understanding, he understood.

He took my hand and pressed it against him. I felt him throbbing. I started to kneel down, unbuttoning his pants. But he grabbed my hand. A light flashed. His whole body shivered and leaped away from me. I turned and saw a circle of light bobbing along over the bushes, sweeping along the river, focusing under the trees.

"Dressed, dressed," he whispered urgently, snatching up my blouse and shoving my bra into his pocket.

The light was coming closer, closer. "Not be afraid," he murmured. "Trust."

He helped me button, his hands shaking. I felt the tips of my breasts erect, painful.

They came closer, the light moving surely, discovering us together, our hands at our sides, under the tree. Then the light was in my face. I was enraged and terrified. What did it mean? What had we done? Why was Tolya so scared? What would happen?

They came over to us, two of them, a young man and a woman. I saw their feet, the heavy shoes. I couldn't make out what else they were wearing. Tolya was talking to them in a quiet voice, explaining. He was in control, very dignified, and I felt proud of him. He was showing them his papers and I heard him say, *"Amerikansky devoushka,* American girl." The light flashed back over to me. *"Mir y drugba,"* I said boldly. They studied my face, my skirt and blouse. I wasn't carrying my passport and Tolya explained that I was staying at a hotel in the Agriculture Exhibit. The light moved off, back to Tolya. Again, it moved over and focused on my feet. They said something to one another and I felt that they believed him. I looked down, wildly fond of my American sandals. How could I have known when I was buying them at the sandal maker in Venice Beach that these trivial objects would one day get me out of a serious scrape? And then they were going away. The man called out something over his shoulder to Tolya, and laughed suggestively. The light bobbed and swept and focused and vanished.

We were alone, silent. Shivering. I was ashamed. "What was it?" I asked him finally as we walked back out of the park, toward the street. But he didn't answer.

At the corner of my hotel Tolya said, "Don't worry. No problem. You American girl. I, Soviet boy. No problem."

"What do you mean? *Ya ni panemayou.* I don't understand."

He flicked his fingers against his neck. "If Soviet girl, American boy, big trouble."

"What trouble? What would happen? Why?"

He raised his shoulders. Again, that silence. Retreat, a door closing.

I watched him, walking away, without turning to wave to me. I knew I'd never see him again. I didn't love him. It didn't matter. But I felt I was losing someone who might have explained things to me. Who, because I was his girlfriend, might have told me the truth. And then, when he was out of sight, I remembered he had my bra in his pocket. But then, very bitterly, shaking my head, I began to laugh, alone on that cold corner of a world tarnishing.

There were only a few days of the festival left. And now every morning, at one or two o'clock, when I returned to my hotel, there was a young Scotsman, standing among the other boys, wearing his kilt, waiting to walk with me through the streets of Moscow.

On those walks, in the early morning, I felt as if I were going back to my earliest childhood. Or further back still, to a time beyond memory, when this was my home. And for this reason perhaps I was so deeply impressed by an event which occurred on my last night in Moscow.

The young Scotsman and I found ourselves in a strange part of town, on a street with only a few lights and with small wooden houses. The twentieth century was not visible here and we had, I imagined, wandered into Old Moscow. The street was cobbled, there was an unusual atmosphere about the place, not because of its poverty, but because of its age. I felt myself holding my breath as we approached a little field, on which there stood a single dwelling, a small, ramshackle, makeshift affair, put together from old wood and crates, with a tiny broken window in which we saw a light. As we were passing, a young man came to the door, a large board nailed across the entrance. He stood there for several minutes and then he waved to us.

We went over to him and stood smiling. We spoke only a few words of Russian, he spoke no English, and it would never have occurred to us to bring out the festival slogan. This was something different. Finally, he stepped back and made a deep bow, inviting us in.

Inside, the little house was dark. There was a mattress on the floor, a small table with a candle burning on it, an accordion in the corner, and piles of books on the floor.

The young man was tall and very slender, with long blond hair that fell over his face as he talked, while we sat and listened to him, without understanding a word he said. After a time he brought two glasses, a bottle of vodka, insisted that we take a little drink, and offered us a piece of bread.

And then he sat there quietly. When it grew light, he blew out the candle, played a song for us on the accordion, and indicated that he would have to return to his writing. A notebook was open on the table, the candle stood next to it. When we left, he stopped me suddenly and pushed a book of poetry into my hands.

Years later, studying Russian, I read this book and was astonished. This young man had pushed into my hands a book which contained the first words I knew in Russian. Poems by Lermontov, recited to me, when I was a little girl, by my mother.

~ ~

That day, a few hours later, I left for China. I was excited by this trip; we crossed the Soviet Union on the Trans-Siberian Express, entered Manchuria, and began our six weeks of travel in the People's Republic of China. I was impressed with this vast new land that had raised itself, by its own effort, into the twentieth century, overcoming a tyranny of tradition which, I then still insisted, could only be overcome with violence.

Yet, during all those weeks in China, I remembered the young man who had given me Lermontov's poems. And when I returned to Moscow I tried to find him again. I went out many times, by myself and with Russian friends, but I never again found the old neighborhood.

I did, however, find a mood that has returned to me many times over the years. It was a feeling of extreme desolation and sorrow that arose from the fact that I had lost the Communist vision I had shared with my parents and was indeed quite alone in the world without that dream. I was in mourning, but I could not admit it.

I went out looking for the young man one more time on my last night in Moscow and I walked until early in the morning. For me, that young man represented a lonelier, more intrinsic apprenticeship than Tolya's friends. In his isolation he seemed to live out a world view I could only vaguely grasp; but I felt instinctively his was the sort of life my parents would have referred to as "bourgeois decadence." They would worry about someone who intended to build a life on self-reflection and the shaping of words.

Yet that is precisely the way I presented myself when I returned to California. I had by then spent several months in Poland and in East Germany. I had been to many poetry readings, and had begun to love sitting in coffee shops. I had let my hair grow and I had a certain carefully cultivated way of tossing back my head to get my hair out of my eyes.

I had developed an enthusiasm for abstract art, had begun to read Sartre, and came home talking about existential angst.

My parents sat at the table during dinner and listened to me in silence. Of course, they did not understand that by advancing this image of myself to them, as an explanation for what had happened to me in Moscow, I was trying to save them from a confrontation with my own doubts and disillusions about Communism. How could they? I myself refused to understand. Once, in a wild moment, I screamed at my mother about my change of heart. But usually, I never mentioned it.

"Don't tell me about Marx," I shouted. "Or Lenin. Or any other of their theories. Lenin is to Marx what the New Testament is to the Old. It's a completely new departure. The most revisionist doctrine in the world."

"Listen to her, will you listen," she yelled back, banging the door to the refrigerator. "She's unlearned everything we taught her."

My father stood in the doorway, looking nervous. This sort of yelling match was not for him. Later, I knew, when I'd gone to bed, he'd knock at the door to my room and want to talk to me. But now he stood there, shaking his head and looking mournful.

"The revolution cannot take place in one country," I yelled, advancing an idea I had worked out for myself, in an effort to explain what had happened in the Soviet Union. "We will not have socialism until revolutions take place all over the world, simultaneously." At the time, this was as far as I could go.

"Hah," my mother shouted, pointing her finger at the ceiling, "so there it is. That's what has happened. She met Trotskyists."

"Trotskyists? What do they have to do with anything? You think I get my ideas from other people?"

"Ideas? You call this nonsense ideas?"

"Why talk to her?" I shouted, whirling around and facing my father. "Is this what you have tried to reason with all these years?"

" 'This' she calls me. Did you hear her, Paul? She calls her mother 'this'?"

"Enough," he said, speaking to both of us. "Who can come to understanding through a tone like that?"

I had only a few weeks with them before I left for the university in Berkeley. Most of the time I spent out of the house, running around with my old friends. Because I was in the first group of Americans to go to China after the revolution, my picture had been in the newspaper; there had been a television segment of me on the ABC news. I had become a minor celebrity and everyone was happy to know me now. I stayed out late, made lists of all the boys who called me for dates, and briefly I fell back into my old way of distracting myself from whatever troubled me.

But now, because I was older, it was harder to pretend. I knew that something had happened. Something had changed me. I had become a poet. By the time I came home from college for Easter vacation I had perfected my new rôle.

"These clothes," my mother would say, watching me with her hands on her hips. "You're going to a costume party, maybe?"

I always played dumb. "What's wrong with them? Everybody dresses like this."

"Show me please this everybody."

The next time I came home for a visit, one long weekend toward the middle of my freshman year, I wrote poetry with soap all over the mirror on my dressing table. Then, I began to recite poetry as I walked about the house, doing my chores. Poetry consumed me. I barely ate a meal. I learned a poem by Walter de la Mare and repeated it at every opportunity. "Very old are the woods;/And the buds that break/Out of the briar's boughs,/When March winds wake,/So old with their beauty are/Oh, no man knows/Through what wild centuries/Roves back the rose."

"What's this?" my mother would say. "Can't take anything into the mouth but poetry now?"

One night, when my mother invited me to a political rally where she was going to speak, I said I had to stay home and finish a poem I was writing.

And so we had an argument which was repeated, again and again, without much variation over the years. You could have heard it the night before my wedding, or the day my husband and I left for Oxford, a year or so later. When I finally moved back to America after four years of living abroad, I spent the summer in Los Angeles. And of course the argument broke out again.

In retrospect, I see that it was a separation ritual, a way we had evolved to speak the central issue between us. For, whatever else we shouted or declaimed, a single idea was at the heart of our quarrel. I mean of course the fact that we thought different thoughts, and experienced the world differently. That we were no longer the same person.

That night, when I was not yet eighteen years old, she stood at the door to my room with her hand on her hips. She was dressed very nicely, and had put on make-up for going out. It seemed a sudden impulse to invite me casually to come along. My father was already driving the car out of the garage and she said, "So, why don't you come along? You'll see a lot of people you didn't see for a while. It'll be good for you."

I was lying on my bed, writing in my notebook. "I'm busy," I said, "I'm writing. It's not something I can interrupt for a meeting." I think the tone of my voice, so superior and contemptuous, must have fired her off.

"Too busy? Too busy for a meeting? The world in a state like this and she's too busy with her poetry?"

She had a way, when she was very angry, of referring to me in the third person, as if I were no longer worthy of direct discourse. And I, if I were angry enough, would pick up her style.

"Yes," I yelled, and I hoped my father would hear me, "SHE'S writing a poem. And someday this piece of paper with HER words will mean more to the world than all your picket lines and mass meetings. Yes," I shrieked, even louder, as she gestured to the ceiling, calling upon the world to witness the folly of her only child, "these words will live long after the Communist Party of America has been forgotten."

"These words? Would you believe it? This paper? Live? Longer than the Party, yet?" Her voice had reached the absolute top of its register, an anguished F-sharp of consternation. And now it suddenly changed color. "That I should live to hear it. I, from my own daughter."

I was on my feet, gesturing with my notebook. I was beside myself. I had become a malevolent creature whose sole intention was to wound. I saw that the same thing had happened to her. We stood a few inches from each other, screaming the worst insults. It was, as I say, the same argument and it played itself out over and over again for the next twenty years.

"You want to know something else," I shouted that night as she stood at my door, and the echo of it went forward and reverberated through the next two decades of our life, "even if no one ever read a single word of what SHE has to say, she'd rather be here forever with her notebook than spend ten boring minutes listening to you make another speech. You think anyone listens anyway? You think you're going to change the world?"

"What's happened to her?" she cried out, genuinely stricken. "Is this the daughter I sent off to Moscow? Is this the child I raised?"

"No, she's not. She's not. She'll never be again, and that's what you've got to understand. I'm eighteen years old. (I'm twenty-three years old. I'm almost thirty. I'm thirty-six now.) I'm a poet. I'm not a political person. Politics just doesn't mean anything to me. Can't you see? I'm not you. I'm my own self."

"A poet." The words ringing with so much contempt they made me shiver. "A poet, this one a poet. That's all we need, another poet, and the world at the edge of a holocaust."

"Who are you to say what the world needs? You're God maybe, you know what's going to save the world?"

And so it would go, until my father came into the house, that familiar look of forbearance on his face, and his deep compassion. It was his particular torment, I now see, that he could understand both points of view, but couldn't find the way to bring about an accord between us. We were both stubbornly locked into our outrage. I should have followed in her footsteps, she believed. And I, although I did not admit it, felt that her revolutionary vision had betrayed me.

That night, she walked out of the house and banged the front door. I could hear her get into the car. My father stayed behind for a moment. "You know," he said, "we always admire a poet. She especially. You know that. But you provoke her. You make her think you have turned against everything she stands for."

284 In My Mother's House

"Maybe I have."

"No. You haven't."

"You're so sure?" But I wasn't yelling now. Somehow, I hoped he was right.

"You're coming?" he asked, holding the door open for me. But I shook my head. "I'm sure," he said and went out to the car.

When I returned to school for the end of my freshman year I began to write long, soulful letters to them about the way I'd wasted my youth. I felt, although I did not say it, that I had attended too many political events when I should have been studying literature. I was, by then, a serious intellectual and I spent many hours in the library with a young man named Peter Minkov. He was a philosophy student and he'd been to Cal Tech. He was also very brilliant at languages. He used to read to me from Rilke in German as we walked about on campus. Together, during the lunch hour, we would go up to the periodicals room and thumb through the copies of the Viennese newspapers. Peter always knew what operas and chamber works were being performed in Vienna; he loved Mahler and told me stories about the way he carried his sister Justi up several flights of stairs to their apartment when she was ill. He was a very romantic-looking boy, with dark hair and the most soulful eyes I'd ever seen. I also thought he was more intelligent than I was. Certainly he was far better educated.

Today, at forty-four, he is a successful doctor, the head of emergency medicine for one of the major counties of northern California. But then he was twenty years old, intense and highly intellectual; he was an aesthete, an ascetic, with a genuine passion for ideas. He took me to my first art films on Telegraph Avenue, where Pauline Kael still owned the Telegraph Repertory Cinema. The films changed daily and there you could get an education, Peter said, better than what was available on campus. He had a circle of friends who met in North Beach most Friday nights. After dinner, we'd go down to the Trieste, a coffee shop with murals on the wall, where you could play arias from La Boheme and Rigoletto on the jukebox.

My new friends were mildly interested in my trip to the Soviet Union. Although we were very young, we felt that we had seen through many illusions that had held our parents captive. We did not believe in God, we had seen through the fakery (we said) of the Moral Law, we were all vaguely socialist, but we no longer held that the end could justify the means. What really excited us however were questions about Art. I remember one night when we discussed Thomas Mann's *Dr. Faustus* and I argued that it was "inherently flawed" because of the narrator's sentimental attitude toward the artist's struggle. It was a debate that kept us up until morning and then we went out and walked past the bakery we knew on Taylor Street and reached into the broken window and pulled out a hot loaf of French bread. We were scornful about grades and never admitted that we studied. But by the end of my freshman year I was on the dean's list and Peter had graduated with highest honors in philosophy.

One weekend, just before the end of finals week, Peter and I drove down to Lost Angeles in his parents' car.

At breakfast, Peter told my father he'd gone to Cal Tech, and my father told Peter he'd always wanted to study science but had chosen engineering so that he could make a living. My mother and I had never heard that before and it made me see just how much, all our lives, we'd neglected him.

Peter felt at home with us the way he did not in his own family. He did not like his father's business ethic and his family's preoccupation with money. My father's revolutionary idealism made him feel very comfortable, and Peter said more about himself on that first day with my family than I had ever yet heard from him. He rarely ate very much, but when my mother offered him a second helping he accepted it, smiling. That night Peter and I went out into the garden. "Your father," he said, "is the first truly moral man I've ever met. Your mother is an authentic revolutionary. You can't judge their life by the Russian Revolution. They almost make me want to become a socialist."

For many years after that Peter claimed that it was my father who had made him a moral person. And even years after our divorce, he always asks in great detail about my mother. But how else could it be? He became part of our family within the first few hours of knowing them. On Sunday, when my Aunt Lillian "dropped by" at lunchtime, I heard my mother whispering with her. I couldn't catch all of it but I heard the words, "future son-in-law." And she was right. Six months later, Peter and I got married. It was December 24, 1958. I was eighteen years old and I wasn't sure that I loved him. But I knew for certain that he and our friends made sense of the world to me. They gave me a way to become myself without ever confronting my mother and father about the failure, as I saw it, of the Communist dream. To us, in our youthful arrogance, politics and the social world simply were beneath us. We lived, we said, for Art and Ideas, and we were not quite foolish in that passion. We did not see that we were a generation deeply affected by the failure of God and the revolution in the decades that preceded us.

When Peter and I left for Europe in 1960 my mother and father drove us to the airport. We turned back as we climbed the steps to the plane and waved to them. And that time, suddenly, I saw them both look very frail, with their white hair, their eager, nervous expressions, holding each other by the hand, two ancient little people who might well have been my grandparents. They stood there for a long time, even after the door to the plane had closed. We waved to them, but they couldn't make us out through the small windows. And then we watched them, my father leaning over slightly to talk to her, as she gestured with her right arm and brought her hand to rest against her heart.

We arrived in Oxford late in the fall and found ourselves a small flat in the Iffley Road. Leaves were falling; the undergraduates were walking about in their short gowns. As a graduate at University College, Peter was soon wearing a long robe and we were invited to tea in the rector's rooms. I was given a peculiar designation as an "extraordinary student," which meant I could attend lectures in any college of my choice.

I wrote long letters to my mother that first term. Although I wouldn't admit it to myself, I missed her terribly. The mail was delivered twice a day and I would run downstairs in the afternoon, as soon as I heard the postman. If there was no letter from her I would go out and buy several bars of chocolate and gobble them down in rage. Then, after a few weeks, I met a group of young men from Trinity College who wrote poetry and I began to take long, ecstatic walks by myself along the river. That was, I suppose, my fatal error. It started me off again writing poems on little scraps of paper I carried in my pockets. And then one night I showed them to Peter who criticized them mercilessly. I remember looking out at the church across the street from our apartment, refusing to cry. But a few days later I shouted at him for not studying. I knew that his parents wanted him to become a doctor. His mother had told me that when he was three years old he had taught himself to read by climbing up to the bookshelves and taking down his uncle's medical books. But I wasn't thinking about that when I began to insist, still in a very loud voice, that he abandon philosophy and take up medicine instead. I was worried about him, but I did not know why.

I remember the letter he wrote, in which he told his parents how much I loved English literature and how I had found what I was looking for. Philosophy, he felt, had become insular, self-referring, indulgent. In medicine, he said, he could combine his interest in science with his desire to do something worthwhile for humanity. It was a very moving, impressive document, the kind that only can be written when you are very young. But it was certainly wrong about me. Frequently, although I did not talk to Peter about it, I felt terribly lost and alone. The way I was living that first term in Oxford made me seem strange to myself. My sense of what was fitting and normal came to me from my mother. Because I could not imagine her walking for several hours along the river I felt as if I, in being there, was engaged in a nefarious and suspect activity. If I walked into a concert I would think, in my mother's voice, So how many people could afford such a price for this seat? Even the clothes I wore made me think of my mother. Once, on a whim, I bought a dress for fifty dollars, which was a lot of money in those days. I brought it home in a reckless mood, egged on by a friend. But the first night I put it on, and looked at myself in the lace gown, with its velvet ribbon threaded around the bodice, I remembered that my mother still bought most of her clothes from the yearly People's World Bazaar, where she could pick up a woolen dress for ninety-five cents, or a beautiful coat for a dollar. Although I was thousands of miles away from home, my mother seemed to be living alongside me. I had put this immense distance between us so that I could have the freedom to be and do what I chose. But now I discovered that I had brought her with me, in the form of a pervasive and intractable judgment against myself.

~ ~

I was twenty-two years old, and we had moved to Dublin, when we decided to have a child. It was, on both our parts, a conscious effort to save our marriage. More and more, over the years, we had continued to drift apart. I was, as Peter told me once, in a rare, confidential moment, still as passionate and enthusiastic as I had always been. But something, he said, had been closing down in him.

"You're just braver than I am," he said to me, "I simply don't have your courage."

Between us, a sullen and hostile silence had grown up and was broken only by my outbursts of rage. One night, in a terrible fight, I lifted a knife and waved it menacingly in his direction. And he said, in a cold, very controlled voice, that he'd rather have me sleep with any other man he knew than have to sleep with me himself.

By then I was pregnant with Larissa. It was a difficult pregnancy, during the coldest winter in Europe for thirty-five years. It snowed in Dublin, the pipes froze, and it was impossible to keep warm. It was the winter, I later found out, that Sylvia Plath committed suicide in London. And I, walking about with my dream of becoming a poet, one day, on a cold morning, four months pregnant, suddenly began to hemorrhage badly. Since I had lost a pregnancy a few months before, I was put to bed and stayed there for the next four months. When the time came to go to the hospital I took two volumes of Proust with me. I knew that I had been born quickly and that my mother had not cried out. I, too, wanted to be brave, but the baby had its head in the wrong position, the delivery was slow and long and painful, my childbirth exercises didn't seem to work, and suddenly I was terrified and alone, clutching a volume of Proust and weeping. I thought I was not the woman my mother had been. I wept tears of self-contempt and loathing. I did not know that in America, with a birth like this, I would have been anesthetized and the baby delivered with forceps. Finally, I began screaming and I yelled out all my rage and disappointment until the midwife came to give me instructions. Then, suddenly, I grew calm, I did what she told me, and I had the overwhelming feeling that I was at the hub of the world. I knew that God existed, tears were pouring down my face, my pain seemed transfigured and I wept because I knew that I was giving birth to my new self.

Larissa stayed in the room with me from the moment she was born. The nurses brought me large glasses of stout and carried Larissa around to show her off in her American pajama suit. I missed my mother then more bitterly than I had for years. By the time she'd given birth to my sister, at the age of twenty-five, she already was what she would continue to be for the rest of her life. And here I was, a student who could not decide upon a major course of study, a would-be poet who was no longer sure of anything in the world. What did I have to pass on to my daughter, what vision or dream of the future would I whisper to her, rocking her in my arms?

The first time I held her against my breast I hummed a Russian lullaby my mother had sung to me. And of course I went on to sing all the other songs I had learned from my mother. The "Internationals," "The Peat Bog Soldiers," "Meadowlands," "Joe Hill," the old union songs. They moved me deeply; through them I could remember the years of my childhood when I was still loyal to everything my mother believed. But I also felt wrong and fraudulent, singing them to my little girl. What right did I have? For me, these songs had become sentimental and nostalgic. But when my mother had sung them to me they were part of a world, a system of belief she intended to impart. Wouldn't it be better to take this little girl home and let my mother sing to her?

Larissa ate and grew round. Her hair came in golden and her eyes were gray. At five months she said her first word. And then, at eleven months she took her first steps.

We had returned to America by then and were sitting in the garden of my parents' house. It was Independence Day, July 4, 1964. My father was picking schav for our dinner, Peter was reading a medical journal, my mother and I were sitting on a blanket, playing with Larissa. We'd begun to quarrel already, of course, now that I'd turned religious. But that day, in the heat, wearing cotton dresses and sipping ice tea, we were suddenly peaceful. Larissa kept getting up and falling down, and then my mother held out her hand. "Lara," she said, very quietly, with her habitual authority, *"koom aher . . . come here."* And sure enough, wobbling and weaving, with a look of deep concentration on her little face, Larissa walked. One step, another, my father turning from his work, reaching up to stroke his mustache, my mother's hands reaching out to her.

It was a good summer; Peter and I got along well, our decision to have a child seemed to have worked out for us, and we rarely quarreled. But my mother and I could always find something to quarrel about. One night we argued about the meaning of Kennedy's assassination. She saw it as a right-wing conspiracy, I saw it as the death blow that rings in a time of chaos and despair. "A mystic," she'd shout, "even about politics. An age of chaos, yet, that's what you believe? And you say it so calmly? A bloodletting, and after this we'll have a new world order? Where does she get these things? Paul, Peter, do you understand the things she says?"

They, of course, were silent. They left us to ourselves, and after a few weeks I stopped talking about my "new vision." She stopped nagging me to become politically active. Maybe in our own way we knew it was the last summer we would spend as a family, together.

And then, during the next two years, before my father died, I gave even him cause to worry about me because of the way my life seemed to be going. Peter and I separated; we never talked about why. After we left Los Angeles we rarely talked at all. One night he didn't come home until two or three in the morning. I knew that he was having an affair. When he walked through the door I began shouting. I remember him saying, "I just don't love you anymore," and then I was holding the door open, telling him to get out. A week later I got a job teaching remedial reading to adults. I took care of children after school in the playground of Larissa's kindergarten. Peter began to pay child support when our savings ran out and I lived from month to month, terrified at times by a sense of insecurity, but at times elated by the first real freedom I had known.

Then, for several months I spent most of my time walking about in Golden Gate Park. Once or twice during my long walks I actually went down on my knees to worship . . . God, or something nameless that seemed to be looking out at me from everything I saw. But kneeling there, I would suddenly become aware of my mother's attitude toward such things and I would scramble to my feet.

In those days I was not yet a good mother to Larissa. I was far too absorbed with myself and I brought her along with me, whatever I was doing. Before she was three years old she'd attended concerts and been to museums, hung out in coffee shops and strolled around bookstores. Twenty-five years earlier my mother had wheeled me in my baby carriage to political demonstrations in the Bronx. Now my daughter and I went regularly to the Japanese Tea Garden, where we would have long and serious discussions. I began to feel that, with her, a rare treasure had been entrusted to me. I was determined to make of her what I myself wanted to be. Without fully understanding my own behavior, I tried to cultivate in Larissa the qualities my mother had always feared and disapproved of in me. It was an act of protest against my mother's influence and power, part of my long and troubled struggle for separation. But it was also, I fear, too great a burden for a small child to carry. One evening, when we'd been playing late at the beach, she danced wildly by herself in the waves and when we drove home I put on the radio and there suddenly was Mahler. She listened with an acute concentration that reminded me of Peter and finally she threw her hands over her ears and began weeping. I stopped the car, to put my arms around her. "What, what is it?" I asked, turning off the radio. "Was he dying?" she said. "No, not then. It is an early symphony." But she insisted, "He was, he was Mama, even then."

For several months when she was almost three years old, she began to wake up frightened at night. Then, I learned how to go and sit with her and soothe her. I told her stories, about my mother's life, and rocked her in my arms. She'd fall asleep, against my breast, sucking her thumb. And I would weep silently with loneliness and tenderness, with all the confusion of my life, and with an indescribable sense of hope.

It was, by then, 1965 and in Berkeley, across the Bay, the Free Speech Movement had begun. I went over there one day out of curiosity and watched the strike that emptied the classrooms and the libraries. But now, as a generation of students turned political, I found myself refusing to do what I knew my mother would have done. While the others marched I went into the library and sat there for several hours, reading Nietzsche and listening to the muted sounds of the students chanting outside the window.

During those months it was my father who called me regularly. Sometimes, my mother did not even get on the telephone. Every time we talked now we'd begin to shout and quarrel and one weekend, when she came for a visit with a friend, to "see her granddaughter," as she said, I told her I never wanted to see her again. What had she said to me? What terrible wound did she inflict? I can't even remember. I knew only that with every year we seemed to be moving farther apart, as I moved farther away from the radical past we'd shared. I was lost and confused, but I was also deeply serious in my quest for something distinctive, something of my own. I remember one ridiculous argument, when I shouted at her over the phone. "I'm a lover of God," I yelled, "that's what I am." She sucked in her breath and was silent. And then I heard her say, "You talk to her, Paul. She's just gone crazy. That's all."

He understood me. I don't know how or why, but he understood. Sometimes, he'd call me quite late at night, when he was at home alone. I once told him that I was reading about Saint Theresa and I thought I was a little like her. He answered, "For us, Marx expressed the truth when he said religion was the opiate of the people. But you, it seems, are a poet. We know, for a poet the world is different. In the Soviet Union I knew a man who claimed he could talk to the birds. Of course, everyone laughed at him, how else? But I did not laugh. Maybe, I thought, he can talk to the birds. How should I know?"

Perhaps he understood that I was, during that first year of my separation from Peter, working out the style of life I would live; hanging up pictures of Rilke and Lou Salome and Jesus in my study, aggravating my mother, bewildering myself, a woman in her middle twenties who did not seem to be growing out of her youth; who wrote and wept and laughed and ran about with men, and became solitary again. And who managed, briefly as I say, to communicate something of all this to her father, who never judged her.

Then, one Sunday in June, in 1967, on the last day of the Six Day War between Israel and the Arabs, when Larissa was almost four years old, I got a call. It was my father's doctor, and closest friend, telling me that my father had been killed in an automobile accident. He had been on his way, with my mother, to the Festival of Nationalities.

"No," I said, "it can't be."

Murray was silent.

"She's fine?" I asked, knowing she was.

"Not a scratch," he said, "although, you know, she was sitting beside him."

I grieved then, for the passage of a very gentle soul; he had lived his whole life according to a simple wisdom of the heart. He found it easy to love, he had never hated anyone. He once said to me, "I am a socialist man in a land where socialism has not yet been accomplished." He seemed to regard that as a sufficient statement about his life, and I agree with him. If we had buried him that would have been a good epitaph, although he spoke it in a rare, melancholy moment. His life had been for the most part characterized by a serene cheerfulness that made him puzzle deeply, I know, about the trials and tribulations of the two women he loved. We were cut from such different cloth, and were, I imagine, in our unappeasable struggle and antagonism, the only real sorrow in his life. The death of my sister, my mother's arrest, the persecution of Communists in the United States — these he accepted. But the rancor between my mother and me he always felt was unnecessary. "Two people, just alike," he used to say, "so why do you have to quarrel?"

He was cremated and my mother held a memorial for him. To my surprise, hundreds of people came. Who would have thought this quiet man had touched so many hearts? We sat together, in the front row of the hall, and people filed past, many of them weeping, to shake our hands and embrace us.

That night, at home alone, after our guests had gone, she sat in bed and I came to sit beside her. "You know," she said, "I heard today from Uncle Max. Your father left me very well provided for."

"He did? You didn't expect it?"

"Did he ever talk? It was his great dream, that he could take care of me after he was gone. He always told me he would do it, but money he didn't mention."

"I'm so happy for you. I'm happy he was that kind of man."

"His kind," she said, "you don't see much in the world anymore. Sometimes, I wonder, would it be better never to know a man like this, so you didn't have to suffer so much if you lose him? I'm sixty-four years old. Who knows how long I'll live? But you can be sure, another Paul Kusnitz, I won't find."

She had cried before, but now she wasn't crying. She sat straight up in bed. By then, each time I saw her, I thought she had grown smaller. Now, I looked at her little hands, bunched into fists.

"We did not make life easy for him," she said. At first, her voice was tense, caught somewhere between guilt and accusation. But then she repeated herself and I heard tenderness. "We didn't make his life easy, I tell you."

Maybe our reconciliation dated from that moment. We still had many difficult years ahead of us, an untold number of violent arguments. She would have to live through my religious phase with me, and then come to understand the hope and promise I saw in feminism. I, in turn, would have to let her go on being loyal to the Soviet Union, and not share my concern for the plight of the Soviet Jews. Together, we would hold our breath as Larissa became an adolescent, and then did not trouble us, as we'd feared, by rebellions and turbulence. She was not like us, in that respect. She'd found a way to be exactly what she was, without drama or upheaval. And both of us drew a sigh of relief at that.

But here, of course, we have come to Larissa's story. For me, the narrative is almost at an end. Those years, after her birth, belong to my daughter and must be told, if ever, in her voice. That, after all, is the pattern my mother has established.

But I can say, in truth, on that night, sitting beside my mother in the bedroom she had shared with my father since we moved to Los Angeles twenty-two years before, I felt the first sense of something peaceful between us. No doubt, my own prolonged youth came to an end that night. I was twenty-seven years old and for the first time in many years I put my arms around her.

"Well," I said, "we don't exactly make life easy for ourselves either." And then we both laughed and rocked each other and wept.

And she said, looking up sideways from my embrace, "So, who said it's too late to learn something?"

Epilogue
In My Mother's House

August 1981

S he calls us on the telephone two times the day before we are due to arrive in Los Angeles. The first time she says: "You know that spinach loaf I make? You think Larissa would like it?" "The spinach loaf? With carrots and wheat germ? She'd love it." "Good," says my mother, "I already baked it."

Our second conversation is like the first. "I found a recipe," she says. "I made kugel. Just like Mama used to make. But now the question is, should we go out instead for dinner maybe?"

Her third call comes the next day, a few hours before we are leaving. "Maybe we should go out after all," she says. "How many times in a life does a person get accepted to Harvard?"

"Mama," I say, "are you kidding? I told Larissa about that spinach loaf. We didn't eat since yesterday morning. Just to have a big appetite when we arrive."

"You don't say," she sighs, "since yesterday." And then she realizes I'm kidding. "You," she says, "you can't fool me. Didn't you just tell me you were cooking breakfast?"

On the way to the airport Larissa is silent. She drives fast, moving the car easily between the trucks and buses on the Bayshore Freeway. I remember teaching her to ride the bus alone, going back and forth with her between home and school. As we are passing the Coliseum, she says, "What if I have a boy someday?"

"We'll love him, of course. It goes without saying."

"But what will happen to our pattern?"

I try hard to keep my voice casual. She doesn't like it when I get melodramatic. "I've heard it takes four generations to make a gentleman," I say. "Maybe it takes four to make someone really at home in a new country."

"Me? The goal of all these generations?"

She has a way of jabbing at my inflations. I like it, but it doesn't keep me from talking. "I've been to Europe at least six times since you were born. I've been to Israel. Always looking for my 'real home.' When I first got interested in feminism, I had the feeling every time I went to a women's event that I'd found a homeland. I've never been able to settle in."

"I didn't like it when you went to Israel," she says, ignoring my outburst.

"You could have come. I wanted to take you."

"Peter Minkov told me there was a war. I was afraid." She always refers to her father in this way, formally.

"You were eight years old, the war had ended at least five years earlier. And anyway, why didn't you just tell me?"

"Because I was eight years old."

She turns the wheel sharply, moves out into the fast lane, and passes a few cars.

"You remember that time we went back to Dublin and you left me there with Moira?"

"Yeah?"

"You didn't say good-bye. How old was I then?"

"Five or six. I'm not sure. Why?"

"You told me you'd wake me up from my nap. But when I got up you were gone."

"I let Moira convince me. I thought it would be easier that way."

"How did I know you'd come back?"

She reaches up to adjust the rear-view mirror, giving me a pointed look. But then her mood changes and she begins to reminisce. She can, when it pleases her, set aside her sophistication and chatter like a much younger girl. It's one of her most lovable traits, and I find myself hoping she will never lose it. "Moira told us she was a witch. I guess I was only five. She said she was two hundred years old. And we believed her."

"You wouldn't believe something like that at the age of six."

"Did you ever think," she says, "all that work to make the fourth generation into an American? And I was born in Dublin."

Her laughter reminds me suddenly what it is like to be this young. There is something in it, still so trusting of life.

"I don't think I want to be a writer," she says, changing her mood.

"What then?"

"I don't know. Science is a dead end. There's nothing left but smaller and smaller particles. Maybe philosophy. I want something . . ." She takes her hand from the steering wheel and stretches it out, defining a large space. ". . . Where you can still *do* something . . ." Her voice trails off. "Lasting, original, immense," are the words I hear, but she doesn't speak them. She's the same age I was when I went to Moscow. She's the age my mother was when she left Waterbury and went to New York. I'm glad she, too, is audacious.

"When I tell people I might study philosophy they say I'll end up being a computer programmer. Everyone knows someone who studied philosophy at Harvard and ended up selling stockings in Macy's."

"Don't you believe it." I know I should retreat from this intensity, but I don't want to. "I don't care how many people end up doing nothing. It doesn't have to happen to you. It didn't happen to Grandma. It didn't happen to me. There *are* exceptions. Why not you?"

She raises her eyebrows, mocking me. But finally she says, very quickly, before leaving the whole discussion, "I'm glad you think that. It's a relief."

"Do you believe me?"

She looks at me for a moment, vaguely sardonic. But then she says, "Yes," very firmly, and the conversation is closed.

~~

The plane is late, of course. We hang around in the magazine shop, waiting. She slips her arm through mine and we stroll out to the gate. Twenty minutes pass, a half-hour. We're silent, but our shoulders lean together, almost touching. "Do you think I have a good memory?" she says. It's an airport mood.

"Of course. Are you kidding? You remember everything you read."

"I don't mean that."

"You used to be able to remember things that happened when you were one or two years old. It was extraordinary."

"I can remember all the houses we lived in since Peter Minkov left." After Stanyan Street we moved to Sausalito. Then, to Berkeley, before you went to Israel. Then, I lived with Peter and Susan in Fairfax. When you came back we lived with Bob in Belvedere. Then we lived in the Raleigh house, in the collective. And then you and Bob bought the house on Euclid. Seven houses. Before I was nine years old."

Suddenly, I realize what all this is about. We are separating again, now that she is planning to leave for college. And no doubt it is intensely painful. But I know not to say anything directly. She has her own way with these things, and her own wisdom.

"I gave you a hard time with all those moves, didn't I?"

"That's not what I'm saying."

"Maybe not."

She takes a few restless steps toward the ticket counter. People are beginning to line up for the plane. Then she comes over and puts her book bag over her shoulder. "When I went for my interview they asked me how I was going to make a living if I studied philosophy. Did I tell you? I said I would probably teach and the man said, 'What about getting married?' "

I pick up my overnight bag and look at her. Never again will there be a little girl racing to me across the school playground waving a drawing. "What did you say?"

"Well, I told him it never had occurred to me. And you know, it hadn't."

We wander out across the landing field. A dry wind is blowing. I can feel the drift of something unspoken. "And maybe I don't want to have children," she says, as we climb the stairs to the plane.

"I didn't think I'd have kids. And just look what happened."

"Wish you could change your mind?"

"What? Are you kidding?" My arm goes out and wraps around her. "The way I love you?"

We crowd past the stewardess and enter the plane. Larissa smiles happily, and I see that this burst of feeling was precisely what she wanted.

When we arrive in Los Angeles I look around for my mother. Even while we're waiting for our Avis car I keep glancing around. But when we're driving out of the lot and I take a sharp right and head out along Airport Boulevard, I remember living in this city. And I'm scared suddenly that maybe she's really ill, and not just overworked and exhausted.

"It seems funny that Grandma didn't come," Larissa says.

"You think it was easy to keep her at home? She doesn't listen to doctors. 'I'm almost eighty years old,' she says. 'I figured out how to live this long, so you think maybe I know something more than they do?'"

"You really don't have a great Yiddish accent."

"But you have quite a tongue."

The streets grow more familiar as we turn on Century.

"Are you going to get along this time?" Larissa asks.

"We've never been better."

"The great reconciliation scene?"

"Something like that." I wait, all due respect to her playfulness. "You know what she did when she read my last chapter?"

"Tore her hair? Rent her garments? Covered herself in ash?"

"You're not always the easiest person in the world to talk to."

"I know. Other people have told me that."

Now I'm irritated and it's hard to get going again. "I'll tell you later. I'm not in the mood." But I want to tell her the story.

"I wish you'd try. Really." She looks serious now.

"Well," I say, drawing it out, "I left the manuscript downstairs, the way I told you. The minute I got back to bed I fell sound asleep and I didn't wake up until eight o'clock the next morning. Then, I heard her in the kitchen. And I was scared. I knew it was all right, and then again I didn't know. I went down there. She was making tea, setting out the dishes on the table. The minute she sees me she starts to talk. 'There used to be a bookstore on Fifth Avenue,' she

says. Just like that. 'It was called the Classical Bookstore,' she says.
'I went in there one day. You know how it is, I liked the name. The
owner was a crippled man and that, too, interested me. Later, he
even came to visit and had tea. That was before I married Paul
Kusnitz . . .'

"Then, she stopped talking. Well, I know better than to ask her
questions, so I waited. And finally she says, 'I wanted to get a copy
of Dante's *Purgatorio*. I don't like to read in translations, and I
figured, I've had four years of Latin, maybe I can translate for myself.
I talked to this man, and he found me a dictionary and he found a
copy in Italian. I was working then in a lady's garment shop. But after
work I'd go home and sit at the table with the dictionary and read
the *Purgatorio*.' "

"That's it?" Larissa says, trying to figure it out.

"That's it. She wanted me to know she understood what made me
into a poet."

"You'll never argue again?"

"I'm not saying that. We're both very passionate. Secretly, we
wish anyone we love will think exactly the way we do. For her, the
entire meaning of her life depends on the success of the Russian
Revolution."

"Well," she says, still keeping it light, "isn't that what it means to
be a Communist?"

"I think you can admire her life no matter what you feel about
Soviet Communism."

Larissa looks skeptical, then she says, "When I went for my Harvard interview I told them my grandmother was a Communist."

"Are you kidding? You're lucky you got in."

"They asked if I was interested in politics," she says with a knowing smile. "I started talking about Grandma. I felt proud of her." She
pauses here to think it over. "It's hard to believe my own grandmother has lived that kind of life. When I was little, I used to want
the kind of grandmother who bakes things. But not now."

"You can't imagine what it was like growing up in my mother's
house," I say, overjoyed suddenly to be bringing her home with me.
"We had the most amazing social life. Barbeques in Griffith Park
when the Armenian Community was holding a national celebration.
Korean banquets at the home of her friends. We knew Greeks and

Latvians and Bulgarians. We had a friend named John who wore shorts and sandals even in the winter and rode his bicycle all over Los Angeles. And that, remember, was in the late forties. He brought us a wonderful yogurt culture from Bulgaria. My father used to make it in a huge green crock."

"I remember when you tried to make pickles in that crock. They came out all covered in dill, with no taste. You forgot the salt."

I can see her eyes in the rear-view mirror. They have a fine, deep glow of love in them. Suddenly, she looks right over at me.

"If your mother heard you talk about her life like this she wouldn't be happy? She'd still want you to believe in the socialist revolution?"

"Maybe she's been able to do what she's done because she be-lieves so strongly in something. There are hundreds of people who would have been jailed or deported if it weren't for her. Or some other organizer with the same system of belief. It makes you wonder, should you judge a life by the ideology that inspires it? Or by what that ideology, true or false, inspires the life to do? It's a whole different way to measure truth."

"Or to measure your attachment to your mother."

This time I look at her. She's smiling, and I can see she's uncertain about how far she can go with me on this point.

"I have a feeling you're going to be crying soon," she says, but her voice is much more gentle than she would ever imagine.

~ ~

During dinner the phone keeps ringing. "I can't talk now," my mother says, standing next to the table. "My daughter and my grand-daughter are here."

Then, setting the phone down, she says, "If you would dream a life could you dream something better?"

Larissa goes into the kitchen and turns off the tea kettle. My mother leans over and whispers in my ear. "I'm almost eighty years old," she says. "Look at my life. My mother, the one literate woman in our shtetl. And today, my own granddaughter going to Harvard."

While we are drinking tea she stands up suddenly and goes off into her bedroom. She has moved since Gertrude's death and has bought herself a little house in a beautiful project at the foot of the Baldwin Hills. My high school is three or four blocks away. Now black people are living in those hills we can see so clearly from her patio. All the others have moved away.

She comes back into the room wearing a little pair of knit slippers. The doctor has told her to rest and she is trying. "I have some money for you two," she says. "What do I need it for? At my age, the needs are little. If I get sick I know you won't let me die because of a few dollars."

"I'm glad you know that about me," I say, strangely relieved that she does.

"I know you. A mother knows her child," she says.

After dinner Larissa goes out for a jog. We can see her, in her red running shorts, looping around the lawns, past the roses and camelias, beneath the olive trees. But then we turn back into the room and my mother sits down in her large chair, near the bookcase. I look at her, balancing her checkbook. She has developed a child's very deep concentration. To open her purse, to look through it searching for her glasses, takes time, a deliberate focusing of attention. It removes her from me, sets her apart in her own world, with that serious frown which makes a kingdom out of a sandbox.

She crosses her legs and takes off one shoe. She is the size of a ten-year-old child, but her head is large and her expression very grave; it gives to this woman, born in a shtetl, who has lived her whole life among the people, a curious air of nobility.

Since I saw her last she has entered into old age. The masks have been thrust off and she has regained the ability to pass rapidly from one pure state of feeling to another. Above all, she loves with such intensity that she cannot keep still. And so she cries out, "What shall I do with all this joy? Do you know how happy you have made me? How will I keep it inside?" And then she presses her hand to her heart and squeezes down, her eyes spilling.

At ten o'clock we make up a bed in the living room. Larissa falls asleep quickly but I hear my mother moving about in her room. Drawers open and close, there is a patter of feet and then I see her, peeping in at me, trying to determine if I am sleeping. I wave to her, and she crooks her finger at me, beckoning.

Her room is large and perfectly ordered. There is a bright afghan on the bed, crocheted for her by a deportee from her committee. On the wall near the window a large oil painting of two Chinese women soldiers, sitting with their guns and reading together from a book. On the dresser there are photographs. And then I see something new. She comes over to stand beside me. "That's what I wanted to show you," she says. "I found it. In the drawer with the letters. My friend Anna Gloria is a printer. She made this for you and put a frame on it." She reaches up to take it down from the wall. "So read," she says, pushing it into my hands. Her love for me has taken possession of her face. She shakes me lightly by the shoulder. I remember a large hall; hundreds of people there, at long tables covered in white cloths. I came all dressed up, and I went up to the stage when my name was announced. I talked into a microphone. And even before I opened my mouth I saw the old women, sitting together, nudging and whispering, the handkerchiefs coming out.

"Shall I recite it for you?"

"Oy," she says, pressing her hand to her heart, "would you do that?"

I glance down at the page, but I realize at once that I don't need it. For more than twenty years I have remembered every word of this speech I gave at her birthday celebration after she was released from jail.

> I would like to greet you on my mother's fiftieth birthday, and tell you what her great fight for freedom and equal rights for all peoples has meant to me. All my life she has taught me to fight for my rights and for the rights of other minority groups. . . . My mother has been a guiding light and a strong influence. . . . I also know now that more than anything in the world I would like to follow in her footsteps and earn from you people the love that she has earned.

I stop, remembering how true these words once were for me. And now, as I go on reciting, I can for the first time in my life acknowledge the longing which even then I saw in her face.

She has been sitting on her bed, her legs drawn up and her bathrobe tucked carefully around her. When I finish, she holds out her hand. "There it is," she says, "there it is. Always the people."

I notice that she has taken a small drawer out of her dresser. She pats the bed next to her and I sit. Then, she reaches into the drawer and takes out a little velvet box. "This is my wedding ring," she says, handing me the thin silver band. "And here's the ring your father gave me when we were married twenty-five years." She reaches over and opens my hand. "It's time for me to divest," she says.

My hands shake as I receive the rings. "Look inside," she whispers. "You'll see the dates." I turn it and hold it up to the light. Inside, in a delicate script, it says: *P.K. R.C. June 21, '26.* She is rummaging in the drawer again. She takes out a beautiful silver necklace and hands it to me. "Heirlooms we don't have in our family. But stories we've got." As I put it around my neck she begins to rock herself, her hands gripping her knees. Softly, she hums a tune I remember from many, many years ago. "It's the story of Stenka Razin," she says. "You remember? The great peasant leader. This necklace your father got for me when we were traveling down the Volga."

She goes back to looking in the drawer. "Good, here it is, I thought I lost it maybe." The drawer yields up a pin with a hammer and sickle. This, too, is passed on to me. She brings out a gold pendant in the shape of a triangle. It holds a red stone set in gold and I can see at once that it is valuable. "This one, a lady gave me after a speech. She came up, she took it from her neck and put it on mine. 'Because of the work you've done, Rose Chernin,' she said. You see this inscription? G 12732. That was her number from the concentration camp." She reaches over and puts the pendant around my neck. "You'll take good care," she says. "This is my life here."

I realize that Larissa is standing in the doorway, watching. She has been asleep and she looks very young, her hair tossed about, her cheeks flushed. Is it really true that she is going away from home in a few months? My mother opens her arms and to my immense surprise my daughter comes over, lies down on the bed and puts her head on my mother's lap. I take her feet and hold them, squeezing tightly. My mother says to her, "When you were a little girl you'd come to visit. I'd give you a bath, dinner of course, and then I'd pick you up to put you to bed. And you'd say, 'When I grow up I'm going to carry *you* around. Because *you* are a little Grandma.'"

As she says this I remember a dream. I was walking about all over the world carrying a burden in my arms. In the beginning I was afraid that the burden would be too much for me. But then, as I kept walking, I found that the burden was growing lighter and lighter and I could not tell, looking down, whether it was my mother or my child.

Larissa stretches herself and turns over onto her back. "I remember Grandpa Kusnitz," she says, in a sleepy voice. "He used to spin me around in the air. And I remember Bill Taylor," she says. "He was huge. A black man, and he took me with him one time on the plane to Los Angeles. You remember, Grandma?"

My mother strokes her hair, humming the Russian lullaby she used to sing to me. *"Spe moi angel, moi precrasni, bayoushki bayou. Ticha smotret mesyats yasni, callibel twayou."*

Larissa goes on talking. "I remember walking in a carriage, with Mama and Peter in Dublin. We saw trees and Mama gave me a green leaf with prickly edges."

My mother gestures to me and takes my elbow and pulls me down so that she can whisper in my ear. "Think of it," she says, "a mother and daughter together like this."

Larissa says, "And a granddaughter."

She curls up against me and puts my hand on her head. It's the last time, I think. The last time. It'll never happen again. And my daughter says, "I remember when we came to America. I was one year old. We stopped in New York. In the Bronx. We stayed with Sonia Auerbach and she made me a bed in a drawer."

My mother reaches up for a pillow and puts it under Larissa's head. *"Ticha smotret mesyats yasni,"* she sings. And Larissa says, "I know what it means. The bright moon looks on quietly."

My mother goes on humming, Larissa's eyes open and close. And my mother says, "Did I ever tell you about Zayde?"

We have both heard this story before. She told it seven years ago, when I first began to write down her life.

"Well," she says, taking a breath, "when we lived in the shtetl, Friday was always the longest day of the week. And why? Because, of course, we were waiting for Zayde . . ."

But this time she talks with a voice so gentle it will run, I know, right into Larissa's dreaming.

~ ~

And then it is Sunday, the last day of our visit. Larissa has gone over to see some of my mother's friends who live in the project. A few houses down there is a woman I've known since childhood, a professor of Marxism at the university. Dorothy Healey, who was in jail with my mother, will be moving in next year. Yesterday, when we went out for a walk, an older man came over to meet me. "A comrade," my mother whispered, taking my hand and placing it in his.

These people have lived their whole lives caring about the world. Little by little the dogma has dropped away, and now only the sense of human possibility remains. It makes them tender, in spite of their militancy. And for me they make this housing project strangely like a shtetl.

We are sitting on the little patio behind her house. It is spring, but leaves are falling. A breeze rises suddenly and my mother says, "Do you know the poem by Lermontov? I remember it from when I was a girl."

I look at her, unable to talk.

"Wichaju adin na da rogu," she recites, very grandly. *"Skvoz tuman kremnesti poot blestet/Noch ticha pustenya vnemlet bogu/E zvezda zvezdoyu gavareet."*

She puts her two hands on her cheeks and rocks herself. "Do you know what it means?" I nod, but she translates anyway. "I walk out on the road alone. The path shines through the fog. The night is still. The desert is aware of God. And the stars speak to one another. Why do I feel so lonely?"

There are tears in her eyes. I wonder what she is thinking when she falls silent. I do not dare to say a word and finally she says, "It is as beautiful today as it was seventy years ago."

There are words but I do not speak them. I wonder whether in this struggle to become myself I have become what she was as a girl. I say, "Do you remember when you used to recite that poem to me?"

"Do I remember?" Her eyebrows fly up, her eyes sparkle. "You used to climb into my lap. You'd say, 'Mama, tell me.' 'What,' I'd say, 'what shall I tell you child?' And you, very serious, used to answer, *'Wichaju,* Mama, *wichaju . . .'"*

We do not move. We do not look at one another. But I feel the way something is imparted to me, palpably, passing between us. And then, grabbing my hand, pressing it against her heart, she says, "You remind me of Lermontov. Did I ever tell you that?"

I look around me in this garden behind my mother's house. It has become a wave of light, an affirmation that rises not only beyond sorrow, but from a sense of wondering joy. I glance quickly at my mother, who has fallen silent, and I watch with disbelief the way the distance between us, and all separation, heals over. We are touched by a single motion of forgiveness. Her hand touches my cheek, she calls me by my childhood name, she says, "The birds sing louder when you grow old."

It has grown dark; the breeze is growing cold and yet we sit on here, where the shadows gather, my mother and I together. Above us, on the hills, lights are shimmering in a dusk that seems to be falling earlier for them.

My mother says, "There is a saying I learned in Russia, when I was a child. 'Da nashevo berega, dabro nie daplievot.' Do you want to translate?"

"Nothing good ever swims to our shores."

"Da, da," she says, "a peasant saying. And do you believe it?"

"Not anymore."

"And yet the people are wise."

"Sometimes a life can grow beyond wisdom."

"So it seems. So it seems."

It is late. My mother is tired. She reaches over to hold my hand. Suddenly, she speaks familiar words in a voice I have never heard before. It is pure feeling. It says, "I love you more than life, my daughter. I love you more than life."

Acknowledgments

For a book that has been under way for seven years, thanks are inevitably due those people who managed to go on believing in it.

Susan Griffin edited many versions of this book and inspired me deeply throughout its composition. I know of no way to acknowledge sufficiently my debt to her.

Evi Newbrun was my first reader, and I shall never forget her enthusiasm and encouragement.

Jean Kidwell and Frank Pestana provided their wonderful hospitality during the early stages of gathering stories for this manuscript. My heartfelt thanks to them.

Bob Cantor believed in my work long before there was much to show for it in the world.

Tony Rudolf gave me invaluable support at a difficult moment in the book's evolution.

Lillian Rubin sat up late one night cutting and pasting with her rare combination of tenderness, insight, and tact.

Roz Parenti came running out of her house one day when I drove up, to share with me her enthusiasm for what she'd just read.

Michael Rogin and I have discussed this book so often and so deeply that I've come to feel our friendship is an inseparable part of it.

Tillie Olsen gave me valuable support and detailed, critical commentary.

Valerie Miner listened to me read weekly and offered valuable critical support.

Rachel Nabloch gave me essential help with the Yiddish.

Judy Jackyl read and deciphered and typed difficult manuscripts.

Nan Talese played an essential part in shaping the book's vision and structure.

My agent, Diane Cleaver, has once again, on my behalf, proved her untiring dedication to a work she believes in.

And finally: Elisabeth Scharlatt, my editor at Ticknor & Fields, probably knows every line of this book as well as I do. There is no way to thank her for her immense contribution to both its form and its content.